Civilian Rule in
the Developing World

Civilian Rule in the Developing World

Democracy on the March?

EDITED BY
Constantine P. Danopoulos

Westview Press
BOULDER • SAN FRANCISCO • OXFORD

Copyright © 1992 by Westview Press, Inc.

Published in 1992 in the United States of America by Westview Press, Inc., 5500 Central Avenue, Boulder, Colorado 80301-2877, and in the United Kingdom by Westview Press, 36 Lonsdale Road, Summertown, Oxford OX2 7EW

Library of Congress Cataloging-in-Publication Data
Civilian rule in the developing world : democracy on the march? /
    edited by Constantine P. Danopoulos.
        p.   cm.
    Includes bibliographical references and index.
    ISBN 0-8133-8289-0
    1. Developing countries—Politics and government—Case studies.
2. Civil supremacy over the military—Developing countries—Case
studies.   3. Democracy—Developing countries—Case studies.
I. Danopoulos, Constantine P. (Constantine Panos)
JF60.C548   1992
322′.5′091724—dc20   92-20224
                                                               CIP

Printed and bound in the United States of America

The paper used in this publication meets the requirements
of the American National Standard for Permanence of Paper
for Printed Library Materials Z39.48-1984.

10   9   8   7   6   5   4   3   2   1

To Vickie and our two boys,
Panos and Andreas,
and to the memory of Harry Maroudas

Contents

vii

Acknowledgments

This volume is a collection of original essays specifically prepared for this anthology. As editor, I wish to express my gratitude to each of the contributors who agreed to tackle a difficult and often polemic subject. Researching the military is inherently difficult and even dangerous. Many colleagues and friends read parts of the manuscript and made numerous helpful comments. I am especially grateful to Professors Roy Christman and Richard Lane of San Jose State for their many editorial suggestions. My parents Panos and Athanasia Danopoulos; my brother George, his wife Niki and their two children, Panos and Soula; my aunt Areti Paraskevopoulou; and my *koumbaro* George Nikoletopoulos have provided boundless support and love. Special thanks are also in order for my in-laws Francis and Gladys, Dean James Walsh, and Leticia A. McCart. Vanetia Johnston's expert typing and cheerful disposition contributed to the completion and the aesthetic quality of the book. Amy Eisenberg's patience and sound editorial guidance made my job a lot easier. Last but not least, my wife Vickie and our two boys, Panos and Andreas, deserve special praise for their willingness to put up with my long hours of seclusion and absence from family affairs. Though helpful, none of these people bear any responsibility for any mistakes and deficiencies associated with the project. Responsibility for the accuracy and scholastic quality of what follows belongs to the contributors and myself.

Constantine P. Danopoulos
Fremont, California

About the Editor and Contributors

CONSTANTINE P. DANOPOULOS teaches Political Science at San Jose State University. He received his Ph.D. in Political Science from the University of Missouri, Columbia, and has written extensively on international security and civil-military relations. He is the author of *Warriors and Politicians in Modern Greece* (1984) and editor of *The Decline of Military Regimes - The Civilian Influence*, *Military Withdrawal from Politics*, and *From Military to Civilian Rule*. Dr. Danopoulos's numerous articles have appeared in journals such as *Armed Forces and Society*, *Political Science Quarterly*, *West European Politics*, the *Journal of Political* and *Military Sociology*, *The Journal of Security Studies*, and *Public Administration and Development*. He is Associate Editor of the *Journal of Political and Military Sociology*.

BAFFOUR AGYEMAN-DUAH is Associate Professor and Director of the Division of Social Sciences at Bennett College, Greensboro, North Carolina. He received his Ph.D. from the University of Denver. He has previously been published in such scholarly journals as *African Review*, *Conflict Quarterly*, *Journal of Modern African Studies*, *Armed Forces & Society*, *Comparative Political Studies*, and *Politica Internazional*.

ANGELA S. BURGER is Professor of Political Science, University of Wisconsin - Marathon Campus in Wausau. She has authored *Opposition in a Dominant Party System* (Berkeley: University of California Press, 1969) as well as articles on South Asian security forces and ethnicity. Her Ph.D. is from University of Wisconsin-Madison.

JOHN DAMIS is Professor of Political Science and Associate Director of the Middle East Studies Center at Portland State University. In 1986 and 1987, he was a Visiting Professor at Harvard University. He is the author of *Conflict in Northwest Africa* and a coauthor of *The OAU After Twenty Years*, as well as numerous journal articles and contributions to collective works. He served for

xi

two years as a foreign affairs analyst for North Africa for the State Department. He received his Ph.D. from the Fletcher School of Law and Diplomacy.

RITA GIACALONE (Ph.D., Indiana University) is currently Head of the Department of Political and Social Analysis, and Associate Professor, Graduate Program of Political Science, Universidad de Los Andes, Mérida, Venezuela. Her publications include two books on Guyana and one on the Netherlands Antilles and Aruba (1990), plus articles in English and Spanish on the military in Venezuela, economic integration, and political and social developments in the English-speaking and Dutch-speaking Caribbean.

COBIE HARRIS received his Ph.D. in Political Science from the University of California, Los Angeles. Currently he teaches African Politics at San Jose State University. Dr. Harris's research interests include constitutional development in the post-colonial state in East Africa.

SARBJIT JOHAL received his B.A. from University of Reading, 1974; M.A. University of British Columbia, 1977; and Ph.D. University of California, Santa Barbara, 1984. Currently, he teaches Political Science at Merritt College. His publications include *Conflict and Integration in Indo-Pakistan Relations* (Berkeley: Centers for South and Southeast Asia Studies, 1989) and articles in *Asian Survey, Strategic Studies*, and *Journal of South Asian* and *Middle Eastern Studies*. Dr. Johal's research interests include South Asian regional politics and international political economy.

HAMAD KHATANI is a free-lance writer. He completed his academic studies in the United States and has taught political science in various American institutions of higher learning. Mr. Khatani has participated in many conferences dealing with the Middle East. His research interests include social movements, Islam and politics, and civil-military relations in the Arab world.

DIANE K. MAUZY is Associate Professor of Political Science at the University of British Columbia. She is the author, coauthor, or editor of over a dozen articles and five books, including *The Barisan Nasional: Coalition Government in Malaysia* (1983) and *Singapore: The Legacy of Lee Kuan Yew* (Westview, 1990).

BENJAMIN N. MUEGO is Professor of Political Science at Bowling Green State University (Firelands) and an Adjunct Professor of Southeast Asian Studies at the U.S. Foreign Service Institute in Arlington, Virginia. A well-published specialist on the Philippines, Professor Muego was a Visiting Fulbright-Hays Professor of Political Science at the University of the Philippines-Visayas in 1986-87, an East-West Center Fellow at the Institute of Southeast Asian Studies (Singapore) post- (1977-78), and a Continuing Fellow of the Inter-University Seminar on Armed Forces and Society.

CARL STONE, (Ph.D. in Political Science from the University of Michigan) is holder of a personal chair in Political Sociology, University of the West Indies. He is a newspaper columnist and pollster who has accurately predicted all national elections in Jamaica since 1972. He is the author of eight books on Caribbean and Third World politics including *Power in the Caribbean Basin* (1986), *Class State and Democracy in Jamaica* (1986), *Politics Versus Economics - The 1989 Elections in Jamaica* (1989), and *Understanding Third World Politics and Economics* (1980).

FREDERIC BELLE TORIMIRO (Ph.D., University of Missouri-Columbia) is Assistant Professor of Political Science and Coordinator of the International Studies Program at Ferrum College, Virginia. His publications include "Nigeria: The Uncertainty of a Long Term Legitimation of Political Leadership" in Constantine Danopoulos, ed., *Military Disengagement From Politics* (London: Routledge, 1988) and a forthcoming article on Chad in Karl P. Magyar and Constantine Danopoulos, eds., *Modern Prolonged Conflicts: Wars of the First Kind* (Montgomery, AL: Air University Press). He is a fellow of the Inter-University Seminar on Armed Forces and Society and was recently elected to *Who's Who in the South and Southwest*.

DANIEL ZIRKER is Associate Professor of Political Science at the University of Idaho. He has published extensively on Brazilian and African politics. During the 1989-90 academic year Dr. Zirker was a Fulbright Lecturer at the University of Dar es Salaam, Tanzania.

1

Civilian Supremacy in Changing Societies: Comparative Perspectives*

*Constantine P. Danopoulos***

Military involvement in politics, or praetorianism,[1] has been the primary method of government change and succession in the developing or changing societies of the Third World since the 1950s. A plethora of studies appeared seeking to analyze and understand the causes of praetorianism and the performance of soldiers as political governors. More recently, as military governments began withdrawing to the barracks in favor of civilian rulers, scholars produced an increasing volume of literature exploring the reasons and the nature of disengagement, as well as the future of civilian rule and democratization in the Third World.

*An earlier draft of this essay was presented at an international conference on (The Armed Forces and Military Service in a Democratic State) in Moscow, Russia (then USSR), November 25-28, 1991. The author wishes to thank the following inviting organizations: The Russian Association on Armed Forces and Society, the State Committee on Defense of the Russian Federation, the Committee of the U.S.S.R. Supreme Soviet on Science and Technology, the U.S.S.R. Philosophical Society, the Institute of Europe, the Institute of the U.S.A. and Canada (the U.S.S.R. Academy of Science), and the Soviet Committee for European Security and Cooperation.

**I wish to express my gratitude to James Walsh, Dean of Social Sciences at San Jose State University and Leticia A. McCart, Director of Program Development at San Jose State University Foundation for their encouragement and support.*

This rather pervasive preoccupation with the role of the military among students of civil-military relations belittles the fact that a good number of Third World countries managed to avoid direct military involvement in politics and maintained various types of civilian rule throughout their existence as independent nations. While the number of such praetorian-free developing countries is small, relative to those which have experienced coups and military rule, nevertheless they do not constitute totally isolated and unique phenomena. They are to be found in Asia, Caribbean, South America, the Middle East and Africa. Moreover, the type of continuous civilian rule in these countries ranges from traditional monarchies to multi-party democracies. While most of them display characteristics such as economic malaise, social fragmentation, corruption, and government inefficiency which are often cited as causes of praetorianism, others (Saudi Arabia and Malaysia) are considered economically prosperous. Yet, with the possible exception of Claude Welch's anthology, *Civilian Control of the Military*,[2] there is little in the literature that systematically and cross-culturally analyzes the factors that contributed to the maintenance of civilian rule in portions of the Third World. The present volume seeks to fill this void by featuring a number of case studies focussing on the factors, methods and means of civilian control of the military. The introductory essay seeks to draw generalizations, discernable patterns, and comparisons regarding this phenomenon, while the concluding essay speculates on the future of civilian rule and democracy in developing societies in a changing world environment.

The Case Studies

The countries selected for this volume include: four Asian (Sri Lanka, India, Malaysia, and the Philippines); one South American (Guyana); one Caribbean (Jamaica); two Middle Eastern (Jordan and Saudi Arabia); one North African (Morocco); and four Sub-Sahara Africa (Cameroon, Kenya, Tanzania and Zambia). An effort was made to include at least one country from the different regions of the Third World. A conscious attempt was also made to emphasize those geographic regions with the greatest number of praetorianism-free countries. As a result, Africa and Asia are more heavily represented while Latin America lags behind. Lastly, care was taken to offer examples of civilian control of the military in different types of political systems, ranging from traditional Middle Eastern monarchies to open and highly competitive democracies such as Jamaica and Sri Lanka. Understanding how civilian control was accomplished and maintained in diverse social, political and economic settings will give us a better understanding of the causes of praetorianism and the travails of disengagement, re-civilianization, and democratization that have dominated civil-military relations in the majority of developing societies.

On Military and Civilian Governments

When we speak of civilian or governmental control of the military, or "the subordination of military point of view to the political," as General Carl Maria von Clausewitz would have it,[3] we are not referring to a situation where the military is not a player in the political arena and has no influence on decision making regarding the politics of state security and wealth allocation. To the contrary, modern military organizations are well organized, politically and socially conscious entities capable and willing to be significant players in the political arena, like all other major social groups.

The distinction between civilian controlled governments and praetorian regimes, then, lies in the methods and means employed by the armed forces to promote their views, and the degree to which soldiers are willing to accept and implement the final decisions of the civilian authorities. In societies where the principle of civilian supremacy is accepted, the military is content to exert its influence through "bureaucratic bargaining [and] expert advice..., but [stands ready to] accept overall policy direction from government officials."[4] When the armed forces question the legitimacy and judgement of the civilian authorities and insist on direct participation in the decision making process, the principle of civilian supremacy is violated and the result is a mixed system of civilian-military governance.

Finally, when military officers step in and occupy the top governmental posts and subordinate civilian officials or relegate them to minor roles, we have military control of government, or praetorianism. In the end, the key indicator that distinguishes civilian-led versus praetorian regimes comes down to personnel. Robert Pinkney expresses the views of many scholars (including Finer,[5] Welch[6] and Huntington[7]) when he defines a military regime "as a form of government in which executive power rests within a military junta using the army as its main power base."[8]

The countries selected for this volume were chosen precisely because they had not experienced military control in their governance, although some (Morocco, Sri Lanka, Kenya, Saudi Arabia and Tanzania) experienced failed or abortive coups; while others, from time to time, have included military personnel in policy-making posts. That such plots failed and the military appetite for greater participation was contained can be attributed to a number of factors, including the resilience of civilian institutions, the existence of what Stepan calls a "civil society,"[9] and the circumstances beyond the borders of each state which coalesced to make the social conditions antithetic to intervention and discouraged the military's "capacity and propensity" for praetorianism.[10]

The Setting

Just as coups are linked to a number of factors,[11] civilian control of the military, which implies absence of successful coups, can be associated with certain societal conditions. Although each individual case has its own character, the durability of civilian rule in the countries discussed suggests that a number of generalizations can be made regarding those societal or environmental conditions which explain the establishment and maintenance of civilian control of the military in the Third World.

The single and all-encompassing explanation for civilian supremacy or military subordination involves the existence of congruency in values among different social groups, including the military. Broadly defined, value congruency connotes a basic consensus among different political and military élites on such matters as methods of governing, conflict resolution and leadership selection, foreign and security policy goals, and the ways of generating and distributing wealth. Such a broad consensus signifies that different societal élites and organized groups are committed to and support the existing polity, and are unlikely to resort to illegal means to affect governmental change. Value congruency can lead to regime legitimacy, which is defined as "the capacity of the system to engender and maintain the belief that the existing institutions are the most appropriate ones for the society."[12] Legitimacy is essential to regime survival and civilian rule; an illegitimate or nonlegitimate regime "is not long for this world."[13]

The existence and durability of value congruency depends on a number of important factors: historical background, social and cultural considerations, the presence of a unifying ideology or religion, geopolitical and international considerations, economic imperatives, and the nature of leadership.

Historical and Cultural Antecedents

Historical experiences influence the temperament, values and attitudes of a society. With the exception of Saudi Arabia, all countries included in this volume experienced British, French or American colonialism. In no small measure the very geographic and societal composition of these countries was determined, often arbitrarily, by the colonial power. The nature of institutions that emerged after independence and statehood, as well as the basic processes of government and even political and cultural attitudes, were influenced, if not adopted outright, from the colonial masters.

Many of the countries included in this volume gained their independence from Great Britain peacefully and gradually, through negotiations. Political struggle as opposed to armed struggle for independence meant absence of strong, well organized military organizations demanding an important role in the newly formed nations. The armed forces were rather small and in some cases, commanded by British officers for many years after independence was granted.

The British model of civil-military relations, based on the inviolate doctrine of political supremacy, "was carried into Zambia's postcolonial period," according to Baffour Agyeman-Duah. Neighboring Tanzania and Kenya displayed remarkably similar characteristics, as did India, Sri Lanka, Malaysia and Guyana. In India, for example, the armed forces "played no role in the independence movement,...were weak in numbers, leadership and equipment...and had to be led by British commanders." Under the circumstances, argues Sarbjit Johal, the civilian leadership had no difficulty establishing supremacy over the military. In Malaysia, the small and British trained and officered army, notes Diane Mauzy, "did not become associated or identified with the Malay nationalist movement" and thus could not claim that "it saved the independence revolution," as the armies of Indonesia or Algeria did.

Although circumstances differ, the experiences of Morocco and the Philippines show patterns similar to those just mentioned. John Damis states that during the period when Morocco was a French protectorate (1912-1956) "there was no Moroccan army at all [and] at the moment of its independence in 1956 [Morocco] was a country in need of a national army."

A negotiated and gradual approach to independence meant that the colonial power dealt with those indigenous forces that were "pliable" or enamored of the metropole's political values and practices. Those opposed to a negotiated or gradual approach to independence, in Cobie Harris' words, were "eliminated," "marginalized," or "banned from joining the armed forces." This approach culminated in the emergence of pre- and post-independence élites which favored strong ties to the ex-colonial power, and, in most cases, joined such metropole-sponsored politico-economic arrangements as the British Commonwealth or the French-inspired *Union Monétaire d'Afrique*.

The dominance of pro-western political values manifested itself in the appearance of parties favoring values bestowed by the colonial power. In competitive party states--such as Sri Lanka and Jamaica--all parties supported constitutional democracy, middle class values, universal suffrage, regular elections, and civilian-based government. This was also true in settings where many parties existed but one emerged dominant. Sarbjit Johal, for example, states that all Indian political parties supported Prime Minister Nehru and his Congress Party's political program, the *Congress culture*, which emphasized economic and social development through central planning, democratization by widening electoral participation, nonalignment in foreign affairs and civilian supremacy.

Malaysia's experience is similar. Although mindful not to neglect minorities, the British viewed the Malays as *primus inter pares*, with "special rights," and turned over power to the United Malays National Organization (UMNO) when it became apparent that the ethnic élites could compromise and resolve their ethnic differences and still win votes." British norms, procedures and traditions," states Diane Mauzy, "survived," are widely accepted, and have contributed to the "political subservience" of the Malaysian army.

Many one party states displayed equally strong attachments to the political values inherited from the colonial power, minus commitment to political competition. The governing parties of Tanzania, Cameroon, Zambia (until recently), and Kenya, operating in rather socially diverse settings, managed to survive and govern largely because they practiced the politics of inclusion, compromise and conciliation. For example, the Kenyan regime's "corporatist strategy," according to Cobie Harris, "manage[d] to engender stability and confidence in the government" and has played a major role in keeping the country's military in the barracks. Frederic Torimiro links "the character of civilian control" in Cameroon to the "effective" and "integrative role" played by that country's political party, the Cameroon National Union (CNU).

Although colonialism, in Cobie Harris' words, "effectively destroye[d] the credibility and legitimacy of indigenous institutions," colonial rulers may be credited for the propagation of constitutional and social norms resistant to praetorianism and supportive of civilian rule and constitutionalism. In Jamaica, for example, long exposure to British constitutional political values led to the development of "deep respect...for civilian led regimes, the rule of law and political rights" which, in Carl Stone's words, have "inhibited the development of military intervention in political life." Frederic Torimiro believes that in Cameroon "constitutionalism institutionalizes the subordinate relationship of the military"--a position echoed in Benjamin Muego's analysis of the Philippines.

He writes that "civilian supremacy is firmly rooted in [that] nation'[s] law and tradition" and is "enshrined" in Philippine constitutions. Angela Burger's findings regarding Sri Lanka lend additional credence. She argues that the Wellington model, which is based on constitutionalism and participatory institutions, is rather popular in that island republic and all major political parties and the military support the British inherited political institutions.

Mention should also be made of certain indigenous cultural traits that display negative and even contemptuous attitudes toward the military. The Philippines can be cited as a prime example. The drafters of that nation's first constitution viewed soldiers with "a fundamental distrust" and feared "the military's alleged propensity to resolve conflicts through the application of violence." These feelings are still strongly held in the Philippines today,and Filipinos see their armed forces as "a repressive, bloated, factious, poorly trained and ill-equipped organization." The "pantheon of Filipino heroes," declares Muego, "is dominated by men of letters, humanists, artists and statesmen" and not military men. The low esteem accorded to the military has been credited as one of the most important contributing factors to continuous civilian rule in the face of a worsening economy, mounting social problems and a continuing insurgency problem. Daniel Zirker underscores the importance of indigenous cultural traits, pointing to the "inclusive character of the Swahili culture," and to the "Tanzanian proclivity for peaceful political compromise, and a deep cultural suspicion of military intentions." Similar sentiments are also said to exist in the Caribbean, India, Sri Lanka, and Malaysia.

Social Class and Ethnic Origin

Value congruency can be affected through recruitment patterns which can either lead to a close, incestuous relationship between the dominant social and military élites, or to a pluralistic arrangement where the diversity of a country's ethnic groups making up a country is also reflected in the composition of its officer corps. The former is likely in societies with two or three ethnic groups or where one group is clearly dominant. Familial ties such as common schooling and family or clan ties often tend to be as important as common ethnic background, if not more so. By contrast, in truly multi-ethnic societies in which no ethnic group is dominant, representation by all ethnic groups in the military is strongly emphasized as a way of propagating the multiethnic character of the society and as a means of preventing social and military fragmentation that may lead to praetorianism.

Guyana, Saudi Arabia, Jordan, Malaysia, Sri Lanka, Kenya, and Jamaica seem to follow the interpenetration model which implies that both military and political élites are drawn from the same social class or ethnic group. In Guyana the composition of the Guyanese Defense Force (GDF) was transformed a few years after independence (1966) into "a predominantly black force with a black commander and a black officer corps." Rita Giacalone suggests that this was clearly designed to ensure the GDF's loyalty to the governing party (People's National Congress--PNC). Familial connections are equally strong in Malaysia between the ruling élite and senior army officers. These ties are also reinforced by "strong personal bonds" which are the "result of relationships between their families, and shared experiences" such as common language, schooling, religion, and common ethnic memories and aspirations. Jamaican officers come from the middle class and "tend to be supportive ...of civilian rule which places power in the hands of leadership elements dominated by that class."

The Saudi Arabian royal family chooses officers from loyal clans and promotion considerations are based on loyalty rather than competence. Hamad Khatani states that nearly all command posts are held by members of the Saudi royal family. John Damis is equally emphatic with respect to King Hussein's selection of military commanders. He reports that the Jordanian monarch appoints to "key command positions officers who [are] related to the ruling family or who [come from] traditional background"--considerations that also figure heavily in King Hassan's military promotion criteria in Morocco.

Kenyan recruitment patterns are designed to under represent the Kikuyus, the second largest but most anti-colonial group. As a result the Kikuyus were virtually excluded from the colonial army, and to this day their representation in the officer corps is smaller than their share in the country's total population. Instead, the Nairobi government has promoted the more friendly Karuba, who constitute 11 per cent of the population but occupy 28 per cent of the total number of slots in Kenya's officer corps.

The truly multi-ethnic societies of Tanzania and India represent a different picture, emphasizing a balanced and often meticulous ethnic representation in the officer corps. One of the pillars of continuous civilian rule in Tanzania, for example, is what Daniel Zirker refers to as "the strict formula of balanced recruitment and promotion" practiced in that country. These are echoed by similar patterns in India, Zambia and, to a lesser extent, Sri Lanka.

The Role of Ideology and Religion

The role of ideology, which is often based on religious doctrines, can act as a powerful generator and propagator of value congruency. An ideology can be a catch all vehicle that often serves as a framework for: action, analysis, justification and rationalization; as well as a blueprint for the present and the future. Islam is credited by Hamad Khatani and John Damis for providing the cohesive force that made it possible for the traditional Saudi, Moroccan and Jordanian monarchies to control their military at a time when dynastic rule appeared out of fashion. Making no distinction between civilian and military spheres, Islam combines the role of the political, religious and military leader in the same person. By invoking the precepts of Islam, the ruler "can justify his actions and declare unsanctified any acts that may threaten his supremacy, including military intervention." Khatani believes that Islam "provides the needed legitimacy upon which is based the continued domination of the royal family." By maintaining "virtually complete control" of such instruments of socialization as mosques, schools, and the mass media, the Saudi rulers are able to engender the belief that "moral quality and historical achievements give them the right to rule the country alone."

Damis' account regarding the impact of Islam in Jordan and Morocco assigns religion/ideology an equally compelling role in the maintenance of civilian rule. Kings Hussein of Jordan and Hassan of Morocco hold the title of *Sharif*, i.e., "descendant of the Prophet Muhammad." This gives these two monarchs "Islamic legitimacy in the eyes of traditional sectors" of their societies. In Moroccan (Islamic law), notes Damis, the king is "commander of the faithful, the stewart of God on earth for all matters, religious or secular, which means in effect that he is above the law: his decisions cannot be questioned nor can his person be criticized." Under such widely held and powerful precepts "potential usurpers of power...hesitate before attacking the symbol of national unity and values." In predominantly Islamic Malaysia the *Agung* (king) and the "Rulers" are regarded by Mauzy as "highly pertinent symbols of Malay political control."

In secular settings the influence of ideology or religion may not be as influence but can be of considerable importance as a unifying force and generator of value congruency. Julius Nyerere's successful promotion of nationalism, village socialism and Kiswahili as Tanzania's *lingua franca* is a case in point. President Kaunda's emphasis on humanism, which Agyeman-Duah describes as an ideology which advocated a "human centered society with traditional communal values," became Zambia's "cornerstone of domestic politics [and gave] the President a powerful moral position to draw on and reconcile the various elements" in his society. Finally, the post-colonial state in Kenya managed to escape military intervention by successfully utilizing a pre-colonial developmental model based on corporatism and agricultural commercialization.

International Considerations

Factors or developments beyond the borders of a nation state can contribute either to military intervention or to the maintenance of civilian rule. Great powers -- citing ideological, geographic, and other "vital" interests -- have intervened (directly or indirectly) in the affairs of smaller states to prop up unpopular regimes, help suppress popular revolutions, or bring down "undesirable" governments. History is replete with examples of such interventions. Guatemala, the Dominican Republic, Czechoslovakia, and Hungary are just four on the long list of countries experiencing foreign intervention in domestic politics since World War II. It is questionable whether dynastic rule would have survived in Jordan, Saudi Arabia and Morocco without Western support, and equally doubtful that democratization in Eastern Europe would have taken place without Moscow's consent.

Value congruency between the military and political élites may be fostered by forces operating outside the borders of the nation-state or by that state's efforts to influence or control those outside forces. In the first instance foreign governments may undertake direct or indirect intervention. In the second instance the state may pursue a policy to prevent the loss of a portion of its territory or become involved with its neighbors in a regional dispute.

For our purposes, forces operating outside the borders of a nation-state and efforts made to influence or control such forces may help foster value congruency between the military and political élites. This can take the form of direct or indirect intervention by a foreign power, involvement in regional disputes, or pursuing a policy aimed to prevent the dismemberment of a state or prevent the loss of a portion of its territory.

The towering presence of France is credited by Frederic Torimiro as having played a role in the survival of civilian rule in Cameroon, Ivory Coast, Gabon and Gambia. Under the policy of "no development without security" and strong economic ties, France intervened directly or indirectly in these countries, often at the request of incumbent governments, to quell rebellions or threats against them. French officers "established the Cameroon Pacification Zone" which, in Torimiro's words, was "designed to subdue...internal rebellion against the Ahidjo regime." Cameroonian officers enjoy close contacts with their French counterparts. The French government closely monitors the activities of the Paris-based opposition groups, and the republic's current President, Paul Biya, "continues to maintain strong Franco-Cameroonian ties." Stone sees Washington's role in Caribbean developments in remarkably similar terms.

Damis' analysis of the Moroccan situation supports the view that pursuing a policy aimed at preventing the loss of territory can be an effective vehicle of national unity. King Hassan's efforts to frustrate the secession of Western Sahara, advocated by the Polisario guerillas, created a "broad and genuine political consensus" in Morocco. The king "tapped into a large reservoir of public emotion and used the Sahara issue to forge a common nationalist cause around which all major political parties rallied." This served Hassan well and proved beneficial in his efforts to keep the military under control. The Middle East problem has had similar results for King Hussein in Jordan.

Regional problems in Southern Africa propelled Zambia and Tanzania to the forefront in the struggle against colonialism and racism. As a "Frontline State," Zambia "played a heroic role in harboring liberation fighters and assisting in the search of just peace." This served President Kaunda well and enabled him to get the Zambian people to rally "around their leader who was seen as a helpless victim of aggrandizement by his white neighbors." In Agyeman-Duah's estimation, this policy "has ensured the survivability of civilian rule in Zambia," as did the "dearth" of coups in that subregion.[14] In Tanzania the Nyerere government took a similar stand regarding subregional problems and gave its military "a legitimate foreign mission." The "'momentum' of this policy," argues Zirker, had "salutary domestic effects" and kept the armed forces occupied "in non-threatening and even diplomatically desirable activity."

Regional considerations seem to have played a role in India and Sri Lanka as well. Disputes with China and Pakistan and the desire to preserve "the stability" of neighboring states (Nepal, Bangladesh, Sri Lanka, and the Maldives) heightened New Delhi's concern with "superpower activity" in the area. Of special importance to Indian civilian and military leaders are the lessons drawn "from Pakistan's history of military rule and alliance with the United States....which led the Pakistani military to expand its power relative to civilian institutions." The policies of non-alignment and self-reliance on defense, inaugurated by Prime Minister Jawaharlal Nehru, were designed to meet India's internal and external security. They have survived to this date virtually with no interruption, and are strongly supported by civilian and military leaders. India's nonalignment, geographic location, and the importance New Delhi attaches to Sri Lanka, Angela Burger believes, contributed the "hands off" attitude that Moscow and Washington adopted toward Sri Lanka. This "hands off" policy was a major factor in maintaining civilian rule, for it gave no reason or vehicle to either of the two superpowers to "foment a coup" in that island republic.

Economic Factors

Economic imperatives, i.e., policies relating to methods and means of making and distributing wealth, have long been considered important stimuli to praetorianism. Most analysts of civil-military relations agree that severe economic dislocations cause legitimacy deflation and may facilitate interventionism.[15] While important and well founded, this conclusion is of little help when it comes to explaining why certain developing countries, often faced with overwhelming economic problems, have managed to fend off praetorianism. Poor economic performance factors can stimulate praetorianism, but do not necessarily explain the emergence of value congruency and the maintenance of civilian control. Tanzania's per capita income is actually lower than Ghana's, and the Jamaican middle class saw its purchasing power decline in the 1980s much the same way Brazil's and Chile's decreased in the 1960s and 1970s. Yet while the armed forces of Ghana, Brazil and Chile stepped in and seized the levers of authority, their Tanzanian and Jamaican counterparts stayed in the barracks. The role of economics in the maintenance of civilian rule in the developing world is an important subject that needs to be investigated further. Any conclusions drawn from our findings must remain tentative.

However, one can argue that economic policies which allocate the armed forces a hefty portion of a country's wealth go a long way toward satisfying military corporate interests. These interests include adequate budgetary support which, if affected adversely, can become one of the most powerful interventionist motives.[16] A country's economic health often determines the ability of its government to meet corporate military interests, although this is not absolute. But the issue of corporate interests relates more to the methods and means employed by civilians to control the military than establishing and maintaining value congruency, it will be more fully discussed in the last portion of this essay.

Leadership and Its Implications

Ann Ruth Willner defines leadership as "a relatively sustained and asymmetric exercise of influence by one individual, the leader, over others, the followers."[17] There is little doubt that the quality of leadership exercised by those in key positions can be of great importance in forging and maintaining an outlook and policies that can provide the basis for value congruency. Inspired and effective stewardship can pick the right time, make the necessary concessions, display vision and determination, show compassion, and touch the sensitive rational and emotional chords of civilians and military alike. Leadership, says Thomas Cronin,

> is all about making things happen that otherwise might not happen and preventing things from happening that ordinarily would happen. It is the process of getting people to work together to achieve common goals

and aspirations. It involves the infusion of vision and purpose into an enterprise and entails mobilizing both people and resources to undertake and achieve desired goals.[18]

Besides charismatic leadership which by nature tends to be rare, idiosyncratic, personalistic, thaumaturgical and often messianic and uncompromising, Oran R. Young recognizes three additional types of leadership: *structural, entrepreneurial* and *intellectual. Structural* leadership acts in the name of a firm, a nation, or a well established and legitimate societal structure. This type of a leader engages in institutional bargaining and "leads by devising effective ways to bring" the resources of his or her office to bear in order to gain maximum negotiating leverage for the purpose of working out acceptable agreements. The *entrepreneurial* leader on the other hand, may or may not represent the state, but uses his or her negotiating skills to frame issues and work out deals and arrangements that may not have been otherwise possible. Finally, the *intellectual* leader "relies on the power of ideas" and "produces intellectual capital" which can provide the framework for handling issues and finding acceptable solutions.

However, Young's categories are not exclusive, and it is possible for the same person to possess characteristics associated with more than one type of leadership. Moreover, his framework is based on examples and processes associated with international politics. Nevertheless, it can be used to categorize and understand the role of leadership in domestic politics as well as international relations. Like the latter, the former involves bargaining arrangements, and coalition and institution building. And the diverse, multi-ethnic, and often fragmented character of many developing societies resembles the contentious politics of "regime formation" at the international level. The role of leadership, therefore, can be "a critical determinant of success or failure" in the domestic as well as international arena.

Furthermore, Young's typology can be utilized to classify the role and contributions toward establishing value congruency and maintaining civilian rule by some of the leading protagonists mentioned in the essays that follow. Though subjective in nature and fraught with leader profiles that are less than complete, a classification attempt is worth the risk. The *structural* category includes those leaders who have operated in societies with well accepted components of constitutional government, but which faced daunting economic and social problems after independence. It also encompasses those leaders who have functioned in milieus characterized by long tradition and attachment to widespread religious precepts or ideological dogmas. Kings Hassan of Morocco, Hussein of Jordan, and Ibn Saud of Saudi Arabia and his successors can be classified as *structural* leaders. By their use of Islam and, in Hassan's case, the monarchy's long historical tradition, these rulers managed to forge value congruencies among the major segments of their societies which, in turn, helped them forestall praetorianism. King Hussein's extraordinary dexterity, strength, and acumen are credited by John Damis as perhaps the most important factors in the survival of the Hashimite monarchy in Jordan. Government leaders in Sri Lanka and Jamaica and Nehru's successors in India used the strong and highly legitimate institutional and political arrangements in those countries to make and implement desired policies. They, too, appear to meet many of the characteristics associated with *structural* leadership.

By contrast the *entrepreneurial* category includes leaders who had to operate in societies devoid of broadly accepted traditional values or a unifying religion/ideology. To make up for such deficiencies, leaders such as Kenneth Kaunda and Jomo Kenyatta utilized the sheer force of their personality. Agyeman-Duah praises President Kaunda's "frugality, moderation, and pragmatism" and his ability to "rise above factionalism" and to balance the interests of Zambia's ethnic groups. Kenyatta's background and links to the Mau Mau revolt allowed him "to infuse his tremendous amount of personal credibility into the executive office" with a "teflon" effect. He was never held personally accountable for the shortcomings of his regime.

Besides Kaunda and Kenyatta the *entrepreneurial* category fits the leadership style of Guyana's Forbes Burnham, Cameroon's Alhaji Ahmadou Ahidjo, Malaysia's Tunku Abdul Rahman, and the Philippines' Ramon Magsaysay and Ferdinand Marcos. Often using strong arm tactics, Ahidjo used his skills to present himself as the "nation's father" and to install a governing framework that personalized leadership which, in spite of its many autocratic features, provided his regime with "the capacity to manage the character of civilian rule." Burham employed almost identical tactics in Guyana.

Though he fits this category, the case of Ferdinand Marcos is somewhat unique. Even though he rose to power through legal means, Marcos perverted his nation's well accepted constitutional framework, and governed as a virtual dictator until the overthrow in 1986. During what many regard as the extraconstitutional period (1972-1986), through strong arm tactics, versatility, and sheer cunning, Marcos divided his opponents, forged an alliance with powerful landlords and commercial oligarchs, coopted the military, and managed to maintain civilian but authoritarian rule. Although he was distinctive, Marcos can still be categorized as an *entrepreneurial* type of leader.

Finally, *intellectual* leadership, exemplified by Jawaharlal Nehru and Julius Nyerere, is responsible for giving birth to ideas that provided the binding force that sufficed to keep together the multinational and diverse societies of India and Tanzania. Nehru is viewed as the prime architect of the *Congress culture* which emphasized economic and social development through central planning, self reliance in defense economy and technology, electoral democracy, and non-alignment in foreign policy. Nyerere's literary and intellectual accomplishment--which includes translation of some of Shakespeare's works into Kiswahili, a self-styled village socialism, and the drive to legitimize Swahili as Tanzania's *lingua franca*--coupled with his personal honesty and "adroit nationalistic leadership" played no small part in nation-building and the maintenance of values conducive to civilian rule in Tanzania.

Besides intellectual leadership skills Nyerere and Nehru also possessed considerable negotiating skills and coalition-building abilities associated with the other two leadership types. Likewise, leaders that have been classified as *structural* or *entrepreneurial* also display qualities associated with more than one of the three categories. In addition to his use of Islam, King Hussein is known to possess considerable negotiating skill and intellectual qualities which have made it possible for him to work out deals and find solutions to difficult and seemingly irreconcilable social problems. Kenneth Kaunda's emphasis on humanism and communal values as Zambia's cornerstones of domestic politics are characteristics that fit both *intellectual* as well as *structural* leadership. The same can be said about Tunku Abdul Rahman, Jomo Kenyatta, King Hassan and even Ferdinand Marcos.

The Methods and Means

While value congruency inhibits the military disposition to intervene, specific methods and means of control adopted and carried out by civilians can also hinder the capacity and the will of the officer corps to stage successful coups. The contributors to this volume make it clear that government employ a number of control mechanisms to ensure military subordination and enhance civilian control of the armed forces. Such methods include party penetration and the use of intelligence, civilian command structures, divided command authority, and geographic dispersion, maintaining rival security organizations, satisfying corporate concerns, and allowing for military participation in politics. Let us be more specific.

Party Penetration and Use of Intelligence

Party penetration and extensive use of spying usually takes place in societies characterized by limited democracy, one party government, or hereditary rule. By extending party organization into the armed forces, requiring officers to meet party or ideological criteria for appointment and promotion, or even mandating that officers join the ruling party, the regimes of Zambia, Tanzania, Guyana, Kenya and Cameroon have managed to monitor the activities of their armed forces and to promote those officers least likely to lead coups. In some cases, civilian leaders themselves join the military. Prime Minister Forbes Burnham of Guyana, for example, promoted himself to "general" (even though the highest rank in the Guyanese Defense Force was that of brigadier) and appeared in public ceremonies in military attire.

Penetration of the armed forces by hereditary regimes appears equally pervasive. Instead of political parties being the penetrators, hereditary regimes rely on members of the royal family or clan to play that role. In Saudi Arabia, Jordan, and Morocco high military or national defense posts are occupied by princes, cousins or other members of the royal dynasty. Khatani goes as far to suggest that the ruling family in Saudi Arabia is "the only unofficial ruling party" and "the only member-state of the United Nations whose very name denotes family dominion."

Besides party or royal family penetration, most of these regimes also rely heavily on well organized and omnipresent security networks to keep the military loyal and to destroy possible praetorian activities at their genesis. For example, Agyeman-Duah believes that alleged coup plots in Zambia "could not materialize due in large part to the efficiency of [Kaunda's] internal security system." Damis concurs, saying that the *mukhabarat*, "the renowned loyal intelligence apparatus," and the secret police have infiltrated the military, the Palestinian refugee camps, and all other social organization in Jordan. Democratic regimes, although making protestations to the contrary, are not altogether beyond spying on their citizens, including the military.

Civilian Command Authority

This refers to the imposition of a civilian dominated authority, which includes military participation, charged with responsibility of making decisions relating to defense policy. Such a structure usually involves a civilian led and staffed ministry of defense, as well as a supreme council of national defense consisting of the head of government and other high government officials. Although such organizational mechanisms exist in nearly all civilian dominated countries, they tend to be more prominent in societies with competitive political parties and other democratic features as executive accountability, freedom of press and regular elections. Public opinion and democratic procedures and practices mandate the existence of such structures. India is a case in point. According to Johal, that country's military "finds itself in a subordinate position" at all levels of India's defense organization. Defense policy decisions "are made by civilians in the Political Affairs Committee of the cabinet, which includes the Prime Minister and the Ministers of Defense, External Affairs, Home and Finance." But India is not unique. Similar civilian dominated structures are responsible for defense policy in Sri Lanka, Malaysia, and the Philippines, as well as in less competitive systems of Zambia, Tanzania, and Guyana. They even exist, albeit more circumscribed, in hereditary settings as Morocco and Saudi Arabia.

Divided Military

Another factor that helps ensure government control is to maintain separate and even competitive command structures in the different services, and to keep the armed forces dispersed around the countryside and major metropolitan centers. Such methods are often necessitated by a country's physical geography, geographic location and size, but can also be the result of deliberate decisions on the part of the civilian authorities. Separate command structures engender communication and coordination difficulties and unleash competition with regard to weapons, resources, turf, and responsibility. Successful coups are deliberate but illegal acts which require speed, coordination, secrecy, and precision. Armies that are organizationally divided, physically separated, and led by multiple and often competitive command structures, are not in the best position to intervene and establish praetorian regimes.

The analyses that follow make this clear. Khatani, for example, believes that the Saudi regime keeps its military scattered around the "vast and forbidding terrain" of the Arabian Peninsula in order "to prevent fraternization and the development of cells of disloyal subjects." Furthermore, the regime rotates military personnel very frequently, thus making it "difficult for any commander or unit to launch a coup that could threaten the government." India's "non-overlapping" service structure is further divided into thirteen different regional commands. This coupled with the country's multiple centers of political, economic and military powers "mean that it is not enough to take control of New Delhi." Johal concludes that a "military coup in one or two cities would risk the possibility of countercoups and resistance by other military units or Indian political parties and labor unions."

Another dimension to the physical allocation of military personnel as a method of maintaining civilian control is to require officers to live alongside the population and involve the armed forces in the building and maintaining a country's economic infrastructure, a practice commonly known as civic action. The underlying assumption is that civic action gives the military a non-military focus, allows it to be a direct participant in the nation's economic development and thus share in the successes and failures of such endeavors, and creates a closer bond between the armed forces and the civilian population. Placing military barracks in the middle of civilian neighborhoods renders military conspiracies more difficult to plan and carry out. Although practiced by some governments around the world, the Tanzanian experience is probably the most effective. President Nyerere advocated this policy because he felt that "the military should serve as a socio-economic militia [and] that national development should be its central focus." Zirker believes that the policy was effective for it managed "to suspend the military in civil society, limiting its (military's) political options, and ....potential popular support."

Creating Rival Organizations

Establishing functional rivals that may threaten the prestige and very survival of the military is often associated with powerful interventionist motives.[19] Yet almost every contributor to this volume credits the existence of a militia, a national guard, or a palace guard for acting as a counterweight to the regular military and bolstering the ability of the civilian authorities to control the military. In Malaysia, for instance, the Royal Malay Regiment and the Special Service Regiment are entirely Malay and are considered the "most loyal and most trusted corps." No army take over can occur in that country, Mauzy believes, without their support. The National Guard in Saudi Arabia, under the direct control of the royal family, is drawn from trusted tribes, is very well equipped, and is stationed in key locations around the country, including oil fields and the palace. Khatani feels that the Guard is "an effective counterforce to the regular army" and capable to "deal effectively with internal security problems."

Do the experiences of the case studies included here, contradict the well-supported conclusion that creating functional rivals damages the military's corporate interests and generates interventionist motives? Not really! A lot depends on when such functional rivals are established. If a national guard or a militia predate the creation of the regular army, or the two emerged concomitantly, the level of fear by military officers regarding their corporate interests is likely to be less intense. It is uncertainty about the future role of the military and the officers' professional well being that lead to praetorianism, and not the opposite. A great deal also depends on the extent to which the civilian authorities manage to delineate clear and distinct roles for paramilitary organizations and the regular military. Confusion and overlapping responsibilities can lead to interventionism. It is worth noting that in the case studies that follow paramilitary units either predate the emergence of regular armies or both security forces were created at the same time. Governing élites have also been careful to delineate separate and clear spheres of responsibility between the armed forces and paramilitary units.

Corporate Interests

Professionalization is the single most salient characteristic of modern soldiery. It renders the military into an "autonomous" and highly independent corporate structure," willing and able to intervene in the political process in order to protect its corporate interests.[20] According to Nordlinger,[21] besides protection of the military organization against encroachments from rival institutions and ensuring survival, corporate interests include adequate budgetary support and institutional autonomy to manage internal affairs. Budgetary appropriations "serve as a telling indicator of the political power and prestige of the armed forces." Civilian interference in promotions, assignments, training and strategy formation, "call into doubt the soldiers' identities...and weaken the officers' power to defend their corporate interests." Defending the military's corporate interests constitutes "the most common and salient interventionist motive."

The experiences of the countries under study exemplify this observation. Abortive coups by the Tanzanian, Saudi, Zambia and Sri Lankan military were all inspired by corporate concerns. The speed with which the civilian leaders in these countries moved to rectify these concerns strengthens the view regarding the saliency of corporate interests. With no exception, all contributors assign a great deal of importance to this factor and see the survival of civilian rule in the developing world inexorably connected to the ability and willingness of the civilian leadership to respect military corporate interests and dispense generous salaries and other benefits to their officers. Even in countries like Tanzania, Kenya, Guyana and Jordan where civilian leaders interfere with promotions, they are careful not to go beyond making appointments to the highest posts--a prerogative accorded to almost all chief executives and generally accepted by the military of all countries.

Military Participation in Politics

Finally, consistent but limited participation in politics in the form of bureaucratic bargaining and expert advice is another method used by civilians to keep the military in the barracks.[22] It is widely suggested in this volume that civilian leaders make it possible for the military to have input in defense policy, strategy and even decisions regarding resource allocations. Isolating the military breeds suspicion, resentment and plotting. That governments increased defense budgets following coup attempts or conspiracies, and that officers are given party, and in some cases, cabinet posts can be cited as evidence pointing to consistent but limited military participation in politics, and indicative of the importance civilian leaders attach to the views of their military. Civic action programs tend to accomplish similar goals.

Summing Up

The preceding discussion and the essays that follow support the view that civilian control of the armed forces cannot be accomplished by separating the armed forces from society in an effort to render them "politically sterile and neutral" servants of the state, as Huntington suggested.23 Instead, civilian rule involves the existence of value congruency between different societal groups, including the military. However, value congruency is not a static, changeless "state of things," but a dynamic process that requires constant adjustments, reinforcement, and a lot of give and take between societal participants. Crafting and maintaining value congruency involves group participation and a sense of involvement in the definition of the broad methods and means of governing, conflict resolution, leadership selection, foreign and security policy goals, and the ways of generating and distributing wealth. Exclusionary politics can lead to value variegation between major social groups and resort to illegal means in order to restore or gain access in the process of value articulation.

In the final analysis, civilian control of the military cannot be accomplished through abstract principles and sweeping political pronouncements. Instead, civilian supremacy involves the interplay between military institutions and societal political processes, and can only be maintained through concrete policies and open channels of communication. Let us see the details.

Notes

1. Military intervention or praetorianism is defined as "a situation in which military officers are major or predominant political actors by virtue of their actual or threatened use of force." See Eric A. Nordlinger, *Soldiers in Politics: Military Coups and Governments* (Englewood Cliffs: Prentice-Hall, Inc., 1977), p. 2.

2. While very valuable and path-breaking, this anthology is not based exclusively on the Third World. It also contains at least two cases (Mexico and Chile) where the military have intervened. See Claude E. Welch, Jr., ed., *Civilian Control of the Military--Theory and Cases from Developing Countries* (Albany: State University of New York Press, 1976).

3. General Carl Maria von Clausewitz, *On War* (London: Routledge and Kegan Paul, 1966), vol. III, pp. 424-425.

4. Claude E. Welch, Jr., *No Farewell to Arms?--Military Disengagement from Politics in Africa and Latin America* (Boulder: Westview Press, 1987), pp. 9-14.

5. Samuel E. Finer, *The Man on Horseback: The Role of the Military in Politics*, 2nd Enlarged Edition (Boulder: Westview Press, 1988).

6. Welch, *No Farewell to Arms?*

7. Samuel P. Huntington, *Political Order in Changing Societies* (New Haven: Yale University Press, 1968).

8. Robert Pinkney, *Right-Wing Military Government* (Boston: Twayne Publishers, 1990), p. 10.

9. Alfred Stepan defines a civil society to mean an "arena where manifold social movements (such as neighboring associations, women's groups, religious groupings, and intellectual currents and civil organizations form all classes (such as lawyers, journalists, trade unions and entrepreneurs) attempt to constitute themselves in an ensemble of arrangements so that they can express themselves and advance their interests." See his *Rethinking Military Politics--Brazil and the Southern Cone* (Princeton: Princeton University Press, 1988), pp. 3-4.

10. Samuel E. Finer, *The Man on Horseback*, p. 224.

11. Claude E. Welch, Jr., "The Roots and Implications of Military Interventions," in Claude E. Welch, ed., *Soldiers and State in Africa* (Evanston: Northwestern University Press, 1970), p. 17.

12. Seymor Martin Lipset, *Political Man: The Social Basis of Politics* (Garden City, N.J.: Doubleday, 1960), p. 77.

13. David Easton, "The Analysis of Political Systems," in Roy C. Macridis and Bernard E. Brown, eds., *Comparative Politics: Notes and Readings*, 4th ed. (Homewood, IL: Dorsey Press, 1972), p. 80.

14. Coups in particular countries are often "contagious" and spill over into neighboring states. See Welch, "The Roots and Implications of Military Interventions," p. 17.

15. Nordlinger, *Soldiers in Politics*, pp. 88-90.

16. *Ibid.*, pp. 66-71.

17. Ann Ruth Willner, *The Spellbinders: Charismatic Political Leadership* (New Haven: Yale University Press, 1984), p. 5.

18. Thomas E. Cronin, "Foreword," in William E. Rosenbach and Robert L. Taylor, eds., *Contemporary Issues in Leadership*, 2nd edition (Boulder: Westview Press, 1989), p. xiii.

19. Nordlinger, *Soldiers in Politics* pp. 66-71.

20. Bengt Abrahamsson defines professionalization in terms of a specialized theoretical knowledge accompanied by methods and devices for its application; responsibility, grounded on a set of technical skills; and a high degree of corporateness deriving from common training and devotion to specific doctrines and customs. See his *Military, Professionalization and Political Power.*

21. Nordlinger, *Soldiers in Politics*, pp. 66-71.

22. Welch, *No Farewell to Arms?* p. 17.

23. Samuel P. Huntington, *The Soldier and the State* (New York: Random House, 1962), p. 84.

2

Sources of Political Stability in Modernizing Monarchical Regimes: Jordan and Morocco

John Damis

Jordan and Morocco lie at the opposite ends of the Arab world. The Hashimite Kingdom of Jordan is in the heart of the Mashriq or Eastern Arab world, far from the Kingdom of Morocco, which occupies the western part of the Maghreb or Arab West. Jordan, a relatively small state with a population of some 3 million, is surrounded by more powerful neighbors, while Morocco and its 25 million inhabitants are a force to be reckoned with in northwest Africa. Both these kingdoms are constitutional monarchies in which the king exercises, to all extent and purposes, absolute power. Both kings--Hussein of Jordan and Hassan II of Morocco--have managed to retain the support of their militaries throughout a series of crises and attempted coups. This chapter examines the factors and policies that have enabled these two monarchies to avoid praetorian rule. The analysis focuses on the maintenance of civilian rule in Jordan since the Six-Day Arab-Israeli War of June 1967 and in Morocco since independence in 1956.

JORDAN

Unlike Morocco, Jordan's emergence as a nation-state is a relatively recent phenomenon. Its creation dates from the post-World War I period when Britain and France assigned to themselves mandates over various portions of Arab lands in the Middle East that had formerly been part of the Ottoman Empire. As a reward to the Hashimite clan--the long-time rulers of the Hijaz district of the Arabian Peninsula, who had actively supported the British war effort against Turkey--Britain created in 1922 the emirate of Transjordan (whose territory corresponded to the present Kingdom of Jordan) and then installed as *emir*, Abdallah, the second son of Sharif Hussein, the ruler of the Hijaz. British subsidies and military leadership contributed greatly to the order and tranquility that the modest emirate enjoyed from 1922 until Britain granted full independence in 1946 and Abdullah became king.

This period of tranquility was shattered by the Arab-Israeli war of 1948-1949, a conflict that dramatically transformed Jordan's political system. The war ended with Jordanian forces in control of the West Bank and the eastern part of Jerusalem, including the old city. By 1950, Abdallah had been proclaimed the king of Palestine by a conference of West Bank notables and he formerly annexed the territory, thereby giving the country its present name, Jordan. The new state now had a mixed and largely bifurcated population: on the East Bank (the former Transjordan) was a traditional desert tribal society, while on the West Bank lived mostly sedentary and better educated Palestinians. This mixed population greatly complicated the efforts of the Hashimite ruling family in Jordan to achieve political legitimacy.[1] Jordan's present territory resulted from the loss of the West Bank and East Jerusalem to Israel in the Six-Day War of June 1967.

Civil-Military Relations

Many students of Jordanian politics would agree that the army is, without question, the most important institution in Jordan. Historically, the army has played a key role both in national development and regional policy and has served as the regime's first line of defense against internal and external threats. The quality of the Jordanian military is probably unmatched in the Arab world. Since the 1920's, the Jordanian army has maintained internal security, and its only defeat came against superior Israeli forces in June 1967. [2]

The consolidation of the emirate of Transjordan and its transformation from a desert territory to an organized state was largely the work of the Arab Legion--as Jordan's army was known until 1956--established by a British officer in 1923. The Arab Legion's critical importance prompted one observer to describe Transjordan as "an army with a country attached."[3] The army was initially formed by merging a local police force with a reserve force recruited mainly from among Egyptians, Sudanese, and Palestinians. Sir John Bagot Glubb (widely known as "Glubb Pasha") played a major role in the development and subsequent deployment of the Arab Legion. He formed a desert patrol of Bedouins which, by 1933, brought order to the tribes. Glubb became commander of the Arab

Legion in 1939 and held that key position until his dismissal in 1956. Under the command of British officers, the army provided the essential base of support for the monarchy and traditional forces in Jordan.[4]

The dismissal of Glubb Pasha reflected the growing Arab nationalist orientation of younger officers, especially Palestinians, recruited after the annexation of the West Bank in 1950. The discovery in April 1957 of a planned coup d'état by the chief of the general staff prompted King Hussein, who had ascended the throne in 1953 on his eighteenth birthday, to take steps to ensure the loyalty of the army. To protect his throne from further attempts to install praetorian rule, Hussein strengthened the Bedouin units of the army and the special forces of the palace; he also appointed to key command positions officers who were related to the ruling family or who had a traditional background.[5]

The enhanced loyalty of the army was evident in the aftermath of Jordan's defeat in the June 1967 war. Despite the crushing defeat by Israeli forces, which caused considerable dissatisfaction in the army, there was no organized military move against Hussein. Instead, some younger officers began voluntarily cooperating with Palestinian *fedayeen* groups which carried out guerrilla raids across the Jordan River. By actively pursuing the military struggle against Israel, the *fedayeen* groups attracted widespread popular support in Jordan and throughout the Arab world in the years following the humiliating defeat of 1967. This support involved both financial donations and young volunteers, which greatly emboldened the Palestinian commandos. Within three years, the *fedayeen* groups built up a military structure within Jordan to the point where they formed a "state within a state" that increasingly challenged the authority of the government and threatened the security of the Jordanian monarchy.

The inherent tensions between the *fedayeen* militias and the Jordanian army, reflected in occasional tests of strength in 1968 and 1969, came to a head in open conflict in 1970. During an initial round of civil strife in June, resulting in nearly a thousand people killed or wounded, the loyalty of some parts of the military was questionable. King Hussein responded by dismissing some key army commanders and making other gestures intended to appease the Palestinians and younger officers. The challenge posed by the Palestinian organizations to King Hussein's authority reached a full-blown crisis in "Black September" of 1970. When the *fedayeen* militias refused government orders to lay down their arms and evacuate the cities, the royalist officers and tribal army assaulted the Palestinian urban strongholds. A bitter nine-day civil war ensued, with enormous destruction and some 4,000 deaths. With this forceful government assault followed by a second crackdown in the summer of 1971, the King's army succeeded in driving the Palestinian   guerrilla organizations and their militias out of Jordan.[6]

The September 1970 civil war represented the most serious organized military challenge to Hashimite rule in Jordan and, at the same time, it severely tested the loyalty of some elements within the Jordanian army. In particular, the fighting between the army and Palestinian guerrilla units posed a dilemma for Jordanian officers and soldiers of Palestinian origin. In this difficult situation, some of these officers defected to the Palestine Liberation Organization (PLO), but most remained loyal to King Hussein and their troops carried out orders given by the Jordanian high command.

In the two decades since the 1970 civil war, the Jordanian military has consistently remained subordinate to civilian rule. Its record of non-interference in politics is clearly better than that of the Moroccan military and this subordination to civilian rule is matched in the Arab world only by the armed forces of Tunisia, Saudi Arabia, and the Persian Gulf shaikhdoms.

Civilian Rule in Jordan

Because of frequent political crises--usually stemming from the Arab-Israeli issue or inter-Arab politics--many observers of Jordanian affairs in the 1950's and 1960's viewed the rule of the Hashimite monarchy as precarious. The survival of civilian rule in Jordan into the 1990's has thus surprised a good many skeptics. Much of the credit for continuing civilian rule must go to the personal leadership of King Hussein.

Civilian rule in Jordan is exercised primarily through the power and authority of King Hussein. Though Jordan's current constitution, promulgated in 1952, increased somewhat the authority of parliament, the palace clearly retained the ultimate authority over the legislative, executive, and judicial branches of the government. Thus, though the country is formally a constitutional monarchy, the political reality is that the king holds near absolute power. The autonomy of Jordan's parliament has been minimal; the lower (elective) house--the Chamber of Deputies--was suspended by Hussein from 1974 to 1984. Elections and elective government are discretionary; in many respects this means they are also advisory. If the king was opposed to the actions of a parliament or a government, he has been able to dissolve parliament or change his government. Martial law was in effect almost continuously from 1967 to 1990. After a brief period of activity in the mid-1950's, political parties were banned from 1957 until June 1991.

In contrast to the relative weakness of civilian institutions of rule, King Hussein has managed to acquire a fair measure of personal legitimacy. Like King

Hassan in Morocco, Hussein is a *sharif*, a descendent of the Prophet Muhammad, which gives him Islamic legitimacy in the eyes of traditional sectors of Jordanian society. Another source of the King's popular support comes from the simple fact that he has survived so many challenges. According to Michael Hudson, "By surmounting crisis after crisis, King Hussein has acquired a measure of respect which helps support the system itself."[7] Hussein's personal legitimacy also derives from his strong leadership and the sheer force and intelligence of his personality. Hudson describes the King's impressive demeanor as follows: " . . . although short in stature he is eloquent in Arabic, has a reputation for personal incorruptibility, and is known for his courage and daring. He is an expert marksman, hunter, pilot, and athlete."[8] The king's courage in personally facing down rebellious army units and his magnanimity toward disloyal officers have become part of popular mythology in Jordan. Finally, Hussein cements and reinforces his personal loyalty among an important segment of the Jordanian population through the traditional mechanism of generous patronage to tribal leaders and notables.

In addition to the personal legitimacy and strong leadership of King Hussein, civilian rule in Jordan is supported by instruments of state control. These instruments include the security forces--the military and the police--and the secret police--the *mukhabarat*, the renowned royal intelligence apparatus. The Jordanian secret police are widely perceived within the country as an effective arm of state control. The secret police have infiltrated the Palestinian refugee camps, the Muslim Brotherhood, the university, and professional associations, and Jordanians assume that they are always present in meetings or groups of any nature.

Civilian rule in Jordan depends on at least tacit support from the two major segments of the population, East Bankers and Palestinians. East Bankers are more natural constituents of the Hashimite monarchy. Since 1922, three generations of East Bankers have become accustomed to rule by the Hashimites. There is among East Bankers a sense of gratitude to King Hussein for his crackdown and expulsion of the Palestinian *fedayeen* groups in 1970-1971 (the East Bankers felt that the king was fighting for them when he attacked the *fedayeen*). They concluded that by 1970 the internal situation in Jordan had deteriorated to a dangerous level and that King Hussein did what was necessary at the time to preserve public order. East Bankers do not want to see a repeat of the bloodshed of the 1970 civil war. Thus, they see the necessity of a strong security system. Further, East Bank sentiment solidified around the Hashimite monarchy following the loss of the West Bank in 1967 and the government's victory over militant Palestinian nationalism in the 1970 civil war. According to one account, " . . . the Jordanian government [then] discovered a Jordanian nationalism based on east Jordanian tribal and Islamic values, loyalty to the royal family and to the king's army, and more pertinently, cleansed of Palestinian, pan-Arab, and progressive ideologies."[9]

Attitudes among Palestinians in Jordan are much more complicated. There is even disagreement about the size of the Palestinian population in the Kingdom. Since the loss of the West Bank to Israeli control in 1967, the conventional wisdom has been that Palestinians comprise anywhere from half to two-thirds of Jordan's East Bank population, now estimated to be between 3.1 million and 3.5 million. Hard demographic statistics, however, suggest that Palestinian Jordanians--those who came to the kingdom from west of the Jordan River after 1948 and their descendants--account for a much smaller percentage of Jordan's present population, somewhere between 37 percent and 45 percent.[10] This includes some 300,000 Palestinians still living in refugee camps. Whatever their numbers, Palestinian attitudes toward the Hashimite monarchy range from mild support to suppressed hostility.

From 1950 until the June 1967 war, King Hussein and his government exercised direct control and authority over the Palestinian population of the West Bank. Following the loss of the West Bank in 1967, the king continued to claim authority over, and responsibility for, West Bank Palestinians. With no viable option, Hussein supported the decision of the 1974 Rabat summit meeting, in which the Arab states recognized the PLO as "the sole legitimate representative of the Palestinians." While giving up the right to speak for the Palestinians, the king continued to assert and exercise some administrative responsibility for West Bank Palestinians. Finally, in July 1988, in the context of the Palestinian *intifada*, and after several years of struggle with the PLO over approaches to a peace settlement with Israel, Hussein announced his decision to renounce Jordan's claim of sovereignty over the West Bank and to sever most remaining administrative ties with the territory.

Among the Palestinians who live in Jordan, there is some support for King Hussein because of what he has done for them. The king has tried to make Palestinians welcome in his country, and all have Jordanian citizenship except a relatively small number from the Gaza Strip. Palestinians enjoy the full legal rights of Jordanian citizenship; they have excellent educational opportunities, though when a choice exists in hiring, preference is given most often to East Bankers. Other Palestinians in Jordan are politically neutral. Finally, some in the Palestinian community have reasons to dislike King Hussein: he has not been militant enough on the Palestinian issue, plus there is a bitter feeling among some for the King's expulsion of the *fedayeen* in 1970-1971.

In general, Palestinians in Jordan are not disloyal to King Hussein. Though some resent the King's treatment of the *fedayeen* in 1970-1971, more are aware that the situations for Palestinians in other Arab countries are even worse. Thus they value the stability, security, and economic opportunities available to them in Jordan. Palestinians realize that the regimes in Egypt, Syria, and Lebanon all have let them down, so they do not hold King Hussein especially responsible for their situation.

Support for civilian rule in Jordan, among both East Bankers and Palestinians, was reinforced by sustained economic prosperity from the early 1970's to the mid-1980's. The kingdom averaged an economic growth rate of nine to ten percent from 1973 to 1981, and the per capita gross domestic product doubled from 1977 to 1981, from about $750 to $1,500. For a few years following the 1978 Baghdad Arab summit organized to oppose the Camp David accords, Jordan benefitted considerably from a $1 billion annual subsidy, provided mostly by Iraq. Another large source of income came from remittances from more than 300,000 Jordanians (mostly Palestinians) who worked abroad, 70 percent of them in Saudi Arabia and Kuwait, where they earned relatively high wages.

The economic boom in Jordan began to collapse in the mid-1980's when oil prices fell and the gulf economies contracted. The ripple effect in Jordan was felt in a dramatic decline in both workers remittances and aid. By the late 1980's, the economic slowdown had fueled mounting dissatisfaction with the regime. This discontent exploded in April 1989 following a round of government-imposed price increases required by an agreement with the International Monetary Fund. Five days of rioting left eight people dead and 50 injured. The riots erupted not in the poor Palestinian neighborhoods, but in southern Jordan, the stronghold of Bedouin support for the Hashimite monarchy.

King Hussein responded to the political rumblings by loosening the reins of political control. He dismissed an unpopular prime minister tainted by corruption and gave greater freedom to the press. More importantly, in November 1989, the king held the first parliamentary elections since 1967. The regime was no doubt shocked by the results, when Islamic fundamentalists won 32 of the 80 seats in parliament and a variety of ten leftists won 10 other seats. By taking visible steps to open up the political system, Hussein gained for himself a good measure of popular credit. At the same time, he gave up very little of his considerable power. Thus the king was able to use political reform as a means of gaining popular toleration of an onerous program of economic austerity.[11]

The relative stability of Jordan since 1970 and the ongoing exercise of civilian rule there are, above all, consequences of the professional behavior of the armed forces, which have resisted the temptations and opportunities, so frequently found in the developing world, to use their military power to seize control of the government. A combination of organizational and other factors can be cited to explain the impressive record of Jordan's armed forces. Ellen Laipson and Alfred B. Prados identify three specific factors that have contributed significantly to the professional behavior of the Jordanian military and have aided its development into a respected national institution.[12]

First, the Jordanian military has benefitted from an extraordinary continuity of leadership. At the top of the military establishment, King Hussein himself has been Supreme Commander for nearly 40 years. The king received a military education in Britain as a teenager, and since his ascension to the throne he has closely monitored developments within his own military. Just below the king, only two men have served as Armed Forces Commander-in-Chief for almost the entire period since 1957: Field Marshal Habes Pasha Majali and his successor, Field Marshal Sharif Zeid bin Shaker, one of Hussein's relatives. This same element of stability is also found at lower levels of command, giving the entire Jordanian military establishment a combination of continuity and stability that is rarely present in armed forces in the developing world.

In addition to a high degree of leadership continuity and stability, the government has taken care to incorporate within the military the country's major ethnic and social groups. As a result, the composition of the army has reinforced its national image. Each of the principal tribes and extended families of the East Bank is represented in the Jordanian Army and East Bankers dominate major combat units and the upper command levels. Though Palestinians have always been in the minority in Jordan's armed forces, they do serve in various capacities, especially in the technical branches. The number of Palestinians in the military has increased since 1976, when the government began conscription, but the great majority of conscripts return to civilian life following their two years of obligatory service. Ethnic and religious minorities, especially Circassians, are also represented in the military, which has further enhanced its appeal as a unifying national institution.

Finally, the apolitical nature of the army has enabled Jordan to avoid the destabilizing effects of military intervention in domestic affairs. The record of discipline and loyalty of Jordan's army has been excellent. King Hussein has tried to build discipline and loyalty into the military structure by a deliberate policy of placing Bedouins and non-Palestinians in most leadership positions. At the same time, the king has reinforced military loyalty by dispensing generous patronage, salaries, housing, and other benefits. Like their counterparts in Morocco, Jordanian military personnel have avoided political affiliation or activity. The rare outbreaks of discontent within the military have typically been caused by economic grievances. King Hussein has successfully adopted a conciliatory approach to these problems: he has taken the initiative and interceded personally with the disgruntled officers and resolved the grievances through dialogue. The wide respect that the king enjoys within the armed forces facilitates the rapid resolution of such grievances.

As a weak state surrounded on three sides by much stronger neighbors, Jordan's domestic stability is potentially vulnerable to international factors. In national defense and security, no conceivable level of armaments and military preparedness could enable Jordan, by itself, to withstand a major attack from either Israel, Syria, or Iraq.[13] Fortunately for the Kingdom, it has had strong allies--particularly Britain and the United States--whose readiness to assist and support Jordan in times of peril has deterred potential aggressors, especially Syria. Over the years, these same allies have provided economic and military assistance, including extensive training in U.S. and British military schools, that has helped to solidify military support for the foundations of civilian rule. Jordan's continuing sense of vulnerability was evident in 1989, when it joined with Egypt, Iraq, and Yemen primarily economic in a new regional alliance, the Arab Cooperation Council.

At the same time, Jordan has taken care in its moderate and non-aggressive foreign policy not to offend neighboring states or antagonize potential enemies. Israel, for example, values the moderate civilian rule of King Hussein; its security would be threatened by a coup in Jordan that brought to power a more aggressive military regime. The United States has valued Jordan as an essential element of the Middle East peace process: the kingdom has long been considered as the only possible "bridge" between Israel and the Palestinians. Only the likelihood of Israeli and American protection has deterred Syrian aggression against Jordan on several occasions since 1970. During this same period, Jordan has been able, for the most part, to stay on good terms with the key states of Egypt and Saudi Arabia. During the Iran-Iraq war (1980-1988), mutual self-interest led Jordan and Iraq to develop close and important relations which involved a high level of cooperation in trade, military logistics, energy, industry, agriculture, transport, and oil explorations.[14]

International factors impacted dramatically on Jordan's internal affairs during the Gulf crisis and war of 1990-1991. The combined loss of remittances from large numbers of Jordanian (mostly Palestinian) workers expelled from Kuwait, the Kuwaiti and Iraqi export markets, aid from Gulf states, and revenues from

Iraqi transit trade had a devastating impact on Jordan's economy, which, as noted earlier, was already in serious decline. The government estimated the potential economic damage from the Gulf crisis at $2.1 billion--nearly half of the country's annual gross national product--while the World Bank projected the annual losses at $1.5 billion. Rationing of basic products began for the first time since the 1940's, and unemployment rose steeply--from 15 percent to 35 percent, according to one estimate--with serious potential for destabilizing the country.[15]

During the Gulf crisis, King Hussein adopted a position mildly supportive of Iraq against other Arab states, but primarily against Western military intervention in what Hussein saw as essentially an inter-Arab dispute. While this position greatly complicated his foreign relations with such key allies as the United States, Egypt, and Saudi Arabia, it found great favor within Jordan, where there was widespread enthusiasm for Iraq both in parliament and public opinion. Thus, despite a genuine economic crisis, the King's popularity reached an all time high during the Gulf crisis. And in the months following the end of the Gulf war, Jordan was able to mend fences with Syria and the United states and secure a resumption of American aid.

Future Prospects for Civilian Rule

In the coming years, a number of potential problems could emerge to endanger civilian rule in Jordan. A major consideration in any assessment of Jordan's future stability is the mortality of King Hussein. Although he is only in his mid-fifties and in good health, anything could happen to him in the coming years. There is less loyalty among Jordanians to the monarchy as an institution than to Hussein personally. The king earned this loyalty by his performance; he proved himself in his first ten years on the throne as both a competent and reasonable ruler. No outside force is now operating inside the country, and there have been fewer assassination or coup attempts against the king since 1970 than during the period from 1953 to 1970.

If something should happen to Hussein, a process for succession exists in which his younger brother, Crown Prince Hassan, would become king. Given the fact that so many Jordanians value stability, the succession process should go smoothly. The new king then would be tested and would have to prove himself worthy of the right to lead the country. Crown Prince Hassan, now in his mid-forties, is an intelligent and competent individual and, although lacking the political charisma of Hussein, has been grooming for power for some time. He has cultivated good relations with the East Bank population in general and the army in particular, which will assist him in the event of his succession to the throne.

Over the longer run, the Jordanian monarchy will have to deal with an increasingly broad demand for more democracy, more representative government, and more freedom of expression. King Hussein recognized this demand in 1989 when he took the steps toward political participation noted above. The Gulf crisis interrupted this process toward greater political participation. It was not until January 1991 that Hussein approved a long-awaited "National Charter" which legalized political parties and endorsed pluralism and constitutional government. The process will continue in the 1993 parliamentary elections--a potential safety valve for discontented sectors of the population.

At present, King Hussein retains firm control over decision-making in the defense and foreign policy areas. Jordanians are now widely educated and they cannot be ruled like illiterate peasants. One problem is that King Hussein, having ruled longer than any living monarch, seems unable to embark on a genuine sharing of political power. He thus may be heading toward some eventual confrontation as long as he stays in power. Once the political process begins to open up, limitations on participation cannot always be controlled. If the king begins to lose control of domestic political affairs--as happened in the mid-1950's and in 1970--the military may be tempted to intervene to restore civil order, thereby threatening civilian rule.

A significant challenge to future political stability in Jordan is external. There is no solution conceivable for the Palestinian question that would not pose serious problems for Hussein, including a continuation of the frustrations of the status quo. Any sort of Palestinian entity, either an independent state or a federation with either Jordan or Israel, is bound to inflame Palestinian feelings within Jordan. The one exception--and clearly the solution that would pose least difficulties for Hussein's regime--would be a permanent Israeli takeover of the West Bank and the Gaza Strip, but there are powerful international constraints working against this solution.

There is almost no chance that Jordan will be drawn voluntarily into an Arab-Israeli war. It is unlikely that Syria will attack Israel with Egypt on the sidelines. If Israel attacks Syria, Jordan will not come to the defense of Syria. Hussein knows that Jordan would be badly defeated, and his prestige would suffer. The greater likelihood is that Israel would attack Jordan, perhaps on the pretext of an Arab missile attack against one of the Israeli reconnaissance planes which regularly overfly Syrian, Saudi, and Jordanian territory. It is difficult to predict what would happen in that situation, though King Hussein is unlikely to do anything rash.

The Palestinian population in Jordan has not posed any major problems to King Hussein's regime since the showdown in 1970-1971. Much of the Palestinian leadership in Jordan has been co-opted by the period of economic prosperity from 1970 to 1985. The Palestinian proletariat thus lacks leaders, plus it is restrained by the memory of the bloody suppression of 1970-1971. At the same time, economic preoccupations of Palestinians in Jordan have diverted their attention away from the Palestine problem. Since 1974, many Palestinians have concentrated their thoughts on immediate material objectives like building or furnishing a house. Also, the strength and penetration of the Jordanian security services discourage disloyal activities.

There is a relatively strong Islamic fundamentalist movement in the country. The Muslim Brotherhood has been permitted to operate more or less openly in Jordan, despite the ban on political parties, because of its long-term support for the king. Though the Brotherhood has a modest membership, relatively large numbers of Jordanians have fundamentalist sympathies. There are also some smaller, more radical fundamentalist groups, but these groups have been penetrated by the secret police and some of their members arrested.

Islamic fundamentalists--which include both the Brotherhood and other related Islamic groups--represent a considerable portion of Jordanian society, both East Bankers and Palestinians. Members of fundamentalist groups permeate all levels of Jordanian society, and there are some links between the royal family and the Muslim Brotherhood. The Brotherhood in Jordan, as elsewhere, believes in moving toward a more Islamic state by improving the moral behavior and Islamic orientation of all members of society. Thus the Brotherhood is not an immediate or direct threat to the regime or to political order in general, and its activities are tolerated within bounds. All the Islamic fundamentalist groups in Jordan are penetrated by the government's security apparatus, and they would be eliminated if they made any move that threatened the regime.

Over the long run, Islamic fundamentalists have the potential to increase their strength in Jordan. The fundamentalists, who oppose peace talks with Israel, can attract disaffected young Palestinians. The movement could exploit class differences and the corruption issue. It could also exploit the present economic crisis. Alternatively, the fundamentalists could benefit from the success of Islamic movements elsewhere and from financial support from Saudi Arabia. In time and in combination with other social and economic problems, Islamic fundamentalists in Jordan could pose a serious challenge to the regime. Specifically, the specter of an Islamic government in Jordan could provoke a military takeover. The military might view the strong showing of the fundamentalists in the 1989 parliamentary elections and the inclusion in January

1991, for the first time, of seven fundamentalists in Jordan's cabinet as the first steps toward an eventual Islamic government. It remains to be seen if the palace will always be able to control the fundamentalists or, in the other direction, if the fundamentalists can consolidate their position as an autonomous, if divided, political actor.

Overall, the prospects for continuing civilian rule in Jordan are probably not as good in the 1990's as they were in the 1970's or even the 1980's. The past decade witnessed the growth of alienation and antipathy in reaction to the blatant corruption that was widespread among members of the traditional élite surrounding the king. The 1989 riots in southern Jordan suggested that the loyalty or at least political passivity of the tribes, long considered a bulwark of the monarchy's support, can no longer be assumed. And the composition of the Jordanian military in the 1990's reflects more urban and modernist trends and less tribal and traditional outlooks than in earlier decades.

Against these trends, however, there is wide agreement that King Hussein, having survived a variety of coups and other crises in 38 turbulent years on the throne, is very important in holding the Jordanian political system together. On the external front, Jordan's neighbors are most likely to continue to find that the survival of the Hashimite monarchy is in their best interest. In the coming years, both these factors will help to ensure the continuation of civilian rule in Jordan.

MOROCCO

Whereas Jordan was "created" as a nation-state by Britain in the 1920's, Morocco's origins go back 1200 years to the Idrissid Dynasty, which established control over the territory and an imperial capital in Fez in the eighth century. The Idrissids, a sharifian family from the Arab East, were the first of several successive dynasties based in Morocco that exercised loose administrative control over the settled areas of the territory. In the case of the Almoravids and Almohades, two Berber dynasties that ruled successively from the eleventh to the thirteenth centuries, this control extended far beyond the borders of present-day Morocco. The latest of these dynasties, the Alawis, established their control in 1666, and the current head of the Alawi Dynasty is King Hassan II, who ascended the throne in 1961 upon the death of his father, King Mohammed V.

While the roots of the Moroccan monarchy and the country's evolution as a nation go back more than a millennium, Morocco's modern administrative infrastructure is a twentieth-century product of the French and Spanish protectorates. By dint of its more modern and superior military power, France forced a weakened Moroccan government to accept a protectorate over most of the country in 1912 while Spain established its own protectorate in the northern tenth of Morocco the same year. According to the terms of the protectorate treaty, France preserved and ruled in the name of the indigenous Moroccan government, the Alawi Dynasty. Between 1912 and 1934, French forces were able to do what Morocco's traditional rulers had never done: extend the authority of the central government over the entirety of Moroccan territory, the mountain retreats as well as the coastal plains. Forty-four years of French rule endowed Morocco with a modern administrative and commercial infrastructure.

From mid-1953 on, the French faced an increasingly militant nationalist movement and armed resistance groups within the country, plus in late 1954 a revolution in neighboring Algeria. In the context of these developments, France granted independence to Morocco in 1956 and Spain followed suit later that same year. The city of Tangier was restored to the Kingdom from international status also in 1956. With the subsequent retrocession by Spain of the southern province of Tarfaya in 1958 and the Atlantic coastal enclave of Ifni in 1969, Morocco achieved its present internationally recognized territorial boundaries. Since 1975, Morocco has occupied, controlled, and administered a progressively increasing portion of the Western Sahara. In late 1991, as the United Nations began to organize a referendum to determine the final disposition of the disputed territory, Morocco controlled about 80 percent of the Western Sahara.

Civil-Military Relations

While the Arab Legion played a key role in the formation of the Jordanian state, Morocco at the moment of its independence in 1956 was a country in need of a national army. In pre-protectorate Morocco, the army served the sultan. In times of foreign campaigns by strong sultans, the army was large and, by pre-modern standards, powerful. Most of the time, however, the sultan's standing army was quite small and had to rely on "reserves" of tribal levies in order to mount a serious military campaign. During the protectorate period (1912-1956), there was no Moroccan army at all. Instead, Moroccans served, often gallantly, in the French and Spanish armies.

Morocco's circumstances at the time of independence in March 1956 required the rapid formation of the Royal Armed Forces (Forces Armées Royales)--the FAR. First were the demands of prestige and the new government's need to assert the sovereignty of the nation. Secondly were the necessities of defense and security: to insure that Morocco did not get drawn into the war in neighboring Algeria and to provide effective police power at home. Finally, the FAR was needed to " . . . replace two undesirable elements in Morocco--the French and

Spanish armies and the Army of Liberation--by absorbing some of their members and all of their functions."[16] At the time of independence, Morocco was still occupied by an 85,000-man garrison of the French Army and a 60,000-man garrison of the Spanish Army in the northern zone. The Army of Liberation began operations in late 1955 as a rural guerrilla force of armed bands numbering no more than 600-800 active fighters. When an agreement signed in February 1956 allowed Moroccans serving in the French Army to terminate their services, the ranks of the Army of Liberation quickly swelled to several thousand--*after* the liberation of Morocco had been achieved. Because the leaders of the Army of Liberation were not satisfied by the terms of independence secured by the government of King Mohammed V, this guerrilla force posed a potential security threat.

Crown Prince Moulay Hassan (the present king) was entrusted with the task of establishing and organizing the FAR. Within a matter of weeks, a new army was formed from a small core of former officers of the French and Spanish armies and large numbers of enlisted men plus some officers from the Army of Liberation. By mid-May of 1956, the entire 14,000-man FAR paraded in review in the courtyard of the royal palace in Rabat. Officer training was accelerated at academies in Morocco, France, and Spain, and the recruitment of conscripts continued, so that by 1958 the size of the FAR had expanded to 30,447, including 884 officers and 3,722 noncommissioned officers.[17]

During the 15-year period from Morocco's independence in 1956 to the first attempted coup in 1971, two factors were noteworthy in civil-military relations. The first was the use by the palace of the FAR to quell or intimidate into submission a series of rural revolts that occurred from 1957 to 1960. In one instance, in the northern Rif mountains, disgruntled diehards from the Army of Liberation revolted over the lack of resources allocated to the Rif region. In another instance, in the middle Atlas, a provincial governor revolted against the government when he saw his local power base being undermined. In each case, a show of force was sufficient to end the revolt. The second factor was the frequent use of military personnel for civilian duties, especially in the Ministry of Interior. FAR officers and recruits participated in a variety of civilian projects that ranged from building schools to providing relief for flood victims. From 1961 onwards, FAR personnel worked in the National Promotion rural development program.[18]

Civil-Military relations in Morocco reached a low point in the early 1970's when two attempted coups nearly succeeded in installing praetorian rule. The first was staged in July 1971 by a group of high-ranking army officers motivated by a common distaste for the widespread corruption among Morocco's ruling élite. The second, in August 1972, was attempted by air force officers but was directed by General Mohammed Oufkir, the regime's strongman, who feared that King Hassan had not taken effective measures to address the causes of the first coup attempt. The details of these two attempts to end civilian rule are less important than their outcomes: with considerable personal resourcefulness and some luck, King Hassan narrowly survived and quickly reasserted his authority.[19]

Unlike King Hussein, who has never executed a disloyal or disgruntled member of the Jordanian military, King Hassan dealt harshly with FAR dissidence. In addition to the alleged coup leaders killed during the 1971 attempt, ten other rebel officers ranging in rank from major to general were executed three days later, following intensive interrogation but no public trial. Following the 1972 coup attempt, Oufkir was summoned to the royal palace, where he was summarily executed; in January 1973, following a public trial, 11 air force officers were executed. This pattern of dealing harshly with disloyal officers continued in the 1980's when General Ahmed Dlimi, who had succeeded Oufkir as the regime's strongman in 1972, was killed in an automobile "accident" in January 1983. It is widely believed that Hassan ordered Dlimi's death because of his suspected links to an anti-regime group based in Western Europe.

In the confused aftermath of the second coup attempt, King Hassan announced that he could no longer place his trust in anyone and proceeded to take steps to "purify" the FAR: officers whose loyalty was suspect were retired or sent abroad with an expeditionary force dispatched to Syria in the spring of 1973 to help defend the Golan Heights and then, since 1975, transferred to the Western Sahara; the network of informers within the military was strengthened; FAR troops (except those sent abroad) were deprived of live ammunition; and commanders were required to obtain permission from three different sources of authority before they could move their troops from one province to another.

The King's distrust of his military carried over into the campaign to "recover" the Western Sahara, whose organized military dimension began with the highly successful Green March of November 1975. For the first several years of the campaign, Hassan required his personal authorization before air strikes could be called in against ground attacks by the Polisario Front, the Saharan national liberation movement that has contested Morocco's presence in the Western Sahara. The delays in obtaining royal authorization often rendered Moroccan air power ineffective against Polisario hit-and-run guerrilla attacks. Only in the 1980's, when commanders in the field were given the authority to order air strikes, did Moroccan army-air force coordination reach an effective level.

Since the launching of the Sahara campaign in 1975, the FAR's attention and much of its energies have been focused on the recovery and defense of what the Moroccan public (including the military) believes is an integral part of the national patrimony. On the one hand, this has meant a progressive expansion of the FAR from a pre-1975 level of about 60,000 to a level of about 195,000 in 1990. On the other hand, the active participation of the FAR in a national cause has kept the military's mind on the task at hand and thereby ensured the military's subordination to their civilian ruler.

Civilian Rule in Morocco

Just as civilian rule in Jordan is exercised primarily through the power and authority of King Hussein, so in Morocco it is King Hassan who dominates the political system. But unlike Jordan, where the monarchy as an institution is relatively recent and weak and Hussein depends on his personal legitimacy and the strength of his military as an institution, Hassan's position is supported by a highly legitimized monarchical institution. In Morocco the monarchy is clearly the dominant and, since the mid-1960's, unchallenged institution in the country. I. William Zartman aptly states the central role of the monarchy in Morocco in the following terms:

> The Moroccan political system is a monarchy in evolution. The monarchy is not merely a passing form or phenomenon in an ongoing development of the body politic . . . . It is the historical and continuing institutional framework of politics, the central structure that must deal with important challenges to its integrity such as colonial administration or nationalist movement. . . . [M]onarchial and mass politics are merely hierarchically contending elements of the same political system to which the monarchial institution gives structure and process. The king forms the apex of the system--Great Imam, Great Patron, Great Manipulator--and the people act as parties, military, students, labor unions, and street crowds, as the occasion demands. Within that system, king and people function both symbiotically and dialectically, producing a continually evolving synthesis as the product of their interactions.[20]

As noted earlier, the Moroccan monarchy's roots are deep, going all the way back to the eighth century, and the present royal family, the Alawis, has ruled for more than 300 years. In addition to its deep roots, the Alawi Dynasty enjoys a high degree of religious legitimacy which reinforces the King's political authority. As a *sharif*, the king combines within his person both political and religious leadership. In Moroccan (Islamic) law, the king is "Commander of the Faithful," the steward of God on earth for all matters, religious or secular; thus he personifies both state and church. The King's word is law, which means in effect that he is above the law: his decisions cannot be questioned nor can his person be criticized.

Since the sixteenth and seventeenth centuries, the Moroccan monarchy has encouraged and institutionalized throughout the country the performance of certain Islamic rituals: the celebration of the Prophet Muhammad's birthday, the rite of first marriage, and the sacrifice of a ram by the head of household on the Muslim holiday *'Id al-Kabir*, the fortieth day after the end of the month of *Ramadan*. These rituals have powerful emotional and political significance for Moroccans and have gone a long way to infuse the Moroccan body politic with a unifying and defining religious culture. By fusing communal values and identity with the ruling dynasty, the Alawis have strengthened their political legitimacy and simultaneously protected themselves against potential usurpers of power who hesitate before attacking the symbol of national unity and values.[21]

Notwithstanding the legitimacy of the monarchy as an institution and the religious veneration in which the king is held by large numbers of Moroccans, especially in rural areas, civilian rule in Morocco has faced challenges of some consequence since independence in 1956. The monarchy's response has varied according to the nature of the challenge. The palace's use of the FAR to suppress rural rebellions in the late 1950's was noted earlier. In the political arena, there was a protracted power struggle between the palace and the political parties during the first decade after independence. By the mid-1960's, the palace had emerged as the decisive winner. Through the adroit use of the spoils of patronage, the manipulation and co-optation of individuals, and divide-and-rule tactics, the parties were progressively weakened and marginalized to the point where they could no longer effectively challenge the monarchy's monopolization of power. The monarchy deliberately promoted social pluralism and élite divisions. The palace concentrated power by allowing, and even encouraging, divisions in society to crystallize and partially institutionalize themselves into political parties and factions[22] --a process that continued well into the 1980's.

The continued existence of a multi-party political system in Morocco since independence contrasts sharply with Jordan, where King Hussein banned political parties from 1957 to 1991. At the time of independence, one party, the Istiqlal, which had dominated organized politics during the nationalist movement from 1944 to 1956, was quite strong and somewhat independent of the palace. It was weakened by an internal split that led to the creation of a rival party in 1959, and by the mid-1960's the palace had succeeded in marginalizing the power of both these parties. The evolution of Morocco's multi-party system since 1956 has included both new parties that have split off from opposition parties and other new, pro-regime parties that have formed with the discreet encouragement of the palace. The system thus includes a broad spectrum of political tendencies that ranges from communist, socialist and centrist opposition parties to centrist and right-wing pro-goverenment parties.

Political parties in Morocco are allowed some input into social and economic policies, but the regime generally does not tolerate criticism in the areas of defense or foreign policy. If a party violates the unwritten rules of political behavior or threatens the government's monopoly of power, it is quickly repressed by suspension or the arrest of its leaders. Overall, the multi-party system functions as a safety valve for political energies and frustrations. It is tolerated by the monarchy not because of a commitment to representative government or political pluralism, but rather because the multi-party system operates as a support mechanism for civilian rule.

When challenged by serious urban riots in 1965 and his security forces in 1971 and 1972, King Hassan stood alone in the political arena. To ensure the continuation of civilian rule in Morocco, as well as his own personal survival, the king was forced to broaden the basis of national politics. Thus, according to Zartman, in the decade following the two attempted coups, Hassan " . . . reasserted control over the agenda of politics and restructured its institutional, organizational, coercive, and social bases. . . . [H]e provided a new constitutional framework for politics, and reshaped the political parties and the army . . . and built a social alliance with the urban middle class."[23]

The King's efforts during the 1970's to create a new polity were largely successful. From 1974 on, these efforts benefitted from the broad and genuine political consensus that formed over the Western Sahara issue. When Hassan called in 1974 for the recovery of "the despoiled Saharan provinces," he tapped into a large reservoir of public emotion that had been largely dormant for some time. The Sahara campaign launched in mid-1974 amounted to a national crusade; it provided a common nationalist cause around which all major political parties rallied. The king skillfully used the media and the aroused public emotions to enhance the image of the monarchy as the symbol of the nation's unity. Hassan was thus able, in a fairly short time, to restore a large measure of the royal prestige that had been lost during the preceding decade. With his popularity and prestige greatly enhanced, the king felt secure enough to take steps toward the liberalization of the political system.[24]

By the 1980's, the restructuring of the polity and the broad consensus over the Sahara issue were not enough to prevent serious manifestations of social discontent. After several years of inconclusive warfare against Polisario guerrilla forces, the initial euphoria over the Sahara issue began to wane. This coincided in the early 1980's with the beginnings of protracted economic difficulties. Frustrations among youth living in Morocco's impoverished urban quarters exploded in violent riots in Casablanca in June 1981, leaving over 600 dead, and over 100 people were killed in a second round of "bread riots" in several cities in January 1984. The Casablanca riots were fueled by a variety of factors that included rising prices, especially on basic foodstuffs; unemployment; food shortages; distribution problems; rural-urban migration, especially to Casablanca and other urban centers; disgruntled university and high school students; lack of schools; and miserable housing. Most of these factors were exacerbated by Morocco's worst drought in 35 years.

Thus, Morocco was beset in the early 1980's by numerous internal problems which posed potential threats to civilian rule. Above all, a number of serious economic problems brought the country to the brink of a financial crisis. Bad harvests caused by recurrent droughts, declining phosphate revenues, and a sharp cutback in generous financial assistance from Saudi Arabia combined to produce large current account deficits. This poor short-term financial situation undercut the government's ability to obtain new credits. The economic burdens added to other societal problems, including a growing population of unemployed young people who had little hope for a secure future. To ease the burden imposed by servicing the country's large and increasing external debt, Morocco in 1983 signed the first of several rescheduling agreements with its foreign creditors.[25]

Beginning in 1983, King Hassan moved on two fronts to alleviate the internal problems facing his regime. On the economic front, under pressure from international lending institutions, policies were initiated to restructure the economy along more liberal lines, including less restrictive regulations on commerce and foreign trade, devaluation of the currency, reduction of price-cost distortions, and, in the late 1980's, privatization. The restructuring of the economy since 1983 has created a new middle class in Morocco with a vested interest in the current political system. At the same time, by the late 1980's, Morocco's general economic performance had improved considerably, spurred by three years of record harvests, an economic growth rate of over 10 percent, low inflation, increased exports, and a sharply reduced budget deficit.

On the administrative front, recognizing that such basic causes of social discontent as unemployment and poor quality housing were likely to persist, the palace extended and reinforced its instruments of control. Specifically, government policy emphasized regional differences, including the creation of major regional cultural associations plus new proposals for regional administrative decentralization. In the rural areas, the process of administrative decentralization through the creation of local collectivities, begun in 1976, was accelerated in 1983. The new instruments of decentralization--the local collectivities--are controlled by both the palace and the powerful Ministry of Interior. These bodies, which now have considerable local financial power and thus political patronage, are controlled by local élites who are loyal to the palace. The regime stimulated the growth of regionalism as a means of further diffusing political tensions and of creating a decentralized administration. This represents a further move in the palace's attempts to maintain control of the substance of power while allowing the impression of a democratic constitutional monarchy to develop.

As was the case in Jordan, an essential element in the unbroken record of civilian rule in Morocco since independence in 1956 has been the professional behavior of the military. When considered in the perspective of the 36-year span of national independence, the abortive coup attempts in 1971 and 1972 by two small groups of rebel officers appear as momentary aberrations in an overall pattern of loyalty to the monarchy. This basic pattern of loyalty derives from a variety of factors: the origins of the FAR, the war in the Western Sahara, and organizational changes within the military.

As noted earlier, the leadership corps of the FAR was originally formed in 1956 around senior and middle-level officers who had previously served in the French and Spanish armies. As members of the two occupying armies, some of these officers had been actively involved in repressing the Moroccan nationalist movement and thus risked being viewed as collaborators by the Moroccan public. With no political base of their own in independent Morocco, these officers eagerly accepted commissions in the new FAR. Once in the FAR, the former French and Spanish officers became beholden to the monarchy both for protection and their livelihood. Thus, with the exception of the rebel officers of the early 1970's, the outlook of these officers has been essentially royalist and conservative. This loyalty and conservatism was sufficiently pronounced among the older officers that they " . . . systematically weeded out junior officers smacking of leftist or strongly nationalist opinions."[26] In addition, personal ties developed between many of these officers and Crown Prince Hassan, who organized and formed the FAR and then served as Chief-of-Staff until his father's death in 1961, when he became King and Commander-in-Chief.

Since the Green March of November 1975, much of the FAR's attention and energies have necessarily been focused on the war in the Western Sahara. For some years now, about two-thirds of the FAR have been deployed in Morocco's

Southern Zone where they have been engaged in an essentially defensive holding action against sporadic guerrilla attacks by the Polisario Front. Troops stationed in the Southern Zone receive special benefits of double pay and free transportation home on leaves. Adequate food and regular leaves help combat boredom and contribute to generally good morale. Other factors that bolster morale are the genuine popularity of the Sahara campaign and the security provided by the long defensive sand and dirt wall constructed and progressively expanded between 1980 and 1987 to protect the Sahara's few population centers and rich phosphate deposits.

Throughout Morocco the military establishment is apolitical and loyal to the monarchy. FAR personnel are not very sophisticated politically, nor are their views advanced or progressive. Political activism in the military ended with the purges of the early 1970's; since that time, officers have not held political rank, as General Oufkir and other senior officers did. The overwhelming majority of officers and enlisted men do not hold any particular political party affiliation. Security forces discourage the parties from trying to recruit members or organize within the FAR, and periodic attempts by Islamic groups in the 1980's to influence military personnel met with only limited success. Members of the military have generally been apathetic about Morocco's occasional elections.

Finally, organizational changes and recruitment patterns have made the FAR more representative of Moroccan society as a whole. The original officer corps of the FAR, drawn largely from the protectorate armies, was heavily Berber in composition, reflecting the privileged status rural Berber notables were accorded by the French. By contrast, higher educational requirements for officers trained after independence meant, in effect, that these men came from urban Arab families, which redressed the Berber-Arab balance in the officer corps.[27] The officer corps underwent further restructuring following the 1971 and 1972 coup attempts. Because of this further restructuring, the FAR officer corps " . . . now more closely reflects current élite structures than it did in 1972. The Berberist and rural notable dominance has gone, as promotion has became a consequence of ability. The result is that the representation of the urban élites within the army has become for more significant . . ."[28] Among the enlisted ranks, the large expansion of the FAR since 1975 has involved heavy recruitment of unemployed young men from rural areas. While these trends do not ensure greater loyalty to the monarchy among the military, neither should they promote disloyal behavior, especially when loyalty is reinforced by the efficiency of the security services.

Unlike Jordan, whose domestic stability is potentially vulnerable to international factors, civilian rule in Morocco has been relatively immune to outside forces. Morocco's northern neighbor, Spain, is clearly a more powerful state, but it has never been a threatening state nor have Spanish governments ever tried to intervene in the Kingdom's internal affairs. A potential dispute over the decolonization of the former Spanish Sahara was resolved amicably by a November 1975 agreement that allowed Moroccan (and Mauritanian) administrative control to replace Spain's presence in the territory. Since then, periodic irritations over fishing rights and the small Spanish enclaves on Morocco's northern coast have been well contained within the context of a generally good bilateral relationship.

Morocco's relations with its eastern neighbor, Algeria, have been much more troublesome. During the 1960's, Algeria gave refuge and assistance to the Moroccan opposition. From 1975 to 1988, Algeria provided critical military and diplomatic support to the Polisario Front in its war against Morocco in the Western Sahara. Algeria's support of the Moroccan opposition was never a serious threat to political stability in the Kingdom, and the war in the Sahara, as noted earlier, has been a national crusade that has rallied public support for the regime. Since the restoration of diplomatic relations in May 1988 (broken by Morocco in 1976 over the Sahara issue), the two states have gradually increased their bilateral cooperation in a number of areas, some of them within the context of the Maghreb Arab Union, formed by five North African states in February 1989.

Morocco has generally been quite successful in nurturing and maintaining excellent relations with such important allies as the United States, France, Saudi Arabia, and the Gulf shaikhdoms. These relations have provided important benefits: military supplies (mostly purchased) from France and the United States and large-scale financial assistance from Saudi Arabia and, to a lesser extent, from the Gulf shaikhdoms. These benefits have strengthened civilian rule in Morocco by enhancing the regime's ability to fight a successful war in the Sahara and cope with the variety of economic difficulties that became manifest in the early 1980's.

Despite the general pattern of Moroccan immunity to international factors, the Kingdom was nonetheless impacted by the Gulf crisis. Income fell sharply in the tourist industry, Morocco's biggest single source of foreign currency, and remittances from Moroccan workers in Kuwait ended. King Hassan clearly and publicly opposed the Iraqi invasion of Kuwait and dispatched a "limited symbolic contingent" of 1,300 soldiers to join the international coalition of forces. This policy was quite out of step with the Moroccan public, which was overwhelmingly supportive of Iraq. Public resentment against the government's policy degenerated into serious riots in December 1990 and culminated in a huge pro-Iraqi rally in Rabat in February 1991. The king made a tactical retreat by assuring his people that Moroccan troops would not attack Iraq and criticizing the bombing of Iraq. He then effectively ended the public opposition by banning a further demonstration, planned in Casablanca, and forbidding any further criticism of his policy. With the rapid and overwhelming defeat of Iraq by the international coalition forces, Hassan weathered the Gulf storm with his authority and effective instruments of control very much intact.

Future Prospects for Civilian Rule

Potential problems could emerge in the coming years to endanger civilian rule in Morocco, though to a lesser extent than in Jordan. One begins again with the mortality of the monarch. King Hassan is in his early sixties and in fairly good health. Nonetheless, the strains of the long Sahara campaign show in his ageing appearance, and anything could happen to the king in the coming years. In the event of Hassan's demise, a constitutional process for succession exists in which Crown Prince Sidi Mohammed, the King's oldest son, would become ruler. Crown Prince Mohammed, now in his mid-twenties, does not seem to possess the dynamism or sharp intelligence of his father. On the other hand, he has been given increasing responsibilities of state as a young man and in time may well develop strong leadership qualities. (Hassan, for example, was considered by many to be a playboy as a young man.) This suggests that the longer the succession is delayed, the smoother it will be. In any event, the widespread acceptance of the monarchy as an institution and the regimes's effective instruments of control should ensure a relatively smooth succession, whenever it occurs.

For the foreseeable future, the royal palace in Morrocco will control all aspects of political power. To ensure and operate an elaborate system of control, King Hassan is likely to rely heavily on the powerful Ministry of Interior and the new instruments of decentralization, the local collectivities. To the degree that the king exercises absolute royal power and bypasses the political parties and Parliament, his political legitimacy will continue to be gradually and progressively, but not fatally, undermined. With the vast majority of Moroccans now convinced that there is no viable alternative to the monarchy, the stability of King Hassan's regime and therefore civilian rule seem assured for several years to come.

The most significant potential problem endangering civilian rule in Morocco in the near term is the Western Sahara issue. This critical issue is moving toward resolution in 1992 through a United Nations-administered referendum of self-determination. It is conceivable that if Morocco should lose the referendum, an angry and frustrated military would try to seize power and install praetorian rule. While this possibility cannot be ruled out, neither can it be considered very likely. The regime will do all it possibly can, administratively and humanly, to ensure that a majority of eligible voters in the Sahara referendum opt for integration with Morocco. Secondly, if Morocco fears it will lose the referendum, it will find ways to postpone the voting indefinitely. Thirdly, if Morocco loses the referendum, the military is just as likely to remain loyal to the monarchy even in defeat. Finally, if some officers decide to seize power, there is the probability (and precedent in 1971) that most officers and rank-and-file soldiers--knowing full well the harsh treatment that awaits unsuccessful rebels--will take a wait-and-see position and refuse to support the coup leaders. In addition, it is worth noting that the likelihood of a coup attempt over the Sahara issue is decidedly less now than it was in 1975 or 1980.

The increasing integration of the various components of the Moroccan élite into a powerful support base for the monarchy is likely to continue. This process, however, will be uneven. The traditionalist élite, which has been quite successful in exploiting opportunities provided by the post-1983 economic restructuring, will further strengthen its close ties with the palace; by contrast, the modernizing élite, which has been a good deal less successful in this endeavor, is unlikely to be as solid in its support of the monarchy.

Ultimately, it is the countryside that will continue to be the major support base for the monarchy--and, by extension, for the government and the élite-- because the traditionalist peasantry still recognizes the sharifian authority of King Hassan. Rebellion, then, would be a religious statement as well as a political act. Major rural disaffection is therefore unlikely unless conditions worsen significantly in the countryside, or unless the FAR, which draws many of its recruits from rural areas where there is serious unemployment or underemployment, suffers a major reverse in the Western Sahara.

Although there is considerable disaffection toward the Moroccan government and its associated élites, there is little evidence to suggest that the gulf between the élite and the mass of the population is sufficient to provide the basis for instability and the possible end of civilian rule. Popular resentment is localized and focused on specific issues. There is still a general consensus that the specific form of government in Morocco reflects a valid national historical tradition and that its institutions embody national aspirations. As a result, opposition tends to concentrate on specific issues such as unemployment, poor housing, excessive price increases, and inadequate income levels. Quite apart from the congruence of government and administrative structures with Morocco's political culture, there is no viable alternative that could successfully threaten the present system.

There is little prospect in the coming years that the political parties will expand their present marginal role in the Moroccan political system. King Hassan maintains a high ability to manipulate his political rivals, to co-opt them by his patronage, and to divide various contending factions. He is thus able to keep his opponents weak, divided, and off-balance and thereby maintain a relatively high degree of control over the political process in Morocco. Even in the event of a settlement of the Western Sahara conflict--which presumably would lead to the breakup of the national political consensus that has operated since 1974 and which would allow at least the opposition parties to attack the government on a number of issues--the parties will be unable to compete with the regime's monopoly of power over the economy and administration of Morocco--the classic levers of political patronage. On the other hand, the parties may become more effective in influencing the making of government policies.

An overriding and stabilizing factor is the stake that the political parties have in the present system. Political leaders know that there are many politicians and many generals, but there is only one king. They recognize the important role of the king both as a symbol of national unity and as the one effective figure who can keep the Moroccan system together. Even though some would prefer to reduce the power of the monarchy, the political parties realize fully that they are better off under the existing political system of limited liberalism than they would be if the monarchy were overthrown and replaced by a military junta. If the present system in Morocco were replaced by praetorian rule, the parties would have no role at all.

Like Jordan, Morocco has a number of Islamic movements which seek the establishment of a truly Islamic society. But unlike Jordan, the Islamic opposition in Morocco is quite weak and is incapable of challenging the monarchy. The fundamentalists in Morocco are weakened by internal divisions along traditionalist, mainstream, and radical lines. The active members of the various groups number only in the tens of thousands in a population of 25 million, though there is no doubt a larger number of sympathizers. Thus far, none of the three Islamic movements has been effective in challenging King Hassan's regime. Popular belief in the King's religious sanctity, which is widespread in Morocco, undermines all attempts to legitimate revolt against him on Islamic grounds.[29]

The current divisions within Morocco's Islamic opposition will persist for many years to come, thus weakening the ability of any single Islamic group to challenge the regime. Of the three groups, the traditionalists are closest to popular beliefs shared by large numbers of Moroccan Muslims. This group, however, has never tried to mount a revolution. If this movement were to join forces with the mainstream and radical movements with their more educated supporters in a serious attempt to overthrow the Moroccan government, they might well pose a serious threat to the regime. But it is hard to imagine such a coalition forming. For the foreseeable future, King Hassan has effectively muzzled or rendered ineffective those who seek to remove him in the name of Islam.

Overall, the prospects for continuing civilian rule in Morocco are better than those in Jordan. Morocco's prospects are better than they were in 1980 and much better than they were in 1970, when a widespread sense of malaise soon led to two attempts to install praetorian rule. In the mid-1970's, King Hassan formed a broad political and social consensus over the Sahara issue which abruptly ended the period of malaise and restored a measure of the monarchy's legitimacy by reinforcing its role as defender of the national patrimony. During the past decade, the palace has moved on several fronts to strengthen its various instruments of control.

While Jordan is vulnerable to developments and pressures in more powerful neighboring countries, Morocco is much less affected by external factors. While King Hussein has to contend with a large Palestinian population whose natural loyalty is not to the Hashimite monarchy, King Hassan has no group in his Kingdom with conflicting loyalties. Whereas the Hashimite monarchy, as a twentieth century transplant of British imperialism, has shallow roots in Jordan and relatively weak institutional legitimacy, the Moroccan monarchy's roots are very deep and its institutional legitimacy is very high. The broad and deep consensus in Morocco that supports the monarchy as a valid national historical institution, King Hassan's mastery and high degree of control over the country's political process, and the regime's effective instruments of control will all go far to ensure the continuation of civilian rule in the country for many years to come.

NOTES

1. See Michael C. Hudson, *Arab Politics: The Search for Legitimacy* (New Haven and London: Yale University Press, 1977), pp. 213 ff.
2. Ellen Laipson and Alfred B. Prados, *Jordan: Recent Developments and Implications for U.S. Interests*, CRS Report for Congress, July 11, 1990, p. 11.

3. Quoted in ibid., p. 11.

4. The classic study of the role of the military in creating and supporting the Hashimite regime is P.J. Vatikiotis, *Politics and the Military in Jordan: A Study of the Arab Legion, 1921-1957* (New York: Praeger Publishers, 1967).

5. Abid A. Al-Marayati et al., *The Middle East: Its Governments and Politics* (Belmont, CA: Duxbury Press, 1972), p. 243.

6. Ibid., p. 244; Hudson, p. 218.

7. Hudson, p. 218.

8. Loc. cit.

9. Ibid., p. 210.

10. Valerie Yorke, "Jordan Is Not Palestine: The Demographic Factor," *Middle East International*, No. 323 (April 16, 1988), pp. 16-17.

11. For a succinct account of Jordan's increasing economic crisis in the late 1980s, the 1989 riots, and King Hussein's response, see Stanley Reed, "Jordan and the Gulf Crisis," *Foreign Affairs* 69 (1990/91), pp. 21-35.

12. The following discussion of the three factors is drawn from Laipson and Prados, pp. 11-13.

13. For an appreciation of the degree to which Jordan is militarily outclassed by each of these three states, see the details of the military strength of Jordan, Israel, Syria, and Iraq contained in *The Military Balance 1989-1990* (London: International Institute for Strategic Studies, 1989), pp. 101-15.

14. See, for example, Amatzia Baram, "Baathi Iraq and Hashimite Jordan: From Hostility to Alignment," *Middle East Journal* 45 (1991), pp. 56 ff.

15. Reed, pp. 24-25.

16. I. William Zartman, *Problems of New Power: Morocco* (New York: Atherton Press, 1964), p. 65. This book, pp. 62-117, contains the fullest treatment of the formation of the FAR.

17. Ibid., pp. 67, 77.

18. John Waterbury, *The Commander of the Faithful: The Moroccan Political Elite--A Study of Segmented Politics* (New York: Columbia University Press, 1970), p. 287.

19. The best accounts of the 1971 and 1972 coup attempts are John Waterbury, "The Coup Manqué," *Fieldstaff Reports*, North Africa Series 15 (Hanover, NH: American Universities Field Staff, 1971), and "The Politics of the Seraglio," ibid. 16 (Hanover, NH: American Universities Field Staff, 1972). For an alternate view of the abortive military coup of July 1971, see Frank H. Braun, "Morocco: Anatomy of a Palace Revolution that Failed," *International Journal of Middle East Studies* 9 (1978), pp. 63-72.

20. "King Hassan's New Morocco," in Zartman, ed., *The Political Economy of Morocco* (New York: Praeger, 1987), p. 1.

21. M.E. Combs-Schilling, *Sacred Performances: Islam, Sexuality, and Sacrifice* (New York: Columbia University Press, 1989). This book argues persuasively and at length the importance of the performance of Islamic rituals in Morocco.

22. The monarchy's progressive monopolization of power in the decade after independence is analyzed in depth and with great insight and skill in Waterbury, *Commander of the Faithful*, cited above.

23. "King Hassan's New Morocco," p. 2.

24. See John Damis, "The Impact of the Saharan Dispute on Moroccan Foreign and Domestic Policy," in Zartman, ed., *Political Economy of Morocco*, pp. 201-10.

25. By 1983, Morocco's debt service ratio had reached 42 percent. For a good overview of Morocco's economic problems in the 1980s, see Ahmed Rhazaoui, "Recent Economic Trends: Managing the Indebtedness," in Zartmen, ed., *Political Economy of Morocco*, pp. 141-58.

26. Waterbury, *Commander of the Faithful*, p. 288.

27. Loc. cit.

28. George Joffe, "Morocco: Monarchy, Legitimacy and Succession," *Third World Quarterly* 10 (1988), pp. 225-26.

29. The various works of Henry Munson, Jr., provide an excellent analysis of the Islamic movements in Morocco and their relative weakness; see, for example, "Morocco's Fundamentalists," *Government and Opposition* 26 (1991), pp. 331-44.

3

The Preservation of Civilian Rule in Saudi Arabia

Hamad Khatani

The modern history of the Islamic Middle East is a tale of colonialism and praetorianism. For instance, from 1947 to 1972 military coups occurred on average once every three months.[1] However, the Arabian Peninsula, save Yemen, managed to escape this pattern. Saudi Arabia, the largest and wealthiest country on the Peninsula, has witnessed very few and unsuccessful incidents of military intervention and no praetorian rule. What makes this case even more unique is that Saudi Arabia has the largest royal family in the world (the House of Saud) with about 5000 members. This powerful family has had complete control over political, social, economic, and even military affairs. Throughout its rule, the family has been successful in keeping the military out of politics. The royal family was able to impose its supremacy over the military for a variety of reasons, as we will discuss later. Because of these various factors, Saudi Arabia is arguably a representative case for most of the Gulf states.

In light of the recent Gulf crisis, the Saudi Arabian military has been under close media scrutiny, particularly because of the modern technology it has acquired. In spite of this attention, very few serious efforts have been made to evaluate the Saudi military and its functions. Moreover, despite the extensive literature on civil-military relations regarding both democratic and authoritarian systems, there has not been a single authoritative study on this important Western ally. There is clearly a lack of data and of precise information of any kind in this area, due in large measure to Saudi secrecy, suspicion and virtual censorship on everything relating to the military in that country.

Due to the strategic and economic importance of the Arabian Peninsula, the West has been willing to help in the development of Saudi Arabia, especially the modernization of its military. This impressive modernization raises an important question: is the process, which includes extensive training of the Saudis by westerners, both inside the kingdom and abroad, likely to produce a military officer corps that will be prone to intervene in civil rule under certain circumstances? Even more importantly, how has the Saudi regime managed to keep the military out of power and hence preserve their civilian rule in the first place?

Explaining the overthrow of a civilian government is easier than determining how that government is maintained.[2] Yet, it is still difficult to separate the two issues. An examination of how civilian rule is preserved requires some reference to the reasons that encourage military intervention in the first place. This is particularly germane to the case of Saudi Arabia. It is well-known that Islam, which is a way of life, does not recognize a separation between military and civilian rule.[3] The idea of such a separation is incomprehensible within the framework of the traditions and attitudes of Islam.[4] The Saudi rulers have used this idea of non-separation during the creation of their state, but they were able to adopt an opposing view in later years. How they adopted and maintained this separation, and hence preserved their civilian rule, is the aim of this discussion.

As mentioned above, a thorough examination of the preservation of civilian rule requires at least some reference to its stark alternative: intervention by the military in civilian rule. This chapter will therefore examine theories of military intervention in the Third World, or rather, theories associated with the prevention of military intervention as they apply to Saudi Arabia. The discussion will focus on political, economic and organizational factors and their impact on military intervention and civil-military relations.[5] However, to better understand the preservation of civilian supremacy in Saudi Arabia, an historical background of the country's civil-military relations would be necessary.

A Brief History of Civil-Military Relations

The roots of the modern or third Saudi state's army dates back to 1902 when Abdulaziz (Ibn Saud, father of the current King Fahad) led forty tribal warriors to capture Riyadh. Dar'iyya served as the capitol of the "first state" (1744-1818) and Riyadh as the center of the "second state" (1824-1891). A series of military victories followed. By 1906, Abdulaziz's forces controlled most of central Arabia.

Understanding the nature of his rivals, Abdulaziz saw the need for more supporters. He tried to encourage the Beduins (*Ikhwan*) to settle down in communities of brotherhood (*Hujar*), which made it easier for him to mobilize them when needed. For the sake of Islam the *Ikhwan* would supply him with warriors to help him unite the Arabian Peninsula under the banner of Islam. In theory, at least, the common denominator for Abdulaziz and the *Ikhwan* was their willingness to fight for God and the unification of the country. As Beduins, the *Ikhwan* were well-trained in desert warfare and were a strong force capable to mobilize in a very short time.[6] Furthermore, they were known for their bravery and dedication to Islam, something which Abdulaziz's rival forces lacked.[7]

With the help of the *Ikhwan*, Abdulaziz won virtually all of his battles. By 1925, Abdulaziz sent his army, which consisted mostly of the *Ikhwan*, to conquer Hijaz, the stronghold of Abdulaziz's remaining rival, Sherif of Mecca, Hussein bin Ali, the Great Grandfather of the current King of Jordan. By that time almost all of the Arabian Peninsula was under his control except for some of the British protectorates in the east, the north, and the south. This meant that for Abdulaziz the "territorial shaping of his kingdom was completed."[8] This arrangement was in contradiction to the beliefs of the *Ikhwan* who saw it as antithetical to the idea of *Jihad* or holy struggle. The duty of every Muslim, as the *Ikhwan* interpreted it, is to fight in the cause of God to make Islam the supreme ruler over the world. By refusing to make *Jihad* against the infidel, Abdulaziz was said to be contradicting the teachings of Islam, and hence should not be able to expect total obedience from the *Ikhwan*.

Upon achieving his tactical goals, Abdulaziz came to regard the fighting force of the *Ikhwan* as a potential threat to his rule, and proceeded to build up the small army he had set up earlier as a counter force.[9] The *Ikhwan* disregarded Abdulaziz's order to stop their *Jihad* against the northern areas of the Arabian Peninsula, which nominally were under the British Mandate. By the late 1920s a growing series of confrontations between Abdulaziz and his former military ally, the *Ikhwan*, reached a peak. Abdulaziz, with the help of British aircraft and pilots, was able to defeat the *Ikhwan*. By 1930 he had managed to eliminate them "as an organized military force."[10]

The *Ikhwan* military forces had, in essence, come to represent a kind of military intervention. The explanation of this intervention rests upon the nature of Islam itself. On this point Be'eri described the attitude of Islam toward political and military power as "not one of negation, disassociation or suspicion,

، of complete affirmation."[11] As a military force the *Ikhwan* felt they had an obligation to intervene in civil rule to defend their interpretation of Islam and to stop any more violation of it by the rulers. They used in their support the well-known words of the Prophet Mohammed, who said, "There is no obedience for a creature in the disobedience of the creator."

Furthermore, the *Ikhwan* expected that Abdulaziz would appoint *Ikhwan* leaders to high governmental positions. For example, Ibn Bijad and Al-Dawish hoped to be the General Commander of the Saudi forces and the Governor of Al-Madina, respectively.[12] Instead, they were punished when they decided to confront Abdulaziz because of his collaboration with the British, whom they regarded as the infidel. After the defeat of the *Ikhwan* revolt, Abdulaziz jailed their leaders and contained their military supporters. He consolidated the remaining *Ikhwan* under his aegis, and incorporated them into the White Army -- a militia designed to "counterbalance" the regular army.[13]

In 1932, Abdulaziz proclaimed the establishment of the modern state of Saudi Arabia. His need for cash led him initially to grant American oil companies concessions. By the late 1930s and early 1940s, Saudi Arabia was exporting oil and receiving revenue. With the arrival of this wealth, the Saudi regime began developing the country's armed forces. This development led to the establishment of the Ministry of Defense in 1944, headed by Prince Mansour Ibn Abdulaziz. After Mansour's death, his brother, Prince Mishal, became the Minister of Defense and started reorganizing the ministry, but made little serious progress in developing the defense establishment or the armed forces.[14]

By 1951, the close Saudi-U.S. military relationship led to renewal of an agreement which allowed Washington to lease the base in Dhahran for five years.[15] This renewal, coupled with the rise of Arab nationalism and economic problems, led to unrest in the eastern provinces, triggering an ARAMCO workers' strike and a subsequent attack on the vehicles of the U.S. Air Force in Dhahran.[16] These pressures persuaded the king to appoint Crown Prince Saud as commander of the armed forces; he later became king after the death of his father in 1953. In short, Abdulaziz's strategy to maintain historic civilian rule was "based on deterrence, diplomacy, and blandishment."[17]

King Saud's decidedly uncharismatic personality and lack of administrative abilities only reinforced his rivalry with Crown Prince Faisal, and ultimately caused a split within the royal family. The rivalry, combined with the problems described above, contributed to a precipitous decline in the army's support of King Saud. By 1955, a mutiny among a group of army officers took place in Taiff.[18] Intelligence reports also confirm that a plot against the regime was discovered.[19] This incident led Saud to take stern measures to secure his reign. He executed one officer and ordered the creation of an internal security system.[20]

Saud's rivalry with other princes, and his fears of the army as a source of disloyalty and conspiracy, caused him to divert financial and manpower resources away from the regular army and into the hands of the Royal Guard and White Army.[21] To strengthen his political and military power, he appointed his sons to important positions: Bandar and Mansour (nephews of the first Defense Minister) became commanders of the Royal Guard,[22] and Khalid served as the head of the White Army.[23] Furthermore, he dismissed his brother Mishal as Minister of Defense and replaced him with his own son Fahad.[24] Saud extended his control, insofar as possible, over all aspects of Saudi society, and this included the military. Nevertheless, external factors intervened. A deterioration in relations with Gamal Abdul Nasser of Egypt led to another coup attempt. This plot was discovered in May 1957, and was followed by mass deportation of pro-Nasser foreigners. Many suspected Saudis were arrested. Evidence subsequently revealed that the plot was organized by an Egyptian military attache in Jiddah.[25]

Saud's problems with Nasser may have contributed to his ineffectual management. Corruption and inefficiency delayed the army's development programs.[26] King Saud used funds form the defense programs to gain political favor and to strengthen his political position against his rival, Crown Prince Faisal.[27] Despite this rivalry, however, the king, under intense pressure from internal crises and outside threats, periodically called upon Faisal to take part in the management of the country's affairs.

In the late 1950s, King Saud, faced with external problems involving Nasser and internal crises within his royal family, transferred most of his power to Crown Prince Faisal, who adopted a new defense policy. To appease Nasser, Faisal discontinued the buildup of the Saudi army, and paid far greater attention to the development of the internal security forces. Faisal was finally removed in 1960, although he was returned to power in 1962, after the military coup in Yemen and the intervention of Egyptian military in support of that coup. Crown Prince Faisal quickly revived the buildup of the Saudi armed forces, simultaneously removing all of King Saud's sons from his newly formed cabinet and appointed his brother, Prince Sultan bin Abdulaziz, as the new Minister of Defense. Sultan continues to hold this position to the present. Faisal reinforced his efforts toward reform by creating a new Supreme Defense Council. The White Army became known as the National Guard, with Abdullah bin Abdulaziz as its head.[28] According to *Al-Hayat* newspaper, Saad, the son of

Saud and the Commander of the National Guard, was dismissed along with six of his brigade commanders.[29]

The war with Yemen in 1962 demonstrated to Saud and Faisal the potential, if not actual, disloyalty of elements of the armed forces. The defection of some Saudi pilots to Egypt, for example, confirmed earlier intelligence reports that most of the air force officers were secret sympathizers of Nasser.[30] The Saudi regime thus responded by grounding the air force and dismissing many officers. Although King Hussein of Jordan sent a squadron of Hunter fighters to Saudi Arabia in support of Saud, the situation continued to deteriorate when the commander-in-chief of the Jordanian air force, along with a few pilots, defected to Egypt. This defection meant that the whole squadron had to be recalled to Jordan.[31]

A key civil-military crisis occurred in 1964 following a worsening of the struggle between Saud and Faisal. The old rivalry had finally escalated to the point of military confrontation, with Saud mobilizing the Royal Guard around his palace and Faisal ordering his brother Abdullah to call out the National Guard.[32] Major Othman Al-Humaid, the Commander of the Royal Guard, favored Faisal and helped in the arrest of the Chief of the Royal Guard, Saud's son Mansour, King Saud's last military supporter.[33] With the help of the *Ulama* (religious leaders) and the senior princes, Saud was deposed and the Royal Guard was incorporated into the army. Major Al-Humaid became, in later years, the Chief of Staff of the armed forces and, after that the assistant to the Minister of Defense, a position that he continues to hold.

Despite Faisal's firm control, the sixties were a decade of turbulence. Signs of this included growing demands for constitutional monarchy;[34] the outbreak of civil war in Yemen (which resulted in a confrontation between Saudi Arabia and Egypt); the defection of Saudi pilots to Egypt; the establishment of a group of "Free Princes" who criticized the Saudi regime from Cairo; and finally, growing political activities among civilians and the armed forces by leftist and pan-Arabist groups, arguably the most dangerous of the developments. In 1963-64, six ranking military officers were jailed for their political activities; Major Abdullah Mashayt was imprisoned for years for distributing anti-regime leaflets to his men.[35] Furthermore, Nasserites were apparently responsible for a series of explosions which destroyed important military posts.

Popular resentment toward the regime increased. In June of 1969, a coup attempt was initiated; however, it was discovered and a wave of arrests followed involving civilians, military officers and enlisted men. More than 130 members of the military, including sixty air force officers, were put behind bars at this time. Many of these were senior officers. The plot involved the director of the air force academy in Dhahran, the director of military operations, the former head of the Ministry of Defense, the former commanders of both the Al-Hassa and Mecca Garrisons, and the commander of the air force.[36] The Saudis ultimately "liquidated" the air force for these reasons,[37] leaving only the royal princes on duty.[38] That same year, in order to liberate the Saudi frontier post, al Wadiah, after a surprise attack by South Yemen, Riyadh had to hire British pilots, led by Commander Tony Winship.[39] Even though most of the coup plotters were from Hijaz, which is west of Saudi Arabia, the plotters' aim was to establish a republic in the Arabian Peninsula. As always, the Saudi government denied that these events ever occurred. However, four years later in an interview with *Al-Hawadith* magazine, the Saudi Defense Minister confirmed the existence of the 1969 coup attempt.[40]

Although most of the plotters were Arab nationalists, as Hijazis, they felt they were often discriminated against,[41] and had become dissatisfied with King Faisal's political and economic reforms.[42] As a reaction to this serious coup attempt, the Saudi government purged the armed forces of radicals while reducing ethnic discrimination against Hijazis. Promotion in the lower ranks became based on merit for non-royal members of the armed forces. Salary increases were also approved, although no political reforms were considered. There is no doubt that the limited character of these reforms reflected Faisal's distrust of the armed forces.

These limited changes did not prevent the military from further plotting against the government. In mid-1977, Saudi military intelligence discovered another plot at Tabuk Air Base.[43] According to published reports by the *International Institute for Strategic Studies*, seventeen officers and many civilians participated in it, and three air officers fled with their airplanes to Iraq.[44] As a result, the Ministry of Defense temporarily forbade all military aircraft to carry any ammunition, and limited their flying range and time to thirty minutes by restricting the supply of fuel.[45]

Although there was a decrease in salaries and benefits for the armed forces in May 1976, a year later salaries doubled.[46] There were no indications that the doubling of salaries was the result of the minor coup. However, the 1979 uprising of the Grand Mosque at Makkah and the Shia disturbance in the eastern province may well have given the Saudis warning that more reforms were necessary. Subsequent evidence of improvements in the armed forces in the early 1980s included an obvious acceleration of military construction, improvements in training and family housing, the replacement and transfer of many senior officers[47] and, perhaps most important, the doubling of salaries in 1981.[48] Up until this historical point, such steps, coupled with other security measures, could plausibly be regarded as the best way to appease the armed forces while containing them within the limited range deemed appropriate by the civilian government.

The Preservation of Civilian Rule

During this general period, the overthrow of several Arabian monarchies by their armed forces alerted the Saudi royal family of the potential danger to the military establishment of the regime. The Saudis tried to avoid military coups of this ilk by controlling what they perceived to be the primary sources of such intervention. There is extensive literature on this topic. Although there are many different theories and explanations of the causes of praetorianism, such factors as political activity within the military,[49] economic deterioration[50], internal organization structures,[51] past military coups,[52] internal disruptions,[53] defeat in wars,[54] professionalism,[55] as well as many others are usually mentioned. Saudi sensitivity regarding the danger of the military coup led the government to do everything possible to keep control over the armed forces even at the expense of military preparedness.[56] For example, military promotions to senior positions have always been based on loyalty rather than competence.

Political Factors

One of the primary sources of military intervention is, broadly speaking, political activity, especially that relating to the questions of legitimacy, political culture, and external conflicts. For many students of military intervention, legitimacy is the critical variable that explains military intervention;[57] at the very least, it is clear that legitimate governments face a significantly lower threat of military intervention. Furthermore, the "legitimacy enjoyed by a government affects the political role of its armed forces far more than any other environmental or internal factor."[58] To gain such legitimacy the regime's leader must find an ideology that is acceptable to most of the people.[59] The Saudi royal family used the ideology of Islam as the central legitimizing vehicle, something which cannot be employed by the military. The usage of Islam is conducive to the idea of *Walee Alamr*, or the head of the Islamic state, which requires obedience to *Walee Alamr* as long as he is applying Islam and the *Shariah*. This means that all power legitimately rests in the hands of the royal family. In turn, this gives it the moral and legal right to dominate everything in Saudi Arabia, including the military and political establishments. Put differently, the Saudi political system easily became "a family bazaar" or, politically speaking, the only unofficial ruling single party, small wonder Saudi Arabia has become "the only member-state of the United Nations whose very name denotes family dominion."[60] This full domination dictates that virtually any political process--such as voting, political parties, unions, and other vehicles of popular participation--is prohibited. The non-participatory political culture is further buttressed by the mentality of the royal family members themselves, who "believe that their moral quality and historical achievements give them the right to rule the country alone."[61]

The royal family clearly understands the implications of this process of domination, and hence employs a variety of techniques to ensure its survival. Important among these is its monopoly over the socialization processes. In Saudi Arabia, the royal family and its institutions control virtually all instruments of political socialization, including mosques, schools, and media, and use them in the interests of maintaining the political *status quo*. No political opposition or criticism in the press is permitted. Furthermore, even public criticism of government by private individuals is forbidden; this is justified by the well-known Saudi proverb, *Asheiookh Abkhass* which means the royal family knows better and there is no need for any criticism. Based upon this, Sheik Al-Awdah, a prominent religious leader, was banned from preaching and lecturing because he preached politics.[62] This phenomenon has increased since the Gulf war.

The prohibition of critical politics is rigorously extended to members of the armed forces. Written regulations prohibit military involvement in politics. In fact, officers are not allowed to join any association and if they receive any political pamphlets, even through the mail, they are required to report them directly to the military intelligence office.[63] In Saudi Arabia, then, political culture produces politically docile military officers, which, it is hoped, means their complete uninvolvement in politics. The logic of this is straightforward, if not entirely valid. Limited political awareness of military officers, it is thought, will result in limited political aspirations, and hence less of a rationale for intervention.[64] Lowering the armed forces' political awareness has required the Saudi government to separate the military from society. This has been accomplished by isolating them in military cities, far removed from urban population centers.

Another variable political scientists recognized as a source of danger for military intervention is external conflict or wars.[65] Members of the royal family realized that if they engaged in any war and were defeated, that defeat might well encourage the army to intervene. This reasoning was behind the government's invitation to British pilots in the 1962 war against Yemen and Nasser supporters and, more recently, the American war against Iraq. Furthermore, the Saudi rulers have tried to reduce external conflict because they know that their likely enemies in such conflicts would encourage the Saudi military to intervene, just as Nasser did in coup attempts in the 1950s and 1960s. In view of this, the Saudi rulers utilize the bulk of their petroleum dollars to coopt and contain possible threats. Their list of potential enemies in the past included Nasser, and more recently, Saddam Hussein, Hosni Mubarak and Hafez Asad. The politics of containment helped the Saudis to reduce the source of this threat and hence keep the military out of politics.

Economic Factors

The literature of political violence has shown that economic decline may affect both military and civilian institutions and their members. As such economic difficulties may "engender legitimacy deflations"[66] and political instability, eventually leading to military intervention. According to Fossum, the occurrence of coups increases at times of economic deterioration.[67] In Arab and African countries, "coups are most likely to be linked to conditions of economic decline."[68]

Oil exports make up Saudi Arabia's main source of government revenue. Sharp oil price increases since the mid 1970s propelled the desert kingdom into a powerful financial force in world politics and allowed the government to modernize the country's economy, dramatically improving living standards. Schooling and medical care are completely free. Personal income is not taxable and modern amenities as running water, electricity and housing are heavily subsidized by the government. Reduction in oil prices in the last few years had relatively little impact on the regime's ability to provide these benefits.

Knowing that economic decline may induce military intervention, the Saudi rulers have managed to control this potential danger by doing their best to please the military economically. After the 1969 and 1977 attempted coups, the regime started a massive program of economic improvement, which included the doubling of military salaries in 1977 and again in 1981. In addition to high salaries, the Ministry of Defense provides the military with plush houses and facilities. According to David Wood of the *Herald Tribune*, the housing of a middle-ranking Saudi officer would astonish any American soldier.[69] The only thing these officers need when moving in to a new villa or apartment is the key. The ministry supplies the villas with everything from needles to beautiful bedroom sets. Along with the furnished housing, the "military cities," are equipped with facilities like mosques, super markets, recreational facilities, and more.

The costs for such policies are, predictably, exorbitant. According to the report of *International Institute for Strategic Studies*, the defense expenditures of Saudi Arabia in 1982 were about $27 billion, and its military manpower in 1983 was 51.5 thousand.[70] Dividing defense expenditures by the total number of men under uniform, the average cost per soldier would be $524,427 a year. This is a huge expenditure per each military individual. In fact, as evident in *Table 3:1*, the cost per Saudi soldier appears to be the highest in the world.

TABLE 3:1

**Comparative Defense Expenditures and Military Manpower
1982-83**

Country	Military Expenditures $(Millions)	Numbers In Armed Forces (Thousands) (1983)	Military Expenditure Per Soldier (Thousands)
Bangladesh	177	81.3	2,177.1
Brazil	1,838	274.0	6,708.0
Britain	24,296	320.0	75,925.0
Cameroon	97	7.3	13,287.60
Colombia	420	69.7	6,025.8
Egypt	2,495	447.0	5,581.6
France	22,522	492.3	45,748.5
Indonesia	2,870	1,120.0	2,562.50
Iraq	8,127	517.3	15,710.4
Japan	10,361	240	43,170.8
Jordan	462	72.8	6,346.1
Kenya	240	16.0	15,000.0
Libya	709	73.0	9,712.3
Nigeria	1,671	133.0	12,563.9
Poland	6,234	340.0	18,335.2
Saudi Arabia	**27,062**	**51.5**	**525,475.7**
Tunisia	239	28.5	8,385.9
Turkey	2,755	569.0	4,841.8
U.S.A.	196,345	2,135.9	91,926.1

Source: Military Balance (London: International Institute for Strategic Studies 1984-1985)

Because the armed forces might intervene on the basis of protecting their interest, which is mainly budgetary allocations, the Saudis have always allocated one-fourth of their budget to the military. In 1987 Saudi Arabia ranked second among 142 countries in the percentage of military expenditure of GNP.[71] Even in 1992 the defense allocation represented about 30 percent of the entire budget. Despite all this spending, the efficiency of the Saudi armed forces remains poor. The Gulf war demonstrated that most officers who enjoy all this financial security and luxury are seriously lacking in physical training. Some of these officers enjoy a pleasant existence, indulging in such prohibited pursuits as whiskey and women. The apparent presumption of the government is that as long as military men are well paid, and receive so many benefits, the chances of their intervention to challenge the *status quo* is very slim.

Organizational Factors

As Welch and Smith note, "Many aspects of military organization affect the possibility of coup d'état,"[72] or at least the members' political attitudes and their sense of competition with other social groups[73] (such as the government) may be affected. Some of the important aspects of military organization include the mission and purpose of the army, and its internal structure.

Even though the main mission of Middle Eastern armies is the defense of their respective countries from outside enemies, there are still other functions they perform, such as maintaining stability and participating in modernizing the country.[74] The Saudi military's main function is, like that of most of the armies of the Middle East, to defend the government from internal threats.[75] To accomplish this, the Saudi leadership needs to recruit officers who are loyal to the regime. As such, the royal family has opted for voluntary membership rather than conscription, because "the latter would create more internal unrest than external security."[76] Moreover, the distrusted Shias and other opposition groups have been excluded from the military. In general, the Kingdom's officer corps is drawn mostly from the middle class. Different groups such as Nadjis, Hijasis, and Janoobis, the latter from the southern province, are well represented. Loyalty to the regime is the most important criterion, and it is reinforced through recruitment patterns. Background examinations are required for anyone wishing to enter Saudi military academies. The size of the army is kept small for it is thought a smaller army is easier to control, and creates fewer problems. To make up for this possible deficiency, the Saudis maintain a contingent of about 40,000 foreign advisors[77] and thousands of Pakistani troops,[78] ostensibly to help the regime in case of internal problems or attempted coups.

The Saudis have organized their military forces with a primary view to protecting their regime. From the beginning, Saudi trust in the army was low. Because of this, some members of the royal family have always supported the National Guard, expecting that it would serve as an effective counter-force to the regular army and would be able to deal efficiently with internal security problems. The Saudi National Guard, which is a totally separate organization from the Ministry of Defense, recruits all of its well-paid members from loyal tribes. The majority of Guard members are stationed in key locations where problems might arise, particularly around Al-Qasim and in the eastern province, where they can keep watch over the Shia population and at the same time protect the oil fields.

Crown Prince Abdullah (half brother to King Fahad and Prince Sultan, the Minister of Defense), who heads the Guard decided to modernize it in ways which suggest that his primary intent was that it become an effective force capable to counter the armed forces. He equipped the Guard with anti-tank guided missiles, anti-aircraft guns and other modern equipment.[79] There have even been some attempts by Prince Abdullah to purchase squadrons of helicopters and heavy tanks.[80] The competition between Abdullah and Sultan has led to rivalry within the royal family.[81] This competition has expanded to include the "Sudairi Seven" or "Al-Fahad," a clan which is comprised of King Fahad, the Deputy of the Minister of Defense, the Minister of the Interior and his deputy, the governor of Riyadh and other junior princes. In 1983 rumors erupted that the Al-Fahad faction would replace Abdullah backers in the National Guard and that Abdullah had warned of "a National Guard-backed coup."[82] Although these rumors proved to be somewhat exaggerated, this rivalry in political and military affairs affected budget allocation decisions and appointments to important political and military positions, such as the resignation of General Khalid Ibn Sultan.[83]

Each faction, having formed alliances with certain sectors of society, has sought to pursue its interests by appointing and promoting its supporters.[84] For example, most commanders of operations within each branch of the armed forces are also members of the royal family; such appointments, based on nepotistic considerations, tend to insure that the current regime will remain immune form most conspiracies within the military. As Cordesman notes, promotions are based on familial ties and "loyalty, not military proficiency.[85] This is shown in the case of Prince Mit'ab Ibn Abdullah, a major in the National Guard who was promoted in a few years to the rank of general and of Deputy Chief of the military organization of the National Guard.

As a bureaucratic entity, the Saudi military has a highly centralized command, which regulates and controls the movements of military personnel.

Notification from Prince Sultan, or his deputy, (his full brother) Prince Abdulrahman, is required prior to any movement or action by troops. As a result of the bureaucratic nature of the military hierarchy, it would be highly difficult for any group of officers to organize a covert operation of rebellion against the government. Furthermore, because intelligence officers in each brigade are required to report directly to the head of military intelligence, who is under the command of the Minister of Defense, even a suspicion of a coup attempt would be easily detected and the suspects dealt with immediately and harshly.[86]

Yet another precautionary measure concerns the logic of the siting of bases; in a vast country where urban areas are few and a forbidding terrain precludes easy travel, Saudi military bases are scattered. This isolates military personnel from civilians. Also, to prevent fraternization and the development of cells of disloyal subjects, military personnel are frequently rotated. This scattering of armed forces personnel supposedly makes it "difficult for any given commander or unit to launch a coup that could threaten the government."[87] As a further reinforcement, the regime has placed air defense units in urban areas, and major air bases under the army, to ensure "that the Saudi Air Force could not be used in a coup attempt."[88]

The Aftermath of the Gulf War and the Future

The Gulf war revealed the vulnerability of the Saudi political and military institutions, as indicated in part by the public outcry at the disappointing performance of the armed forces. Fear of death and lack of fighting competence led some pilots who are members of the royal family to plead illness in order to escape combat during the war.[89] A Saudi journalist observed that "August 2, 1990 was a turning point. We discovered that we were talking about no defense, no power--nothing."[90]

The weak performance displayed by the Saudi military, as best exemplified by the political leaders' call for Western military units to defend the country, caused some in the reform movement (led by 500 religious leaders) to issue a call for political changes, most notably the establishment of an independent consultative assembly, greater press freedom, and a stronger defense capability. This collective call for reform was a new phenomenon in recent Saudi history, and as a Western diplomat pointed out, it was "significant and virtually unheard of in Saudi Arabia."[91]

The government responded to these demands by temporarily blacklisting the protestors, banning their international travel, and demanding an apology; simultaneously, a campaign was mounted to draw new recruits into the armed forces, suggesting a new desire to increase the overall number of military personnel. It is interesting to speculate on the impact such recruitment might have on political attitudes, particularly if future recruits are drawn from the population of students who have studied in Europe and the United States, and if, at the same time, officers currently serving in Saudi military units are sent in greater numbers to the United States for military training.

The Gulf war also revealed the precarious state of discipline within the ranks. During the war, one pilot escaped with his plane into neighboring Sudan,[92] while other pilots discharged their bomb loads into the waters of the Gulf, rather than on Iraqi targets.[93] These actions were widely interpreted as stemming from religious feeling, specifically the Islamic prohibition in the *Q'uran* about killing innocent people.

The recent Gulf crisis affected negatively the Saudi economy. To ameliorate the problem Riyadh responded by sharply increasing oil production. Nevertheless, the 1992 budget showed a large deficit. It remains to be seen whether and to what extent post-war economic and strategic realities will affect long-term military spending, especially in light of the Arab-Israeli talks and the possibility of an arms control agreement regarding the Middle East. A lot will depend on the nature and the fate of post-war security arrangements and the possible reactions of conservative Muslim forces in Saudi Arabia and in neighboring countries. It should be noted that Khomeni's Islamic Republic threatened the stability of the Saudi Arabian's regime in the 1980s. While the outcome of the Gulf war proved beneficial to Riyadh's short-term interests, it did little to ameliorate concerns regarding Saddam Hussein's future intentions and those of his supporters in Sudan and Yemen. To counter possible dangers, the Saudi regime is planning to build a $2.9 billion electronic surveillance system along the Saudi-Yemeni border.[94] At present, the greatest concern of the Saudi regime centers on the increasing popularity of the Islamic movement,[95] and the potential for confrontation which could result in a popular uprising and subsequent military intervention. This likelihood is increased by the absence of any signs of reform under the ailing King Fahad. Although many Saudis are looking to his successor, Crown Prince Abdullah, to initiate change, he will be constrained in confronting the stronger presence of the Al-Fahad clan. Thus, for the near future at least, any reform is likely to be symbolic, or, at best, minor, unless the Saudi government faces a genuine social or economic crisis. Barring that situation, the current regime may be expected to maintain its strong civilian

68

rule by continuing to provide attractive benefits and strong deterrents to its people, particularly the military.

Notes

1. Gary Bertsch, Robert Clark, and David Wood, *Comparing Political Systems: Power and Policy in Three Worlds* (New York: John Wiley and Sons, 1978), p. 431.

2. Claude E. Welch, Jr., "Civilian Control of the Military: Myth and Reality: in Claude E. Welch, Jr., ed., *Civilian Control of the Military* (Albany: State University of New York Press, 1976), p. 1.

3. Manfred Halpern, *The Politics of Social Change in the Middle East and North Africa* (Princeton: Princeton University Press, 1963), p. 251.

4. Eliezer Be'eri, *Army Officers in Arab Politics and Society* (New York: Praeger, 1970), p. 281.

5. For different studies on a variety of countries see Alfred Stepan, *The Military in Politics: Changing Pattern in Brazil* (Princeton, New Jersey: Princeton University Press, 1971), pp. 172-184; Guillermo A. O'Donnell, *Modernization and Bureaucratic-Authoritarianism* (Berkeley: Institute of International Studies, University of California, 1979), pp. 54-75; Youssef Cohen, "Democracy from Above: The Political Origins of Military Dictatorship in Brazil," *World Politics* 60 (Oct. 1987), pp. 37-45. On the Philippine case see: Gretchen Casper, "Theories of Military Intervention in the Third World: Lessons from the Philippines," *Armed Forces and Society* 17 (1991), pp. 101-210. Also see: Claude Welch, Jr. and Arthur Smith, *Military Role and Rule: Perspectives on Civil-Military Relations*, (Massachusetts: Dusbury Press, 1974), pp. 5-24; Warren Dean, "Latin American golpes and Economic fluctuations, 1823-1966," *Social Science Quarterly* 51 (1970), pp. 70-80; Eric A. Nordlinger, *Soldiers in Politics; Military Coups and Government* (Englewood Cliffs, New Jersey: Prentice Hall, Inc., 1977).

6. This is based on an informal discussion with one of the leaders of the Abdulaziz Army. He told the author about how easy it is to mobilize *Ikhwan*. He said, "Abdulaziz would send me to the leaders of tribes and I would tell them about the time and place where we should meet to go and fight the enemies. Easily, they would be there on time." June 1976.

7. Ayman Al-Yassini, *Religion and State in the Kingdom of Saudi Arabia* (Boulder, Colorado: Westview Press, 1985), p. 54.

8. Ibid., p. 54.

9. Richard F. Nyrop, *Area Handbook for Saudi Arabia, Foreign Area Handbook Series* (Washington, D.C.: American University, 1984), p. 259.

10. Ibid., p. 260.

11. Be'eri, *Army Officers in Arab Politics and Society*, p. 281.

12. Ahmad A. Attar, *Sayr Al-Jazira*, v. 7 (Beirut: Matbaat Al-Hurriah, 1972), pp. 267-70.

13. Nyrop, *Area Handbook for Saudi Arabia*, pp. 260-261.

14. David Holden, Richard Johns, *The House of Saud* (London: Sidgwick and Jackson, 1981), p. 160.

15. Nadav Safran, *Saudi Arabia: The Ceaseless Quest for Security* (Ithaca: Cornell University Press, 1988), p. 67.

16. Anthony H. Cordesman, *The Gulf and the Search for Strategic Stability*, (Boulder, Colorado: Westview, 1984), p. 99.

17. Safran, *Saudi Arabia: The Ceaseless Quest for Security*, p. 59.

18. Robert Lacey, *The Kingdom* (London: Hutchinson & Co., 1981), p. 312.

19. Safran, *Saudi Arabia. The Ceaseless Quest for Security*, p. 104. Alexander Bligh, "The Interplay Between Opposition Activity in Saudi Arabia and Recent Trends in the Arab World" in Robert W. Stookey, ed., *The Arabian Peninsula: Zone of Ferment.* (Stanford: Hoover Institution Press, 1984), p. 67.

20. Lacey, *The Kingdom*, p. 313.

21. Safran, *Saudi Arabia: The Ceaseless Quest for Security*, p. 109.

22. Cordesman, *The Gulf and the Search for Strategic Stability*, p. 105.

23. Lacey, *The Kingdom*, p. 313.

24. Safran, *Saudi Arabia: The Ceaseless Quest for Security*, pp. 104-5.

25. Holden and Johns, *House of Saud*, pp. 194-6. Lacey, *The Kingdom*, p. 317.

26. Safran, *Saudi Arabia: The Ceaseless Quest for Security*, p. 105.

27. Cordesman, *The Gulf and the Search for Strategic Stability*, p. 105.

28. Ibid., pp. 111-12.

29. Alexander Bligh, *From Prince to King* (New York: New York University Press, 1984), p. 77.

30. Safran, *Saudi Arabia: The Ceaseless Quest for Security*, pp. 105, 472.

31. Holden and Johns, *House of Saud*, p. 227.

32. Lacey, *The Kingdom*, pp. 350-1.

33. Cordesman, *The Gulf and the Search for Strategic Stability*, p. 113. Holden and Johns, *The House of Saud*, p. 239.

34. Fatina A. Shaker, "Modernization of the Developing Nations: The Case of Saudi Arabia," Unpublished Ph.D. Dissertation, Purdue University, 1972, p. 307.

35. Ali A. Alyami, "The Impact of Modernization on the Stability of the Saudi Monarchy," Unpublished Ph.D. Dissertation, Claremont Graduate School, 1977, p. 124.

36. For details see Mordechai Abir, *Saudi Arabia in the Oil Era* (London: Croom Helm, 1988), pp. 113-20; Safran, *Saudi Arabia: The Ceaseless Quest for*

Security, pp. 129-30; Cordesman, *The Gulf and the Search for Strategic Stability*, pp. 137-41; Holden and Johns, The House of Saud, pp. 277-80; Lacey, *The Kingdom*, pp. 379-82. For the list of names of those who participated in the attempt see: Ibid., pp. 201-2.

37. *New York Times*, September 9, 1969.

38. Lacey, *The Kingdom*, p. 381.

39. Holden and Johns, *The House of Saud*, p. 281.

40. Bligh, "The Interplay Between Opposition Activity in Saudi Arabia and Recent Trends in the Arab World," p. 73.

41. Cordesman, *The Gulf and the Search for Strategic Stability*, p. 137.

42. Shaker, *Modernization of the Developing Nations*, p. 307.

43. Gwynne Dyer, "Saudi Arabia" in John Keegan, ed., *World Armies* (New York: Facts on File, 1979), p. 620.

44. Adeed Dawisha, *Arabia's Search for Security*, (London: International Institute for Strategic Studies, 1979), p. 7.

45. Dyer, "Saudi Arabia," p. 620.

46. Safran, *Saudi Arabia: The Ceaseless Quest for Security*, pp. 428-29; Ibid., p. 617.

47. Cordesman, *The Gulf and the Search for Strategic Stability*, pp. 227-37.

48. Holden and Johns, *The House of Saud*, p. 533.

49. Eric A. Nordlinger, *Soldiers in Politics: Military Coups and Government* (Englewood Cliffs, New Jersey: Prentice Hall, Inc., 1977).

50. Warren Dean, "Latin American Golpes and Economic Fluctuations, 1823-1966," *Social Science Quarterly* 51 (1970), pp. 70-80.

51. Welch, Jr. and Smith, *Military Role and Rule*, pp. 9-19.

52. Douglas Hibbs, Jr., *Mass Political Violence: A Cross-National Causal Analysis* (New York: Wiley, 1973).

53. Dankwart A. Rustow, "The Military in Middle Eastern society and Politics," in Sydney N. fisher, ed. *The Military in the Middle East*, (Columbus, Ohio: Ohio State University Press, 1963).

54. Ibid., p. 11.

55. Bengt Abrahamsson, *Military Professionalization and Political Power*, (Beverly Hills: Sage, 1972).

56. William B. Quandt, *Saudi Arabia in the 1980s*, (Washington: The Brookings Institution, 1981), p. 102.

57. Nordlinger, *Soldiers in Politics*, p. 92-3.

58. Welch and Smith, *Military Role and Rule*, p. 29.

59. Takukder Maniruzzaman, *Military Withdrawal from Politics* (Cambridge: Ballinger, 1987), p. 4.

60. Michael C. Hudson, *Arab Politics: The Search for Legitimacy* (New York: Yale University Press, 1977), p. 177.

61. Othman Y. Al-Rawaf, "The Concept of the Five Crises in Political Development--Relevance to the Kingdom of Saudi Arabia," Unpublished Ph.D. Dissertation, Duke University, 1980, p. 367.

62. Secret pamphlet dated April 2, 1991, was distributed in Riyadh showing an official order of the government to stop Sheik Al-Awdah form preaching. He was allowed to preach religion again in October, 1991.

63. Informal discussion of the author with an air force major, January, 1991.

64. Welch and Smith, *Military Role and Rule*, p. 20.

65. Frank W. Wayman, *Military Involvement in Politics: A Causal Model* (Beverly Hills: Sage, 1975), pp. 26, 58.

66. Nordlinger, *Soldiers in Politics*, p. 93.

67. Egon Fossum, "Factors Influencing the Occurrence of Military Coup d'Etat in Latin America," *Journal of Peace Research* 3 (1967), pp. 236-7.

68. William R. Thompson, "Regime Vulnerability and Military Coup," *Comparative Politics* 7 (1975), pp. 475-6.

69. Anon, *Saudi Military Expenditures: A Model for Wasting the Muslims' Wealth*, 1983 (no publisher, no place of publication, in Arabic), p. 10.

70. I.I.S.S., *The Military Balance, 1984-85*, pp. 140-1.

71. Ruth L. Sivard, *World Military and Social Expenditures* (Washington, D.C.: World Priorities, 1991), p. 56.

72. Welch and Smith, *Military Role and Rule*, p. 9.

73. Nordlinger, *Soldiers in Politics*, p. 43.

74. James A. Bill, Carl Leiden, *Politics in the Middle East* (Boston: Little, Brown and Company, 1979), pp. 250-1.

75. The two main wars the Saudis fought were fought mostly by non-Saudis, the Yemen War and the Gulf War (against Iraq). Other wars, for example against Israel, the Saudis sent only a symbolic or token military unit.

76. Cordesman, *The Gulf and the Search for Strategic Stability*, p. 199.

77. Ibid., p. 201.

78. Safran, *Saudi Arabia: The Ceaseless Quest for Security*, p. 362-3; Nyrop, *Area Handbook for Saudi Arabia*, p. 267. This was confirmed to the author by a Saudi general in 1984; however, most of the Pakistanis were asked to leave because of the Saudi distrust of the Shia Pakistanis, who represented a large number in the Pakistani military. Since then the Saudis have been shopping around for other foreign troops, for example Turks or Bangladeshis.

79. Nyrop, *Area Handbook for Saudi Arabia*, p. 285.

80. *Makka Calling*, an opposition publication, (January 1987), p. 17.

81. Cordesman, *The Gulf and the Search for Strategic Stability*, pp. 178-9.

82. Ibid., p. 378.

83. General Khalid Ibn Sultan is the son of the Minister of Defense and was the commander of the Arab and Muslim forces in the Gulf War. He resigned because of the pressure of some members of the royal family and military leaders

for his poor performance and his involvement in briberies during the Gulf war. Also, "he was retired by royal decree after he demanded a promotion to Chief of Staff of Saudi armed forces in a direct communication to the King, outside the chain of command," *New York Times*, October 13, 1991.

84. Cordesman, *The Gulf and the Search for Strategic Stability*, p. 380; *Makka Calling* (January, 1987), p. 19.

85. *Time* (September 14, 1990), p. 40.

86. An army captain related to the author an old incident about three junior officers riding together. One of them said jokingly, "If I become the president of this country, I would appoint both of you as cabinet ministers." A few days later, he was tortured and subsequently sentenced to a long period of incarceration, while the second, who had not reported these comments, was tortured and dismissed from the army for failure to report subversive statements; the third junior officer had, of course, reported the incident. August 1988.

87. Cordesman, *The Gulf and the Search for Strategic Stability*, p. 173.

88. Ibid., p. 173.

89. *Time* (September 24, 1990), p. 40.

90. *Chicago Tribune* (May 19, 1991).

91. Ibid.

92. *Al-Gazeera Al-Arabia*, an opposition publication, (January, 1991), p. 28.

93. An informal discussion with Saudi diplomats. June, 1991.

94. *Economic Intelligence Unit, Saudi Arabia, Country Report*, No. 2, 1991, p. 12.

95. In January 1992, the Saudi government arrested about 50 fundamentalists, *Al-Quds Al-Arabi*, January 22, 1992. Furthermore, King Fahed warned "the fundamentalists of harsher treatment if they persist in challenging Saudi foreign and domestic politics," *New York Times*, January 30, 1992.

4

The Military in Guyana: From Party Control to Party Dependence?

Rita Giacalone

Located in the northern part of South America, Guyana is culturally, historically, and ethnically linked with the English-speaking islands of the Caribbean. As such, it presents an interesting case study of a Third World nation where the military has never taken political power into its hands. This case, however, can not be considered a successful experience in civilian control of the armed forces, according to the expectations of most Western academics dealing with this subject. In other words, the reasons why the Guyanese military has not seized, or even attempted to take over the government, have little or nothing to do with concepts like professionalization, "liberalization-democratization," or even the toleration of some level of political competition between civilians. Relations between civilian society and the armed forces in Guyana seem to fit neither the model of its Latin American neighbors (Venezuela and Brazil) nor that of most of the English-speaking Caribbean. On the contrary, the Guyanese model more closely resembles that found in Sub-Sahara Africa, with Tanzania apparently being the most similar experience.

The Guyanese armed forces have had a short institutional life of less than thirty years. There is, however, a prevailing view that the perpetuation in power of the People's National Congress (PNC) from 1964 to the present has been made possible by the creation of the armed forces which, in many ways, have been penetrated and controlled by that party. We will trace here the creation of the Guyana Defense Force from its establishment (1965) and its subsequent evolution, in order to determine whether the party's control has been eroding, and

73

the extent to which the PNC has come to depend increasingly on the military and para-military institutions to retain power.

The Background

The Guyana Defense Force (GDF) constitutes the Guyanese military. There is no separate air force or navy. A small air wing with light aircraft and a marine wing with coastal patrol vessels fall within the GDF's control.[1] The Guyana National Service (GNS) and the People's Militia are para-military forces. The British garrison in Guyana, two infantry battalions and a mixed army/air force helicopter group left the country in October 1966, five months after formal independence. They left behind some senior officers in charge of the police and a small training group for the GDF.[2]

The Guyana Defense Force emerged out of the Special Service Unit (SSU) created in 1964 by the British Governor, Richard Luyt, in an effort to suppress the violent expressions of popular and ethnic discontent which erupted during the government of the leftist-oriented People's Progressive Party (PPP), led by Cheddi Jagan. The GDF was formed shortly after a series of clashes between the two most important ethnic groups: the majority of East Indians (51%), represented by the PPP; and the minority black population (41%), supporting the PNC. Under British organization and training there was "a conscious effort to achieve an ethnic balance in the SSU."[3] Even the successor of the British commander, Colonel Ronald Pope, as head of the Defense Force after independence, was Major Raymond Sataur, an Indo-Guyanese officer trained at Sandhurst, the British Royal Military Academy.[4] But the GDF quickly turned into a predominantly black force with a black commander, Major Clarence Price, and fiercely loyal to the PNC.

The 1964 general elections brought to power a coalition consisting of PNC and the right-wing United Force (UF), a grouping extracted mostly from white Portuguese and Catholics.[5] It is worth remarking that both the PPP and the PNC had started as one party in 1960, committed to independence and the socialist transformation of the then British Guiana. The party split, however, after the British government deployed troops in the colony in 1953 to put an end to the rapid changes initiated by the first PPP government elected by universal adult suffrage. Supported by rural East Indian plantation workers Jagan maintained a more radical stance. Forbes Burnham, leader of the PNC, appealed to the urban black and mixed population and those in the public service and commerce. He espoused a more moderate program.[6] The task of converting the

SSU into the GDF, in 1965, fell to the PNC-UF coalition government led by Prime Minister Burnham.

As Cynthia Enloe has pointed out, the GDF's evolution has been influenced by the fact that it was born "at a time of both accelerating politicization and growing party-encouraged ethnic polarization."[7] It is not surprising, then, that the coalition in power attempted from the very beginning to render the military into a bulwark of support for the government. The parliamentary elections of 1968 convinced Burnham that if the coalition broke up he would no longer be able to stay in power because the number of East Indian voters was on the increase.[8] The British were aware of the Prime Minister's need to draw the military on his side. The Guyanese military forces enjoyed little public support and had to operate in conditions of "endemic insecurity arising from the existence of a racially divided society." The British worried that the GDF would be hard pressed to resist the government pressure to support the party in power and leave to the police the task of maintaining law and order. The emerging role of the military in the Guyanese post-colonial situation was akin to that prevalent in Latin America, and different from the politically neutral role of the army in Great Britain.[9] This may be the reason why the British military advisors did not abandon Guyana until 1968, and why Colonel Pope stayed until 1969.[10]

In spite of the fact that in 1965 the Burnham government had invited an International Commission of Jurists to study the ethnic composition of both the black dominated Guyanese civil service and security the forces, including the police, the same government did little to address the imbalance recommended by that commission. The government even claimed that the GDF had the most equitable ethnic representation in the country. By 1972 the proportion of East Indians within the force had dropped to 10 per cent. All commanding officers were black and came from the mostly urban reservist Volunteer Force and the civil service.[11] By 1973 the GDF had grown enough to consume, together with the police, 7.7 per cent of the national budget.[12]

Redefining the Role of the Force

According to Enloe, the PNC used promotion and recruitment as instruments to penetrate and control the GDF. Prime Minister Burnham himself made all promotion decisions. As chair of the Guyana Defense Board, he had assumed direct authority for all security forces, a responsibility previously held by the Minister of Home Affairs.[13] Even though the independence constitution of 1966 made the President commander-in-chief of the Guyanese armed forces,

Prime Minister Burnham took over the post himself.[14] By 1968, Burnham felt confident enough to discard the UF, won the election held that year and moved to strengthen his hold on the security forces.[15]

Following his victory at the polls, Burnham took more aggressive measures to control both his party and the armed forces. Guyana entered a long period of Afro-Guyanese ethnic dominance. Assisted by a centralised state apparatus, a black minority group monopolized the resources of the state.[16] Burnham's hegemonic control was "rigorously regimented." Using similar recruitment and promotion methods, he imposed strict political control over the political corps. Burnham also weakened the power base of members of Parliament using a system of proportional representation. The Prime Minister surrounded himself with a cabinet of young (mostly black) technocrats.[17] At the same time, a six-month cadet course was established at Timehri, granting the PNC the possibility of being "more politically selective of new entrants into the officer corps."[18] Enloe has posited that

> efforts to tighten relations between the party and the GDF suggest that civilian politicians see the armed forces as crucial for maintenance of power, despite their succession of electoral victories under a proportional representation system that gives the PNC special advantages. PNC attention to the GDF implies also that the reliability of the GDF is not certain without such increased partisan supervision.[19]

Two events, one internal and the other external, prompted the redefinition of the role of the GDF in 1970, and a subsequent reshuffling of senior officers in 1971. The first took place in January 1969, when supporters of the UF in the Rupununi district mobilized the Amerindians settled there in order to stage a revolt against the government and to attempt to secede from the rest of the country.[20] The second was an uprising by the Trinidad armed forces in February 1970.[21] Although suppressed, these rebellions convinced Burnham that if he wanted to maintain control of a racially divided country, the GDF had to become completely loyal to him and his PNC.

One of the first steps to increase party influence over the GDF was the formation of the Education Corps used by ministers and other PNC officials to "discuss" officers and enlisted men with the "philosophy of the government." GDF officers were also included in the Social, Political, and Economic Council (SPEC), a group set up by the Minister of Information on the grounds that there should be more "social analysis" behind PNC's rule.[22] The group was not heard from since 1974 because by then it had completed its mission of weeding out officers of questionable loyalty or those resistant to PNC indoctrination. Most senior GDF officers, though only in their forties or fifties, were sent to retirement in 1971, or placed in positions removed from actual troop command. In addition to pushing aside those who objected to closer links between the GDF and the PNC, Burnham promoted younger officers more prone to accept his leadership and PNC political ideology.[23]

An important element in the redefinition of the military role was the oath of loyalty to the government that officers had to take. Burnham expected that the armed forces be loyal to him personally. He made this clear in an address to the GDF in October 1970:

> I do not share with the British the concept that the army is...loyal to the Government of the day. As Prime Minister, I expect you to be loyal to this Government....It must be a straight forward loyalty from top down, and it must be based on an appreciation of the philosophy of this Government....It is therefore essential that you should understand what this Government stands for if you are to serve in the GDF.[24]

George K. Danns sees this statement as a manifestation of the PNC government's attempt to turn the military into "an organisational panacea for societal transformation."[25] Granted that "military institutions are authoritarian," with a rigid bureaucratic system of delegated authority from the top down, they also tend to be efficient. Danns believes the GDF was the only efficient institution available that could be used as a prototype to start reshaping Guyanese society, as proclaimed by the establishment of the "Socialist Cooperative Republic" in 1970. He notes that "the army has been engaged in building roads and airstrips in the remotest regions of the country's hinterland, performing mercy missions...[and] providing medical treatment..." (i.e., civic action).[26] Danns agrees with Morris Janowitz's, John J. Johnson's and Lucian Pye's[27] argument concerning the armed forces as organizational tools capable of promoting social change through mass mobilization. For Guyana, mobilization was viewed important to the decolonization process.

Percy Hintzen has pointed out that the expanding political role of the army, after 1968, related to an effort by the PNC ruling elite to free itself from the influence of the black and mixed middle sectors; these elements were viewed as hampering the party's decision to accelerate the political transformation of Guyana into a "socialist cooperative republic."[28] Be it part of the decolonization process or of the need to create a new base of support for the PNC program of change, party penetration of the army was and remains a reality. Enloe notes that joining the GDF's officer corps required "explicit PNC affiliation." --

something not altogether unique to the military institution, for patronage has governed most relationships in the Guyanese bureaucracy since British rule.[29]

The extent of PNC control over the Guyanese military can be clearly observed on the occasion of the 1973 general election won by Burnham and his party. Charges surfaced that army units broke up opposition campaign rallies in the East Indian-dominated sugar plantations and of tampering with ballot-boxes on election day. The GDF did not allow anyone representing opposition parties to be present while ballot-boxes were transported from the polling stations to army headquarters.[30] Enloe summarizes these actions as follows:

> it is open to question just how the PNC would have fared had the government not been able to call upon the GDF. It is possible that the PNC still would have won. However, in an open election the PNC might not have been able to capture the two-thirds majority which gave it the ability to amend the Constitution. Furthermore, an untampered poll might have shown a far lower voter turnout, indicating substantial political alienation...[31]

Army loyalty to the PNC was not merely a matter of shared ideology. The government saw to it that the GDF's budget went up by 60 per cent on the eve of the election, followed in 1974 by further increases for defense and internal security.[32] In exchange for these, the GDF had to pledge allegiance to the PNC, at the first biennial party congress held that year.[33] Burnham had himself promoted to "general of the army" and appeared in public ceremonies wearing appropriate military attire. It is worth noting here that the highest rank in the GDF was that of brigadier while the Prime Minister was a full "general."[34] Seeking to enhance "the paramountcy [sic] of the party," the PNC presented itself as more important than the civil government or any other institution, including the army.[35]

From Control to Dependency: The PNC-Army Relationship

Open GDF involvement in the electoral contests since 1973 highlights the degree of control achieved by the PNC and its leader. At the same time, it demonstrates the weakened position of the latter, who increasingly came to depend upon control of the army to stay in power. Perhaps fear of enhanced GDF influence led to the creation of two paramilitary forces: the Guyana National Service (GNS, 1975) and the People's Militia (1976). These moves have been interpreted as efforts by the PNC to form alternative poles of coercive power to counterbalance the GDF.[36]

The formation of strong paramilitary units did little to curtail the GDF's influence.[37] It retained the largest share of the defense budget and its chief-of-staff was named chief of all the security forces -- a position which gave him the top command of the GDF, the GNS, the militia, and the police.[38] The National Service grew out of the Guyana Youth Corps, while the militia imitated the Cuban pattern. The government justified the establishment of the militia on grounds of an imminent invasion from neighboring Venezuela due to a territorial dispute over the Essequibo region.[39] Both organizations (GNS and the militia) were black, loyal to the PNC, and subjected to continuous indoctrination.[40] They were also used to provide employment for the urban black unemployed, as well as vehicles to promote a "national ideology" among the people.[41] Inter-service rivalries developed among the four security forces regarding training, budgetary allowances, and salaries. Danns sees these as remnants of the British strategy of "divide and rule." The Guyanese armed forces, he argues, have become "an institutional and coercive buffer between the people and the ruling power elite."[42]

The formation of the Working People's Alliance (WPA) in 1979 presented an alternative to the PNC and the East Indian-dominated PPP. The WPA emerged as a new urban-based political organization with a socialist program and a strong following among black workers and intellectuals, under the leadership of Walter Rodney.[43] When a party of similar orientation, the New Jewel Movement, took power in Grenada in 1979 by resorting to the use of armed force, the Burnham government forced a major shake-up in the high command of the GDF. The government dismissed high-ranking and popular officers, including the chief-of-staff. The latter was replaced by a police officer, Norman McLean, "a Burnham loyalist who had at one time been the traffic chief." McLean had attended the International Police Academy in Washington, D.C. and had been running the GNS.[44] McLean's promotion was in accordance with the concept of interchangeability of personnel in the four security forces that Burnham had announced earlier that year.[45]

Apparently grumblings had surfaced in the military regarding the advisability of linking the fate of the GDF to a single political party. Officers had also expressed concern about the Burnham administration which, by 1978, had lost most of its popular support and relied almost exclusively on coercion and fraud to perpetuate itself in power. Increasingly, between 1974 and 1979, the army had been called upon to restore order and to break strikes at a time when important areas of the mostly "estatized" Guyanese economy were paralyzed.[46]

The appointment of a police officer as chief-of-staff hardly lessened discontent within the GDF, but it assured a commander loyal to Burnham and the PNC. Ironically, soon after a new socialist constitution was ratified in 1980, the government made "amends by issuing a postage stamp commemorating the 16th anniversary of the GDF."[47] The military coup of 1980 in neighboring Suriname further emphasized the need to control the armed forces, if Burnham and his PNC were to remain in power. In 1980, for example, the government allocated 10 per cent of the budget to the security forces in exchange for support.[48]

The close relationship between the GDF and the PNC was illustrated by the involvement of a GDF sergeant and electronics specialist, Gregory Smith, in the death of WPA leader Walter Rodney in 1980. Sergeant Smith posed as a former GDF member disenchanted with Burnham and ready to cooperate with the leader of the WPA. When a set of walkie-talkies he had given to Rodney exploded in the latter's hands, Smith was flown out of the country, probably by the military. The GDF claimed that there was no member by that name in its files, but the opposition disclosed his army number, photograph and service record.[49]

Commenting on the role of the GDF in the parliamentary elections held in the latter part of 1980, one international observer, Lord Averbury, noted that

> The military['s] presence in certain areas was intimidating. The boxes were collected by military personnel who prevented accredited officials of the opposition, sometimes by force or the threat of force, from accompanying or following the boxes.[50]

The United States Department of State in its *Country Report on Human Rights Practices* for 1982, pointed out that in Guyana the state security forces seemed to have become "the private protectors of the ruling party."[51] The following year's report said that Burnham government's survival "was ultimately based on the security forces."[52] This situation did not prevent the participation of Guyanese officers in the IMET (International Military Education and Training) Program and the purchase of arms and military material from United States sources, in the early 1980s. According to Griffith,[53] this collaboration stopped in 1984, but resumed again in 1988. Rumors of military discontent with Burnham and of an American attempt to destabilize the PNC leader, echoed by the *Financial Times* in 1984,[54] might have been responsible for this change in relations between the GDF and the U.S. military.

In 1985, Burnham died while undergoing surgery and was replaced as President by Prime Minister Desmond Hoyte. The latter reached an agreement with the other two leadership contenders in the PNC (Hamilton Green and Viola Burnham) and was duly elected by popular vote in December 1985.[55] The opposition requested that the GDF be confined to its barracks on election day, but Chief-of-Staff McLean refused, alleging that the army's presence was more necessary when electoral tensions were running high.[56]

President Hoyte's first measures regarding the military included promotion of the most GDF senior officers. In October 1986, the President promoted Colonel Joseph Singh to Brigadier General and named him commander of the GNS.[57] There has been no indication of change in the relationship between the PNC government and the armed forces since Burnham's death. Toward the end of 1987, for example, when the local press reported that the GDF was concerned about the negative effects of a new devaluation of the Guyanese currency "on an already beleaguered population," Brigadier Singh, hastened to refute these allegations.[58]

The internal situation within the ranks of the PNC has been dominated by clashes between President Hoyte and Prime Minister Hamilton Green, a former secretary general of the party. Green is said to have a large following "among the rank and file of the PNC and the security forces."[59] His power base probably affected Burnham's decision to bypass him as his successor in favor of Hoyte.[60] Festus Brotherson feels that Hoyte's strategy has been to try to keep Hamilton Green "away from executive duties in major institutional sources of power such as the military."[61] Thus, when an official report concluded that Guyana had become a transhipment point for cocaine, Hoyte himself chaired the inter-agency committee which included representatives from the army and the police appointed to deal with the problem.[62] It is worth noting that drug trafficking involves large sums of money for Guyana's starved economy. The country's military is allegedly heavily involved in such illegal activities. Even the pro-government *Sunday Chronicle* suggested in January 1989 that "a high ranking Guyanese military or para-military officer" might have known something about a clandestine airstrip (located near the Guyana-Suriname border), and a damaged Rockwell Commander aircraft. Two Colombians and a Guyanese were found nearby engaging in a smuggling operation.[63]

Besides promoting GNS officers to higher ranks, in a period of escalating inflation, Hoyte reduced the GDF's share of the budget (from G$ 118.2 million in 1987 to G$ 100.9 million in 1988) while the GNS's share remained intact.[64] Budget cuts forced the GDF in 1989 to launch a vehicle rehabilitation program. Military aircraft were leased to civilians in order to earn foreign exchange. According to Norman McLean, the GDF could not purchase new aircraft and vehicles for seven years.[65] Most of these happened from the time Hoyte became President. These moves suggest that he is strengthening the GNS in order to counterbalance Green's support among senior GDF officers. Perhaps it is not coincidental that in 1989 more than fifty officers left the GDF. When Norman McLean retired from his command post the following year, he was replaced by Joseph Singh, head of the GNS.[66]

Despite the power struggle within the PNC the armed forces continue to support the government. By the end of 1988, Guyana was facing an acute internal tension manifesting in outbreaks of arson, disorder and street violence. In the midst of all this an exercise, called "Operation Wallop," was launched by Guyanese military and para-military forces in the coastal areas. The officially stated purpose was to test the forces' readiness "to maintain peace and security."[67] In October 1990 the press reported the detention of a former army officer and a senior policeman accused of having links to a group which allegedly plotted to overthrow the PNC by force.[68] But this seemed to be an isolated case.

In spite of this incident, the army continued to be one of the pillars on which the PNC's political power rests. And this has not been lost to opposition groups in Guyana. In a circular made public in April 1989 by both the Roman Catholic and the Anglican Bishops of Guyana, entitled *Bishops' Manifest for Peace*, outlined seven principles to achieve internal peace and national progress. The sixth reads:

> Not only is the responsibility of the State, through the security forces, to protect each and every citizen, but the people must have the confidence and trust that they are being protected.
>
> The security forces must, therefore, publicly affirm their loyalty to the Guyanese nation and the upholding of the Constitution. There can be no suggestion of their loyalty to any group without the alienation of others.[69]

Following many delays, the Guyanese government responded to domestic and international pressure and decided in late September 1991 to hold parliamentary elections. An updated voters list, compiled by the government, was made public. The accuracy of the list was immediately and vigorously attacked by opposition parties. The chorus of protest was also joined by a team of neutral observers representing the Carter Center.[70] Under the circumstances, President Hoyte was forced to postpone the electoral contest scheduled for December 1991. He then proceeded to declare a state of emergency, reconvened the legislature and passed legislation extending the present parliament's life until September 1992.[71] None of the moves seem to have generated any known reaction from the military, implying support for the President's decisions. The PNC managed to extend its tenure in office by an additional year at a time when polls gave the opposition PPP, led by Cheddi Jagan (an East Indian Marxist) a good chance to unseat the incumbent party. It is rather obvious that the PNC has become increasingly dependent an the military to remain in power and the armed forces do not appear prepared to repudiate the party.

Prospects and Perspectives

Will the Guyanese armed forces reconsider their stand? If we accept Griffith's contention that the Guyana case fits the "penetration model" of civilian control, according to which of the armed forces act only as the recognized organ of the single ruling party,[72] then the questions are: will the PNC government accept the results of a fair election if the results run counter to its interest? and what will be the eventual outcome of the personality clashes within the PNC? The first question points to the possibility of a PNC-induced military takeover either to prevent fair elections or to maintain the government in power if the opposition wins. The second may suggest that Green could eventually risk a military coup to gain power. While not discarding the possibility of a PNC military coup to retain power, a clash between PNC factions seems more unlikely. The hemisphere is moving toward elimination of military governments. Guyana has succeeded in preserving the appearance, though not the substance, of democracy since 1968. Given Guyana's dire economic conditions, no government, PNC or opposition led, will risk alienating the chances of attracting foreign investment and financial assistance from international lending institutions. Organizational considerations are also likely to prove an important inhibiting factor. Owing to the division of the Guyanese armed forces into different branches (GDF, GNS, and so on) our attempted takeover by one group may be opposed by another.

Cognizant of Guyana's explosive ethnic divisions, the East Indian dominated PPP is seriously entertaining the possibility of a multi-ethnic coalition with considerable black representation. This means that even if the PNC is voted out of office, the Afro-Guyanese community would still be fairly represented in a PPP led government. Such a government would be hard pressed to provoke a confrontation with the armed forces. Maintaining its autonomy is important to the Guyanese military who enjoy prerogatives unavailable to most of the Guyanese population; if these such prerogatives continue, there would not be much incentive to intervene against a government with black participation. There is also the possibility of an accommodation between the military and non PNC led coalition government with strong black representation and too weak to curb the armed forces' influence in the allocation of Guyana's resources. This, of course, is based on the premise that ethnic affiliation and socio-economic considerations are more important to the Guyanese military than political ideology and/or personal allegiance to a particular party leader.

Contradicting Griffith's position, it appears that the GDF has arrived at a situation of relative power vis-a-vis the PNC. The Hoyte government has abruptly changed the political ideas on which Guyanese officers were indoctrinated in the 1970s, and Burnham's dominating personality is long gone. What keeps the GDF close to the PNC is no longer "congruity of political ideas" and personal allegiance to the party leader, but rather common ethnic affiliation and a hefty share of the country's scarce resources. In other words the PNC seems to have gone from political control of the GDF to a situation where it is highly dependent on the support of the army to remain in power. So far, the prevailing trend seems to be one of maintaining the status quo for both the PNC and the armed forces find cooperation to their mutual benefit. A move by a future PPP government, or even one dominated by blacks outside the PNC, to restrict the military's preferential access to societal resources may prompt the GDF to stage a coup in order to protect its corporate interests.

Guyanese civil-military relations do not conform to the usual Latin American norm of recurrent military intervention, "caudillo" factions within the armed forces, or the myth of a military tradition and culture. Nor do they dovetail with the post-independence experience of the English-speaking Caribbean, where the military establishment is seen as a "transplanted social institution" with close links to metropole patterns and tradition, or susceptible to United States encouragement to maintain some degree of militarization for internal stability considerations.[73]

Following the regional approach posited by Ulf Sundhaussen Guyana looks closer to the Sub-Sahara African experience where, "despite initial democratic constitutions, authoritarian rule has become the norm." This model of civil-military relations is characterized by uncertainty as to "what...constitutes legitimacy [and] the unabated strength of primordeal loyalties of an ethnic/tribal nature." In this sense, it can be said that Sub-Saharan élites, including the military, lack "a commitment to democratic norms..." and operate in a political culture that places emphasis on values like family ties or ethnicity.[74] At the outset of independence civilian leaders in Guyana and Sub-Saharan Africa were not "confronted with established armies that could...challenge their authority." On the contrary, they created armies and managed to exercise full authority over their role and activities.[75]

One might compare Guyana with Daniel Zirker's case study of the structural barriers to military intervention built in Tanzania since the 1964 army mutiny.[76]

Like President Nyerere, the Burnham government "purge[d] the officer corps of potentially charismatic leaders;" incorporated the officer corps into the dominant political party; introduced of "civic action as a major military function," provided the military with a foreign policy "mission" (either expansionist or defensive),[77] and paid attention to military pay demands. Zirker concludes that these measures led to the "politicization of the military and the militarization of civil society" in Tanzania, by means of ideological training and party penetration of the military and the formation of a people's militia in order to counterbalance military power; these were augmented by substantial growth in budgetary allocation for defense.

This is not to say that this similarity is a product of a premeditated decisions on the part of Afro-Guyanese political leadership to copy the Tanzania case. It is worth remembering, however, that Julius Nyerere, leader and founder of the Tanzanian African National Union, was long regarded in the English-speaking Caribbean as a model worthy of imitation. Nyerere endeavored to forge a viable, united black nation from a patchwork of tribal groups, and to resist the penetration of external economic and political forces. These, after all, were the proclaimed objectives of the "cooperative socialist" path pursued in Guyana under Burnham's authoritarian personal rule. Further scrutiny of ideological and other contacts between the Guyanese and Tanzanian experiences would be necessary to fully understand the reasons that account for those similarities.

Notes

1. Chaitram Singh. *Guyana: Politics in a Plantation Society* (Stanford, California: Hoover Institution Press, 1988), p. 76.

2. Anthony Verrier. "Guyana and Cyprus: Techniques of Peace-Keeping," *Royal United Service Institution Journal*, vol. 3 (Nov. 1966), p. 299.

3. Singh, *Guyana*, p. 77.

4. *Ibid.*

5. See Thomas J. Spinner, Jr. *A Political and Social History of Guyana, 1945-1983* (Boulder and London: Westview Press, 1984).

6. *Ibid.*

7. Cynthia H. Enloe. "Civilian Control of the Military: Implications in the Plural Societies of Guyana and Malaysia" in Claude E. Welch, Jr., ed. *Civilian control of the Military: Theory and Cases from Developing Countries* (Albany: State University of New York Press, 1976), p. 82.

8. Verrier, "Guyana and Cyprus," p. 299.

9. *Ibid.*, pp. 298, 301.

10. George Kenneth Danns, "Decolonization and Militarization in the Caribbean: The Guyana Example" (Inter-American Politics Seminar Series, Center for Inter-American Relations, 1978), p. 22.

11. Enloe, "Civilian Control," pp. 84-85.

12. George K. Danns, "Militarization and Development: Experiment in Nation-Building" *Transition*, vol. 1, no. 1 (1978), p. 30.

13. Verrier, "Guyana and Cyprus," p. 299.

14. Singh, *Guyana*, p. 73.

15. Reynold A. Burrowes. *The Wild Coast: An Account of Politics in Guyana* (Cambridge, Massachusetts: Schenkman Publishing Co., 1984), pp. 218-19, 222-23, 234-35. Skillful changes of electoral law combined with control of the registration process by PNC activists explain Burnham's victory in 1968.

16. Ralph Premdas. "The Politics of Preference in the Caribbean: The Case of Guyana" (Montreal, McGill University, Department of Political Science, n/d).

17. Burrowes, *The Wild Coast*, pp. 239-40.

18. Singh, *Guyana*, p. 77.

19. Enloe, "Civilian Control," p. 87.

20. Danns, "Militarization and Development," p. 34; Percy C. Hintzen, "Civil-Military Relations in Guyana and Trinidad: A Comparative Study" (Mimeographed paper, Yale University, 1976), p. 13.

21. For more detail see Susan Craig. "Background to the 1970 Confrontation in Trinidad and Tobago" in S. Craig, ed. *Contemporary Caribbean: A Sociological Reader*, Vol. II (Maracas, Trinidad-Tobago: The Author, 1982).

22. Danns, "Decolonization and Militarization," pp. 25-26; Enloe, "Civilian Control," pp. 87-88. For Ivelaw L. Griffith, "The Military and Politics in Guyana" (XV Annual Conference of the Caribbean Studies Association, Port-of-Spain, May 1990), p. 5. This fits into the penetration model of militarized politics where congruity in political ideas of government leaders and officers removes potential sources of conflict between them.

23. Enloe, "Civilian Control," p. 86.

24. Quoted in Danns, "Decolonization and Militarization," p. 24.

25. *Ibid.*, p. 25.

26. Danns, "Militarization and Development," p. 33, and George K. Danns, *Domination and Power in Guyana* (New Brunswick: Transaction Books, 1982), p. 152.

27. Morris Janowitz, *The Military in the Political Development of New Nations* (Chicago: University of Chicago Press, 1964); John J. Johnson, *The Military and Society in Latin America* (Stanford: Stanford University Press, 1964); and Lucian Pye. "Armies in the Process of Political Modernization" in J.J. Johnson, ed. *The Role of the Military in Underdeveloped Countries* (New Haven: Princeton University Press, 1962).

28. Hintzen, "Civil-Military Relations," pp. 13-14.

29. See Harold A. Lutchman. "Patronage in Colonial Society: A Study of the Former British Guiana" *Caribbean Quarterly*, Vol. 16 (June 1970).

30. Enloe, "Civilian Control," p. 90.

31. *Ibid.*, p. 89.

32. *Ibid.*, pp. 92, 98.

33. Singh, *Guyana*, p. 78.

34. Danns, *Domination and Power*, pp. 149 and 169.

35. *Ibid.*, p. 149

36. *Ibid.*, p. 165.

37. The GDF and the GNS had the same strength in number of members, according to Danns, "Decolonization and Militarization," p. 17.

38. Danns, *Domination and Power*, p. 164.

39. For more detail on the border question with Venezuela see Jacqueline Braveboy-Wagner. *The Venezuela-Guyana Border Dispute* (Boulder and London: Westview Press, 1984).

40. Singh, *Guyana*, pp. 79-81.

41. Kempe R. Hope, "Guyana's National Service Programme" *GUYGRAM* 40 (Oct. 4, 1974), p. 35.

42. Danns, *Domination and Power*, p. 165.

43. Singh, *Guyana*, p. 78.

44. Spinner, *Political and Social History*, p. 172; Humberto Garcia. "*La estrategia militar en el Caribe angloparlante*," *El Caribe Contemporaneo*, No. 11 (*diciembre* 1985), p. 33.

45. Danns, *Domination and Power*, p. 165.

46. Singh, *Guyana*, p. 79.

47. *Ibid.*

48. Spinner, *Political and Social History*, pp. 183-184.

49. *Ibid.*, pp. 184-85; *Caribbean Contact*, February 1987, p. 10; later Smith reappeared in French Guiana and declared that he had been flown out of the country by the WPA because he had been involved in a subversive plot with Rodney, *Latin America Regional Reports-Caribbean* (April 1987), p. 3.

50. Quoted in Spinner, *Political and Social History*, p. 193.

51. *Ibid.*, p. 204.

52. Quoted in *Ibid.*, p. 211.

53. Griffith. "Military and Politics," pp. 14-15. For more detail on collaboration between the two military see Garcia, "Estrategia militar," p. 36.

54. Quoted in Garcia, "Estrategia militar," p. 36.

55. *Latin America Regional Reports-Caribbean*, 23 Aug., 1985, pp. 2-3, and 17 Jan., 1986, pp. 4-5; Hoyte was chosen president, according to the terms of the Constitution of 1980.

56. *Ibid.*, 1 Nov., 1985, p. 3.

57. *Latin American Monitor-Caribbean*, Nov. 1986, p. 357.

58. *Latin America Regional Reports-Caribbean*, Jan. 1988, p. 6. For more detail about the economic situation see Rita Giacalone, "FMI, movimientos sociales y politica electoral en Guyana" *El Caribe Contemporaneo* (Mexico) No. 20 (*enero-junio* 1990), and Roland T. Ely. "Guyana and the International Monetary Fund" (XV Annual Conference of the Caribbean Studies Association, Port-of-Spain, May 1990).

59. *Latin American Monitor--Caribbean*, Jan.-Feb. 1987, p. 382.

60. Franz J.T. Lee. "Involucion del 'socialismo cooperativista' en Guyana despues de Burnham" *Revista Occidental*, Año 4, No. 3 (1987), p. 277.

61. Festus Brotherson. "Hoyte Fully in Charge." *Caribbean Contact*, Dec. 1989, p. 12.

62. *Caribbean Insight*, April 1988, p. 10.

63. *Ibid.*, March 1989, p. 3.

64. *Ibid.*, May 1988, pp. 10-11.

65. *Ibid.*, Aug. 1989, p. 14.

66. *Ibid.*, March 1990, p. 12.

67. *Ibid.*, Nov. 1988, pp. 1-3; *Caribbean Contact*, Nov. 1988, p. 7.

68. *Latin America Regional Reports-Caribbean*, November 8, 1990, p. 3; *El Universal* (Caracas), October 6, 1990.

69. Quoted in *Caribbean Contact*, June 1989, p. 6.

70. *Caribbean Insight*, November 1991, p. 4.

71. *Ibid.*, February 1992, pp. 9-10.

72. Griffith borrows this model from Eric Nordlinger, *Soldiers in Politics: Military Coups and Governments* (Englewood Cliffs: Prentice hall, 1977).

73. In the case of the English-speaking Caribbean there is no developed model or norm of civil military relations at the theoretical level. There are a few recent studies but they tend to stress the impact of U.S. global strategies in the formation of armed forces in this subregion. See Alma Young and Dion Phillips, eds. *Militarization in the Non-Hispanic Caribbean* (Boulder, Colorado: Lynn Rienner,, 1986).

74. Ulf Sundhaussen. "Military Withdrawal and Re-Intervention: Patterns of Legitimacy and Regional Dimensions" (Paper delivered at the International Meeting of the Research Committee on Armed Forces and Society, IPSA, Madrid, July 1990.

75. James S. Coleman & Belmont Brice, Jr. "The Military in Sub-Saharan Africa," John J. Johnson, ed. *The Role of the Military in Underdeveloped Countries* (New Jersey, Princeton Press, 1962).

76. Daniel Zirker. "Structural Barriers to Military Intervention: The Case of Tanzania" (Paper delivered at the International Meeting of the Research Committee on Armed Forces and Society, IPSA, Madrid, July 1990). A revised version of this paper appears in this volume.

77. *Ibid.*

5

Personal Rule and the Search for Political Pluralism in Cameroon

Frédéric Belle Torimiro

The rising tide of activism and demands for political change in several African countries once again draws special attention to the durability of civilian rule in the Third World. Seemingly inspired by the pro-democracy movements in Eastern Europe, there is a growing endorsement of political pluralism and pressure on African leaders to establish a viable democratization program. The discourse of democracy in Africa is increasingly dominated by the saliency of a political structure and system of governance with widespread popular support. The inviolability of one-party rule is now challenged by those seeking to alter its pattern of political monopolies. Some intellectuals and political leaders are revisiting the idea of multipartyism even though Richard Joseph argues that it may not "rescue Africa from its distress."[1] However, Julius Nyerere of Tanzania observes that multiparty political systems increase the chances of conquering "the problems related to the complacency of a single-party system."[2] It seems that *perestroika* in sub-Saharan Africa invokes the need for the people to have control of their destiny.

Cameroon is one of the sub-Saharan African countries experiencing the surge of political pluralism. The pressure to change the political landscape is related to the calls for multipartyism, political liberalization and government accountability. However, the desire for democratization raises several basic questions. Can the current political leadership afford a broadly based democratic system? To what extent does a shift from one-partyism to multipartyism ensure public order? What role does the military play if any new landscaping culminates into a crisis of political order and subsequently increases the chances of public disorder?

This chapter provides a critical analysis of military abstention from politics in Cameroon. The character of civilian control is examined in terms of the democratization efforts influenced by political, economic and external factors. The operant assumption is that the challenge for political pluralism raises the possibility of a domestic power vacuum which could prompt a military intervention. As observed by Morris Janowitz, what is uncertain is whether a politically active military necessarily represents a "fundamental commitment to the emerging values of the society."[3]

Theoretical Propositions on Civilian Control of the Military

The importance of the military in developing countries is related to its capacity to seize power. It has manifested the ability to interrupt civilian politics and to broaden the public's sense of its responsibility to maintain political order. By the same token, the apparent stability of some African countries, including Cameroon, is attributed to civilian control of the military. The theoretical arguments rest on the assumption that there is an asymmetrical relationship in which the military accepts civilian authority and serves as a tool of the state.[4] More substantively, Samuel Huntington's theory of "subjective civilian control" suggests that the maximization of civilian power is enhanced by strong, well-organized governmental institutions or political parties and the presence of a weak military organization. The military lacks the institutional capacity to systematically influence changes within the political system.[5]

Claude Welch concentrates on the idea that the military is not completely disengaged from politics. As a consequence, civilian leaders are forced to institute constraints on the military to ensure its compliance. The extent of civilian control is determined by the capacity of political institutions, such as parties, to delimit and define the responsibilities of the military. Put differently, civilian control is governmental penetration of the military by constitutional and political means entrenched firmly in the political process.[6] By contrast, Samuel Finer and Ali Mazrui in separate analyses emphasize the extent to which the military is satisfied with civilian control.[7] As Auma-Osolo points out, the military is "likely to challenge and possibly remove civilian control" whenever it is no longer deceived by civilian leadership.[8]

Cameroon represents a relatively successful case of civilian control of the military in sub-Saharan Africa. The above theoretical discussion offers an opportunity to understand the ways in which the civilian leaders have controlled the military in order to survive politically and personally. In the light of these arguments, nonmilitarization of politics in Cameroon focuses on three possible propositions.

Proposition 1: *Institutional Performance*
The military will remain disengaged from politics only if civilian political parties and other institutions are equipped to deal with the sociopolitical and economic challenges of the society.

This proposition raises the optimum of the party system, the constitution and political leadership. The effectiveness of these institutional devices helps to explain the scope of military abstention from politics. To begin with, Samuel Huntington argues that the party system is "the principal institutional means for organizing the expansion of political participation."[9] Thus, multi-ethnic societies faced with the challenge of nation-building may be drawn toward the creation of either a one-party or multiparty system. Single-partyism is perceived as an integrative and stabilizing element designed to undermine particularism.[10] Its organizational capacity lends support to the process of conflict resolution as well as the achievement of national loyalty. Correspondingly, the desire for multipartyism suggests that mass regimentation runs contrary to the fundamental principles of democracy. A society that seeks to democratize its institutions must be willing to accommodate diverse and opposing views. The political parties in Nigeria, for example, are not only encouraged to promote discussion and dissent but they are expected to reflect the ethnic diversity of the society.[11] This study of Cameroon links the character of civilian control to the ability of the party machinery to effectively play its integrative role.

The party system is not the only source of civilian control. There is the importance of constitutionalism--with emphasis on the search of adequate constraints on militarism so as to institutionalize the subordinate relationship of the military. Claude Welch writes that "one must recognize that legal prescriptions do help to legitimate civilian control--and this legitimation may give pause to potential coup-makers when they consider the act of intervention."[12] Equally significant, the nature of political leadership is relevant to establishing civilian control over the military. The consequences of political authority are measured in terms of conflict resolution as well as the allocation of national resources and values.

Proposition 2: *The Effect of Economic Development*
Civilian control will collapse if it lacks the ability to promote economic development.

The high priority given to economic development in African states today reveals its importance in the political stability of civilian regimes. The assumption is that military intervention is a likely occurrence when civilian politicians can no longer manage economic growth or crises. Put it in a somewhat different manner, the collapse of civilian control over the military is in part attributable to adverse conditions of the national economy. Militarism or civil-military discord may be precipitated by a weakening economy or the military's perception that any economic misfortune is linked to the poor performance of civilian leadership. At best, this proposition attempts to establish a connection between levels of economic development and military inertia.

Proposition 3: *The Impact of External Influence*
Civilian control will prevail when there is considerable external pressure against military intervention in politics.

This proposition specifically addresses the manner in which the economic and military influence of France in francophone African states impacts on the military's predisposition to intervene. It encompasses explanations based on the relationship between France and its former colonies. There is the possibility of increased external influence to help maintain civilian rule or to protect French hegemony over the destiny of Africans. The flow of economic and military assistance may increase if the potential threat of a military coup undermines the objectives of France's Africa policy. It is explicitly recognized that French policy in Africa has underscored the idea of "no development without security."[13] France has intervened militarily in francophone states on the grounds that the *accord de défense* (security agreement) allows it to maintain the rule of friendly governments or permits African rulers to seek direct security assistance from it. Justification of its claim to such an interventionist role is also enhanced by the special bilateral and multilateral *coopération* agreements which cover important areas such as the economy, defense, education and foreign policy. The French-African relationship nevertheless may be altered by the democratization campaigns in various francophone states. The view that Africa experiences a *déficit démocratique*[14] is increasingly pushing France to review its policies in the continent.

The Dynamics of Political and Constitutional Control

The analysis of military abstention from politics in Cameroon must consider the important changes which accompanied the evolution of a de facto multiparty state into a totally dominant one-party state and then the appearance of *le renouveau* (New Deal) which promises political liberalization. From 1958, Alhaji Ahmadou Ahidjo's *Union Camerounaise* (UC) ruled the francophone majority in East Cameroon with the support of France. The party's hegemony was nevertheless challenged by the *Union de Populations du Cameroun* (UPC). As a radical nationalist party formed in 1948 and banned by 1955, the UPC pushed for socialism and rejected French rule by advocating *unification et indépendence immédiate* (immediate unification and independence).[15] The party resorted to violence when it was prevented, under the *Loi Cadre* (or enabling act), from participating in the electoral process. The UPC's unsuccessful insurgency allowed Ahidjo to spearhead the suppression of multipartyism and the establishment of a one-party system by 1964 in East Cameroon. To broaden the scope of his political power base, Ahidjo entered a *marriage de convenance* (marriage of convenience) between the UC and John Ngu Foncha's Kamerun National Democrats Party (KNDP) which was the governing party in West (anglophone) Cameroon. The agreement resulted in the formation of the Cameroon National Union (CNU) as well as undermining the strong and vibrant tradition of multiparty politics in West Cameroon.

As Aristide Zolberg observes, the dominance of one-partyism is derived from its capacity to propagate an ideology.[16] To provide Cameroonians with apparently a new sense of direction and purpose, Ahidjo placed the emphasis of the party's ideology on *national unity*. The CNU was organized to militate against the forces that threatened the efforts at nation-building. The incorporation of regional parties into a single, ruling party was intended to promote the idea that language, tribal, ethnic, regional and other forms of subgroup differences were obstacles to national unity. Political control through the party was therefore consolidated by immobilizing all forms of opposition and by presenting the CNU as a *parti unifié*. Other political parties were not allowed to take part in elections even though they were never outlawed by the constitution. In effect, the Constitution of 1972, creating the United Republic of Cameroon, provides in Article 3 (Section 1) that:

Political parties and groups may take part in elections. They shall be formed and shall exercise their activities in accordance with the law.

Contrary to this constitutional provision, the CNU operated as the only legitimate political apparatus with the capacity to mobilize the people in the task of political and economic modernization. The *rapprochement* between the party and the society was marked by apparent public loyalty to the CNU and by the ability of the party leadership to maintain, often by coercion, institutionalized unity. The absence of effective political opposition conjured an image of strong public confidence and long-term political stability.

The relevance of a strong ideological base is also evident in Paul Biya's regime. (He succeeded Ahidjo in 1982.) Biya removed the emphasis on unity that essentially defined the CNU's *raison d'être*. Following the March 21-24, 1985 Fourth Party Congress held in Bamenda, the party's name was changed to the Cameroon People's Democratic Movement (CPDM). The stress in what has been called *New Deal* policies to create a *new society* was an important part of Biya's brand of political liberalization. The Bamenda Congress which was chaired by Biya agreed on multiple candidacy within the CPDM to contests seats in the National Assembly. The delegates also supported the increase of the Party's Central Committee membership from 60 to 85, with only 20 of the members appointed by the party chairman. Twenty-eight of the committee members were purged and replaced by intellectuals, businessmen and five women.[17]

The Bamenda Congress provided the party leadership with a chance to alter the public personality of the CPDM. Arguably, Biya's political concessions appeared to be an attempt to weaken, if not avert, the call for a multiparty system. The CPDM party leaders looked anxious to take the lead in democratizing the political system. The party's aura of legitimacy in the post-congress period was therefore prolonged by vigorously pushing the idea that unity, peace and democracy could only be achieved in a one-party system. Its claim to political preeminence in Cameroon was affirmed by the support of militants and by the ability of the leaders to advocate a meaningful "transformation of the political principles and institutions" salient to the pursuit of national policy goals.[18] No doubt, the emergence of strong civilian movements favoring political freedom, anglophone rights and multipartyism present a real test to the dominance of the CPDM. Cameroon's experience with the push for political pluralism raises speculation on the ability of the CPDM to remain the governing institution without increasingly relying on the military.

Karl von Clausewitz asserts that the military should accept the responsibility and the right of civilian politicians to control and conduct the affairs of the state.[19] The idea of subordinating the military to civilian control in Cameroon is bolstered with specific constitutional prescriptions. The 1972 constitution recognizes the principle that all power rests with the people. Article 2 (Section 1) reads:

> National sovereignty shall be vested in the people of Cameroon who shall exercise it either through the President of the Republic and the members returned by it to the National Assembly or by way of referendum; nor may any section of the people or any individual arrogate to itself or to himself the exercise thereof.

The last phrase suggests that any possible claim to power through military intervention would undermine popular sovereignty. Section 3 of the Constitution also states that: "The authorities responsible for the direction of the State shall hold their powers of the people by way of election by universal suffrage, direct or indirect." The implication here is that ascension to political power is achieved through accepted conventional practices. The legitimacy of the government is therefore a function of people power vested in the political leadership.

It is also evident that civilian control of the military can be derived from the leadership role of the head of state in security matters. The President of the Republic of Cameroon is recognized in Article 9 (Sections 1, 10, 11) as "head of the armed forces" with the responsibility to "appoint to civil and military posts" as well as "ensure the internal and external security of the Republic." However, Welch aptly points out that "as long as the head of state is drawn from a civilian background, his personal command over the military provides a veneer of civilian control."[20] The specific constitutional constraints are useful as long as there are no military officers determined to intervene in politics.

The Personalization of Political Leadership

The formula of political leadership in Cameroon has been autocracy. The supremacy of the president is supported by constitutional provisions which appear to erode the power base of the other branches of government. Article 9 (9) of the Constitution gives the president "the power to issue statutory rules and orders." This lawmaking power has allowed the executive to obscure the jurisdiction of the National Assembly. For the most part, the National Assembly has been relegated to function "almost entirely to rubber-stamp decisions taken by the executive."[21] The constitution in Article II also provides:

(1)   The President of the Republic may where circumstances require proclaim by decree a State of Emergency, which will confer upon him such special powers as may be provided by law;

(2)   In the event of grave peril threatening the nation's territorial integrity or its existence, independence or institutions, the President of the Republic may proclaim by decree a State of Siege and take all measures as he may deem necessary; and

(3)   He shall inform the nation by message of his decision.

These provisions draw attention to the broad security powers exercised by the President. The chief executive has the power to detain or restrict the movements of Cameroonians without any institutionalized opposition.   Under these circumstances, the preventive detention laws tend to foster willful arrests. As Olesegun Obasanjo, a former military ruler in Nigeria, puts it:

...most of Africa's inheritors of political independence spent inordinate time not only "establishing" themselves to ensure personal and political survival, but also hunting down and dealing with "enemies," real and imagined.   The kind-hearted allowed their opposition to go into exile or put them in prison; others put theirs under the soil.[22]

In Cameroon the idea of a loyal opposition is hostile to the one-party state and incompatible with the personal ambitions of those seeking to stay in power. A political opposition is therefore perceived as a *political enemy* that must be removed from center stage.

Ahidjo's ability to personalize leadership was marked by the absence of political opposition and the elimination (by jail terms and self-exile) of rivals seeking control of the state.   In depoliticizing the regime, Ahidjo sought to cultivate the image of a patriarch who represented the will of the people (his 'children').   This approach to personal rule was assisted by the maintenance of a police state.   Ahidjo personally controlled the *Sûrété Nationale* (National Security) and the *gendarmerie* (constabulary) which were used to coercively mold public opinion.   The armed forces were also within the control of the President since it was headed by Sadou Daoudu (a trusted friend and advisor).   To achieve compliance, Ahidjo was able to demand and receive pledges of loyalty from party and government officials, coopt some of his viable opposition into the regime, as well as detain for long periods of time those who displayed an unwillingness to acknowledge his political supremacy.   Patronage was therefore a means used to secure the dependence of potential political opposition.

In 1982 Ahidjo unexpectedly resigned after twenty-two years in office. The decision to hand over the reins of the government to Biya posed a serious challenge to the identity of thought and outlook between the political leadership and the people. It was necessary for Biya to develop an image that would assist in defining his own political direction. President Biya moved to dismiss in a major cabinet shuffle the "older politicians who owed their office simply to tribal connection or loyalty to Ahidjo."[23] He brought young technocrats into the government and further consolidated his power by assuming leadership of the CPDM after a special election in September 1983. The name of the country was also changed from the United Republic to the Republic of Cameroon (Law No. 84-001) on February 4, 1984.

These actions gave rise to tension between Biya and Ahidjo, and subsequently led to an attempted putsch in April 1984 by presidential palace guards reluctant to be reassigned to outposts far removed from the capital city. The insurrection was eventually quelled by loyalist forces in the military after two days of fighting and close to 1,000 casualties.[24] Biya used the coup attempt to strengthen his support base in the country. Not only did the 11,600 man armed forces (including the *gendarmerie*) remained loyal to him, but Biya was able to present the coup attempt as the work of "a minority of ambitious men thirsting for power" rather than a sign of nationwide disapproval of his regime.[25] This approach seemingly helped Biya to galvanize public support since most Cameroonians, at least publicly, were displeased by the outbreak of violence. The coup aftermath also revealed that Biya's leadership style reflects a deliberateness and orderliness in planning. The movement of the government toward *political renewal* has since produced some political pluralism within the one-party system and a growing opposition pushing for a much faster process of democratization.

The Implications of Economic Development

Political stability in Cameroon, so important to military abstention, may also be the result of the state's capacity to foster economic development. The overall economic growth has been strongly influenced by oil resources. Following the discovery of oil in 1978, production output gradually increased to 185,000 barrels a day by 1985.[26] Oil revenues contribute approximately 17 percent of total gross domestic product (GDP) and about 45 percent of total government spending. The oil economy has also raised the per capita income from $500 to an estimated $800, reflecting a 6 to 7 percent GDP growth rate annually in terms of local currency.[27] Equally significant, oil policy has reflected the government's determination to downplay the potential of the production capacity. This cautionary policy is aimed at avoiding mistakes similar to those of countries like Gabon, Nigeria and Zaire where a boom in mineral production and export earnings resulted in a neglect of other sectors of the economy. Oil revenues placed in *comptes hors budget* (off-budget accounts) are used discreetly for special industrial projects and for payments of the total external debt estimated at $1,974.6 million in 1985. The service ratio is merely 12.2 percent--a figure considerably lower than that of most other African countries.[28]

Agriculture remains the mainstay of the economy. The agrarian sector occupies about 80 percent of the domestic workforce. As Ahidjo accurately observed, "before petroleum there was agriculture, and after the petroleum era there will still be agriculture."[29] Besides assuring higher export earnings and total self-sufficiency, diversification and expansion have been intended to prevent a rural-urban migration. Accordingly, Biya's attempt to liberalize the economy has emphasized the growth of the agricultural sector. In the sixth five-year development plan (1986-91), the government has committed 25 percent of its budget to the rural sector.[30]

Of related interest is the nature and level of foreign investment in Cameroon. Evidently, the government has seen the need to diversify its trade partners. By 1986, Cameroon had trade agreements signed with several West European countries, Canada, China, the Soviet Union and the United States to fund projects and furnish grants and loans to local financial institutions. A new liberal investment code and the creation of *free zones* emphasizing tax and custom-free incentives, just to name a few policies, are designed to lure foreign investments. However, the government recognizes the need to promote local entrepreneurial activities. Foreign investors are encouraged to 'Cameroonize' their personnel and their projects must reflect the needs of the local population.

Manufacturing is now identified as the weak link in the national economy. The significant growth realized from 1978 to 1982 is currently tempered by a slowdown. The decline has been related to "shortages of raw materials, rising labor costs, and high import bills for imports."[31] It is also a result of the poor performance of government parasatals like CELLUCAM (cellulose pulp plant) and ALUCAM (an aluminum smelting firm). Nevertheless, the government's economic liberalization policy has targeted the development of light and medium-size companies like breweries and textiles as well as initiated plans to improve the communication and transportation infrastructure in Cameroon.

These improvements are recognized by Biya's government as a way to increase foreign trade, investment and tourism.

The French Connection

The influence of France remains relatively strong in the economic and political realms. Economically, France is Cameroon's main trading partner especially for imported manufactured goods. The institutional cooperation of both countries is most evident in the stability of the monetary system. The creation of the Franc Zone subsequently led to Cameroon's membership in the *Union Monétaire d'Afrique Centrale* (UMAC). The activities of UMAC are organized through the *Banque des Etats d'Afrique Centrale* which supplies the CFA (*Communauté Financiere Africaine*) with a recognized convertibility value. Not only does the currency flow freely among the member states without any restrictions but it is based on a fixed exchange rate in terms of the French franc. The regional monetary union also ensures price stability for Cameroon exports and maintains a strong financial support from France. Quite simply, these financial arrangements underscore the basic institutional influence of France in Cameroon.

From a political and military perspective, France's promotion of the idea of "no development without security" is obvious in its intervention in the political development of Cameroon. The UPC insurgency in the 1960s was quelled with the involvement of French troops. Under the principle of *Force d'Intervention* (Intervention Force), French officers and NCOs (non-commissioned officers) established the *Zone de Pacification du Cameroun* (Cameroon's Pacification Zone) designed to subdue the internal rebellion against the Ahidjo regime.[32] Cameroon continues to receive approximately 41 percent of its arms, which include Mirage F-1 and Magister weapons training aircraft, from France.[33] While 69 French officers served in 1988 as technical advisors there were 169 Cameroonian military officers upgrading their professional skills in France.[34] More recently, the French government has closely monitored the activities of Paris-based groups like the Cameroon Organization to Fight for Democracy (COFD). The COFD party members, for example, were denied the right to organize what they referred to as "a national discussion between Cameroonians abroad."[35] Although Cameroon no longer participates in the annual summits of Francophone leaders, Biya continues to maintain strong Franco-Cameroonian ties.

The Mechanism of Civilian Control

The absence of a successful *coup d'état* in Cameroon does not suggest that the military is completely disengaged from politics. It would seem that its "political role is a question, not of whether, but of how much and what kind."[36] The scope of *how* and *what* is determined by the political, economic and external factors discussed in the preceding section. In this sense, the disposition toward what Janowitz[37] calls "reactive militarism" becomes evident when civilian institutions reveal weaknesses and there are "pressures by civilian groups to expand" the military's role in dealing with domestic political problems. In other words, coups represent a "military response to political decay."[38]

In the political realm, it has been hypothesized that the nature of party politics, constitutional constraints and strong leadership is related to military nonintervention. As already observed, one-partyism continues to play a dominant role in Cameroon's political life. The party copes with mass public mobilization by displaying some political tolerance. Its capacity to immobilize opposition groups, bring the military under the wing of the party, and to broaden popular support prevents any serious challenge form the army officers. Furthermore, the public's aversion to violence implies that there can be a successful military coup only if government and party officials are inept.

The interest in constitutional constraints also lends support to the legitimacy of civilian rule. As Welch reveals, the legitimation of civilian control "may give pause to potential coup-makers when they consider the act of intervention."[39] In the case of Cameroon, preserving a regime of nonmilitarization through the Constitution is fostered by provisions for a strong and almost imperial executive with the capacity to manage the character of civilian control. The impact of popular sovereignty is diluted by constitutional declarations which allow the president to arbitrarily exercise power on national security matters. Nevertheless, it must be made understandably clear that constitutional restraints on militarism acknowledge the willingness of the military to play a subordinate role or accept civilian control.

In addition, the durability of civilian political authority may depend on leadership style. The twenty-two years political dominance of Ahidjo reflected a preoccupation with the centralization of the one-party state against potential insurgent movements in the society. By advocating toughness and accommodations--tolerance for political involvement--as the rules of the game, Ahidjo did not have to rely heavily on the military. Similarly, Paul Biya's *New Deal* approach has conjured the image of a leader whose tools of political control are connected with a grassroots mechanism. The idea of political liberalization suggests the need to create a channel for the articulation and representation of differing views. Again, this form of participation is only allowed within the one-party system.

The civilian leaders have also sought to preserve the professional image and social prestige of the military. The *Armed Forces Day*, for example, is an occasion when promotions are announced and servicemen decorated. It is also an opportunity for the civilian leadership to praise the military or to provide psychological reassurance of the latter's status. Both Ahidjo and Biya have used this day to remind the military of their service to the nation under the control of the party state. It is noteworthy that the 1984 attempted coup was obviously not a reflection of the military's dissatisfaction with civilian rule. Biya demonstrated shrewd leadership by being able to portray it as the action of "a minority of ambitious men thirsty for power."[40] In this case, the emphasis was not placed on the army which remained loyal to Biya, but on disgruntled presidential palace guards loyal to Ahidjo.

On the economic level, a relatively effective management of the national budget and self-sufficiency in food has so far prevented direct military involvement in Cameroon politics. For the present economic problems (increasing urban unemployment, the low productivity of some of the parastatal industries, 20 percent inflation, and government corruption) to inspire a military challenge, the public must have lost complete confidence in the government. The government is now trying to reduce its involvement in the economy by promoting private enterprise and joint ventures. Equally important, the military's budget has not been drastically reduced. In terms of current budgetary expenditures (in CFA francs), the defense budget rose from CFA 19.23 billion in 1980/81 to CFA 45.84 billion in 1984/85.[41] In fact, the 1989/90 allocation to the military was increased to CFA 51.977 billion in order to strengthen the defense capacity of the military as well as the facilities of the *gendarmerie*.[42] It is, however, noteworthy that the national economy has not been seriously burdened by the military. Total defense expenditure in 1987, $160 million, accounted for 6.9 percent of government spending.[43]

The civilian control mechanism is also strengthened by the French influence. Cameroon's dependence militarily on France was demonstrated when French troops under General Briand were invited by Ahidjo to suppress the UPC revolt. If the relative political stability of Cameroon since the late 1960s has precluded a French military intervention to save the government in power, France's influence has been evident in other ways. To some extent, it can be argued that France's economic and foreign policy interests make it rather difficult for the Cameroonian military to seriously challenge the civilian leadership.

However, there is not enough empirical evidence to support or adequately evaluate the impact of this influence on military abstention from politics and the maintenance of personal rule in Cameroon.

Vers Le Pluralisme Démocratique?

The apparent *passage du monolithisme au pluralisme* (transition from monolithism to pluralism) was initiated when the National Assembly voted on December 5, 1990 in favor of multipartyism.[44] Approved by President Biya two weeks later, the legislative action drew strong speculation that the institutional dominance of the CPDM would be replaced by a wide popular-based political process. The urgent political need in Cameroon's democratization effort is to dismantle the one-party apparatus and substitute its components of centralized authority with competing party organizations. Equally important, there is growing impatience and skepticism about the democratization movement since the government party seeks to dictate the terms of political change. The notion that multiparty state activities or the new institutional landscape would occur under the aegis of the CPDM compels some critics to describe the effort as *multipartisme de facade* as well as *la démocratie truquée* (democracy betrayed). As Celestin Monga, an economist and former reporter of *Jeune Afrique* magazine, puts it: *"les députés d'un parti unique ne sont pas qualifiés pour organiser le multipartisme et la concurrence"* (the representatives of a single party are not qualified to organize multipartism and competition).[45] This reaction from the political opposition, including the Social Democratic Front (SDF), *Le Mouvement National pour la nouvelle Démocratie* (UPC), and *L'Organisation Camerounaise de la Lutte pour la démocratie* (the Cameroon Organization for the Struggle of Democracy), reflects the government's continuing reliance on coercion to ensure its hegemony. The harassment of opposition leaders, for example Yondo Black, and the disruption of gatherings by the opposition suggest that there is limited tolerance of political pluralism in Cameroon.

Moreover, the principle of political pluralism discloses the anglophones' demand for greater political and economic participation. Their definite signs of political awakening and aspirations for democracy are evident in the push for genuine press freedom and a return to the tradition of multiparty politics. Even the anglophone university students are challenging the instructional supremacy of French in their classes.[46] Furthermore, there is increasing demand for greater government attention to the infrastructure (roads, seaports, industries) and distribution of foreign investments. The SDF and other opposition groups constantly assume that the ideas defining democracy in Cameroon take into account political accountability, freedom, distributive equity and a system of governance that is viable.

It is safe to say that the stakes in political pluralism are high. The civilian leadership cannot afford to ignore the pressure to broaden the political system. Expanding public rejection of the CPDM's claim to organizational autonomy and dominance is matched by the call for a political system relevant to the needs and aspirations of Cameroonians. A focus on cosmetic changes would increase the likelihood of popular unrest and destabilization of the political system. In other words, the abandonment of democracy in Cameroon raises the possibility of military intervention.

Conclusion

This chapter has drawn attention to some of the elements which may explain the stability of Cameroon, the movement toward political pluralism and military abstention from politics. In investigating the nature of party politics or the role of the party in maintaining civilian control, the stress has been on the party's capacity to galvanize the people by idea of unity and political liberalization. Military nonintervention is also maintained by the legitimacy and actions of the party leaders. They derived their right to govern from the commitment to maintain values such as political stability, economic development and political freedom as part of the party ideology. Needless to say, the durability of one-partyism and the scope of presidential power is tested by the call for multipartyism and democratization of the political system.

The study has also shown that there may be a connection between economic development and civilian control. The government must deal with the widening problems of official corruption, a bureaucracy unresponsive to the public, the revitalization of the manufacturing sector, and the need to create jobs for secondary and university graduates if it seeks to maintain public support without a heavy reliance on force. Finally, the potential impact of French influence in Cameroon cannot be ignored. It would appear unlikely that the French, given their economic and political interests, would allow the decay of the political system. However, the umbilical cord tying both countries may be severely damaged if the Cameroon leadership ignores the need to remedy what has been described as a *déficit démocratique* in most francophone African states. It may also be necessary to examine the effect of the new European Community on

France's relationship with its former colonies. In short, to what extent can France maintain the current exchange rate of the CFA amidst the growing opposition from other European Economic Community members? It is possible that the special bilateral cooperation agreements may be influenced by a movement of both countries toward multilateralization or a change in interests.

Notes

1. Richard Joseph, "Partnership," *Africa Report* 35 (September-October 1990), p. 30.

2. Collen Lowe Morna, "Pluralism: A Luxury No More," *Africa Report* 35 (November-December 1990), p. 34.

3. Morris Janowitz, *The Military in the Political Development of New Nations: An Essay in Comparative Analysis* (Chicago: The University of Chicago Press, 1964), p. 102

4. Karl von Clausewitz, *On War* (Princeton: Princeton University Press, 1976); R.C. Snyder and B. Sapin, *The Role of the Military in American Foreign Policy* (New York: Doubleday, 1954); Samuel P. Huntington, *The Soldier and the State: The Theory and Politics of Civil-Military Relations* (Cambridge: Harvard University Press, 1957); Morris Janowitz and Jacques van Doorn, *On Military Intervention* (Rotherdam: Rotherdam University Press, 1960).

5. Huntington, *The Soldier and the State*, pp. 80-85.

6. Claude E. Welch, Jr., "Civilian Control of the Military: Myth and Reality," in *Civilian Control of the Military: Theory and Cases From Developing Countries* (Albany: State University of New York Press, 1976), pp. 2-24.

7. Samuel E. Finer, *The Man on Horseback: The Role of the Military in Politics* (New York: Praeger, 1962); Ali A. Mazrui, "Political Hygiene and Cultural Transition in Africa," *Journal of Asian and African Studies* 5 (January-April 1970), pp. 113-15.

8. Agola Auma-Osolo, "Objective African Military Control: A New Paradigm in Civil-Military Relations," *Journal of Peace Research* 17 F(1980), pp. 38-39.

9. Samuel P. Huntington, *Political Order in Changing Societies* (New Haven: Yale University Press, 1968), p. 298.

10. James S. Coleman and Carl G. Rosberg, Jr., "African One-Party States and Modernization," chap. in *Political Parties and National Integration in Tropical Africa* (Berkeley: University of California Press, 1964), pp. 655-80.

11. See Frédéric Belle Torimiro, "Nigeria: The Uncertainty of a Long-Term Legitimation of Political Leadership," in Constantine P. Danopoulos, ed., *Military Disengagement From Politics* (London: Routledge, 1988), pp. 94-96.

12. Welch, "Civilian Control of the Military," p. 9.

13. Pierre Lellouche and Dominique Moisi, "French Policy in Africa: A Lonely Battle Against Destabilization," *International Security* 3 (1979): pp. 108-33.

14 Mamadou N'Diaye, "The Horse and the Jockey," *Africa Report* (September-October 1990), p. 33.

15. Ali A. Mazrui and Michael Tidy, *Nationalism and the New States in Africa* (London: Heinemann, 1986), p. 131.

16. Aristide R. Zolberg, *Creating Political Order: The Party-States of West Africa* (Chicago: Rand McNally, 1966).

17. Mario Azevedo, "The Post-Ahidjo Era in Cameroon," *Current History* 86 (1987), p. 219.

18. *Cameroon Tribune*, 3 April 1990, p. 27.

19. Clausewitz, *On War*, p. 87.

20. Welch, "Civilian Control of the Military," p. 6.

21. Mbu Etonga, "An Imperial Presidency: A Study of Presidential Power in Cameroon," in Ndiva Kofele-Kale, ed., *An African Experiment in Nation Building: The Bilingual Cameroon Republic Since Reunification* (Boulder: Westview Press, 1980), p. 146.

22. Olesegun Obasanjo, *Africa in Perspective: Myths and Realities* (New York: Council on Foreign Relations, 1987), p. 8.

23 . *Africa Confidential*, 3 August 1983, pp. 1-2.

24. Frederick Scott, "Biya's New Deal," *Africa Report* 30 (July-August 1985), p. 58.

25. Quoted in Azevedo, "The Post-Ahidjo Era in Cameroon," p. 218.

26. Richard Everett, "Cushioning the Shock," *Africa Report*, 31 (May-June 1986), p. 77.

27. World Bank, *Cameroon Country Economic Memorandum*, 19 February 1987, p. 2.

28. *Ibid.*, p. 38.

29. Howard Schissel, "Cameroon Survey," *African Business*, 52 (December 1982), p. 57.

30. Azevedo, p. 230.

31. Everett, p. 80.

32. John Chipman, *French Power in Africa* (Oxford: Basil Blackwell, 1989), p. 123.

33. *The Military Balance 1988-1989* (London: International Institute for Strategic Studies, 1989), p. 120.

34. Chipman, *French Power in Africa*, pp. 132, 147.

35. *Africa Research Bulletin*, 15 March 1985, p. 7603.

36. Claude E. Welch, Jr., and Arthur K. Smith, *Military Role and Rule* (North Scituate: Duxbury Press, 1974), p. 6.

37. Janowitz, *The Military in the Political Development of New Nations*, p. 16.

38. Thomas S. Cox, *Civil-Military Relations in Sierra Leone: A Case Study of African Soldiers in Politics* (Cambridge: Harvard University Press, 1976), p. 16..

39. Welch, "Civilian Control of the Military," p. 9.

40. Azevedo, "The Post-Ahidjo Era," p. 218.

41. World Bank, p. 122.

42. *Cameroon Tribune*, 7 July 1989, p. 7.

43. *The Military Balance*, p. 225.

44. Michel Epée, "Le 'Oui Mais' A La Démocratie," *Jeune Afrique*, 9-15 January 1991, p. 26.

45. Celestin Monga, "La Démocratie Truquée, *Le Messager*, 27 December 1990, p. 5.

46. François Misser, "Cameroon: Grudging Pluralism," *New African*, February 1991, p. 21.

6

The Preservation of Civilian Rule in Tanzania

Daniel Zirker

The overwhelming tendency in sub-Saharan African countries during the 1970s and 1980s to drift into military intervention and dictatorship stimulated a variety of explanations in the literature of comparative politics regarding the causes of praetorianism. Authors stressed *internal* and *external* political and socio-economic variables such as elite political behavior,[1] a national history of previous coups,[2] the "imitation" of neighboring systems,[3] the buildup of military "power"--but not necessarily *size*,[4] the growth of "interventionary professionalism,"[5] and many others.

These explanations have arguably yielded at least some insight into why the military has tended to intervene in particular cases. Nevertheless, the breakdown of civilian rule in Africa is primarily idiosyncratic in character, and the centrally defining importance of the "element of chance," as one observer labels it,[6] reinforces the argument for most case studies. In the midst of the diffusion of East European political shock waves,[7] and what Goran Hyden has called "perestroika without glastnost in Africa,"[8] it is increasingly useful to examine those African countries that successfully resisted over the decades the military "man on horseback."

The following is an examination of the maintenance of civilian rule in one of the relatively few sub-Saharan African countries that has openly, and largely effectively, controlled military influence and intervention throughout its thirty years of existence. Tanzania, in fact, considered abolishing the army at independence, or placing it under the direct command of the United Nations.[9] Julius Nyerere, Tanzania's founder and first president, argued in 1961 that "if an

African country is armed then, realistically, it can only be armed against another African state,"[10] a point that he was to prove, ironically, nineteen years later with his invasion of Uganda. Nyerere, incidentally, remained ambivalent on the general subject of international military forces: while he opposed the establishment of joint East African armed forces, he long argued the merits of a unified African army.

Despite a brief army mutiny in 1964, Tanzania and Guinea appeared to one observer, at least, to be the only two African countries in the late 1960s that were likely to remain somewhat "immune" to military takeover because of their implementation of concrete policies, including the stimulation of political participation within the military rank and file, and the association of the army with the "aspirations and . . . machinery of the mass party."[11]

Background

The historical background of the cultural and political units that now comprise the United Republic of Tanzania suggests the likelihood of a future filled with perpetual instability, fractionalism and ultimate division. Zanzibar was the capital of the Omani empire and the center for the export of East African slaves in the nineteenth century, many of whom came from what is now the Tanzanian mainland. It was also an area of slave-based agricultural (clove) production. After the Berlin Conference of 1884-85, it formally became part of British East Africa, along with Uganda and Kenya, while Tanganyika, mainland Tanzania today, was part of German East Africa until the end of WWI. German colonial rule was violently resisted in Tanganyika because of its implementation of forced agricultural production in such commodities as cotton: in the Maji-Maji rebellion of 1905-07 alone, over 100 thousand people are thought to have died. When Tanganyika was placed under British control as a League of Nations trust territory after WWI, British rule tended to reinforce the two most pernicious fractional characteristics of German colonial rule, agricultural commodity production for export, and inter-ethnic tension.

Tanzania is one of the most ethnically diverse countries in sub-Saharan Africa. With more than 130 different languages and a century of divide-and-rule colonial administration, its prospects of evolving into a stable and unified polity seemed initially to be almost non-existent. Several key factors boded well for national integration, however. First, the sheer multiplicity of ethnic identities in Tanganyika, where the largest group constitutes only about eleven percent of the population, the two most powerful only about eight percent each, and the rest under five percent each, created an unusually egalitarian setting. No dominant ethnic group could hope to seize control of the system. Second, the inclusive character of Swahili culture, which established trading links throughout the territory, simultaneously provided an incipient *lingua franca* and a culture of tolerance and cooperation well before the independence era.[12] Third, both the German and British colonial authorities trained civil servants from various ethnic groups, and maintained a practice of transferring them throughout the colony regularly, thereby establishing a tradition of formal interethnic contacts.[13] A structural basis for stable, civilian rule was thus evident, at least to some degree, in Tanganyika well before the 1960s.

Tanzania's thirty years of independent civilian rule nevertheless represents a striking accomplishment in relation to most other African countries, and invites close examination in the context of the *determinants* of military coups. One of the best examples of this focus[14] concluded in the late 1970s that such elements as social mobilization, certain forms of cultural pluralism (e.g., "The presence of a large and potentially dominant group"[15]), and the lack, or significant weakening, of one-party dominance, correlated highly with military coups in Africa. Although earlier studies[16] had argued that such structures as *party systems* were *not* useful, by themselves, in explaining political change in Africa, Jackman pointed out that "multipartyism is particularly destabilizing *when coupled with* the presence of a dominant ethnic group,"[17] and the "social mobilization *and* the presence of a potentially dominant ethnic group" also correlated highly with "instability," i.e., *coups d'état*.[18] With the rapid political modifications in African countries that have followed East European political independence in 1989-90, few African countries can expect to avoid democratization.

Tanzania's much praised progress in nation-building, the entrenchment of its single-party state through popular participation, and its natural abundance of small, compatible ethnic groups, all seem to reinforce the promise of continuing civilian rule. Nevertheless, its history of at least two military conspiracies, one of which was an open mutiny, and its military invasion and overthrow--by its armed forces--of a neighboring country are not entirely compatible with this thesis. Furthermore, the fundamental systemic changes associated with the retirement from the presidency in 1985, and from the chair of the single party, the Chama cha Mapinduzi (CCM, or *Revolutionary Party*), in 1990, of Nyerere, along with the current intensification of internal and external pressures for multipartyism, and the ongoing economic depression in Sub-Saharan Africa, all suggest the utility of reappraising this key case of civilian rule in the Third World.

The Establishment of Stable Civilian Rule

Given that Tanzanians did not experience a successful military intervention during their first thirty years of political independence, and are frequently described as having "one of the most consistently stable governments in Africa,"[19] it seems strange that they display so much anxiety as individuals regarding even the most trivial discussion of coups. This concern, moreover, is pervasive. From the choice of the single Shakespearean play that Nyerere chose to translate into Kiswahili during his successful drive to legitimate the language as a national *lingua franca* (*Julius Caesar*), to the reticence, even of Tanzanian professionals, in 1990 to broach the topic of the viability of civilian rule in casual conversation, it is always evident that there is a perceived, if not real, military threat to civilian rule in Tanzania.[20] In the relatively open political climate of 1990, the topic was almost always avoided in public, in the experience of this observer. Furthermore, Tanzanian scholars have largely ignored it, despite their country's reputation as an interesting case of civilian rule. As a gregarious and outspoken businessman in Dar es Salaam noted, Tanzania is a *free country* as regards speech, although military intervention is the one subject in which voices are always lowered, and words are carefully chosen. It is not, he emphasized, a forbidden subject, but is generally regarded as *dangerous*.[21]

Several major events in Tanzania's military history appear to shed at least some light on this phenomenon, and underscore the protracted character of the country's struggle to maintain civilian rule over three decades. The major events, the army mutiny of 1964, the military invasion of Uganda in 1979, and the coup conspiracy of 1982-83, all point to the potential interventionism of the Tanzanian military, and to specific political moves which have effectively dampened, but never quite extinguished, the threat that this poses. Such policies have been able to prevent an initial instance of successful military intervention, which by itself is probably the greatest single indicator of subsequent coup threats, at least in African systems.[22] Nevertheless, unsuccessful coup conspiracies, and a successful foreign military adventure seem to have contributed to a penchant for secrecy and placation regarding military affairs that is frankly antithetical to the relaxed openness that characterizes other aspects of Tanzanian political culture.[23]

The Tanganyika army mutiny of 1964, which affected the armies of Uganda and Kenya as well, has been examined in a number of works.[24] It was thought to have been initiated as an enlisted men's pay dispute in three British-led colonial armies, although in Tanganyika, which experienced the most serious of the revolts, the central focus was the attempt to block the *Africanization* of the officer corps.[25] This appeared to point to an incipient solidarity, a class-like behavior pattern among soldiers who seemed willing to put their immediate interests in a wider social context, and hence to constitute themselves as an emerging *lumpen militariat*.[26] Bienen argued in this vein that the Tanganyikan mutiny was "intimately related to the Zanzibar Revolution and developed with such suddenness and surprise that it seemed at first to be not indigenous to Tanganyika's political system."[27] The indignity, if not immediate threat, suffered by the government, and by Nyerere himself, appeared to be significant. He went into hiding during the heighth of the crisis,[28] and called in British troops to put down the revolt, a move for which he later publicly apologized.[29] Less than 1000 riflemen had shaken the political foundations of civilian rule in the new nation, and although Nyerere made it clear that he meant to transform political structures to prevent a recurrence of military intervention, as he said in a radio address at the conclusion of the crisis, "it is not easy to disarm an army, especially one which is already intoxicated with the poison of disloyalty and disobedience."[30]

Tanzania's subsequently successful record in preventing military coups probably owes in large measure to policies formulated following the 1964 mutiny, including the disbanding (and total reorganization) of the army.[31] This provided a good opportunity to purge the officer corps of potentially charismatic leaders, the best known of whom was a young Nyassan (his grandparents had been Malawian) who had dramatically raised the Tanganyikan flag on Mt. Kilimanjaro in the famous photo that came to symbolize the country's independence. This emphasis upon the removal of potentially charismatic officers continued, moreover. The first commander of the *New Army*, who was regarded as *highly professional* and, as a Meru, "authentically Tanzanian," was himself later removed in another series of army purges in the mid-1970s, likely because he also had become dangerously popular with officers and enlisted men.[32] The tactical use of retirement and political appointment (out of military command positions) was thus one of the most visible, and apparently effective, policies to ensure civilian rule following the mutiny of 1964.

A second policy mandated the membership of soldiers of all ranks in the single mainland party,[33] and the takeover of the independent trade unions, which were widely blamed for encouraging the mutiny.[34] Despite the failure of an early plan to recruit the new army exclusively from the ranks of the Tanganyika African National Union (TANU) youth wing, soldiers were encouraged to join TANU, and officers were appointed and promoted on political, as well as professional military, criteria.[35] The position of Political Commissar of the

People's Forces was created to ensure a new, *correctly* politicized military establishment,[36] and senior officers were given prominent party positions. The army was later constituted as its own *political region* in the party, with automatic representation on the party's National Executive Committee.[37]

A third policy after 1964 was the introduction of civic action as a major military function. Nyerere argued that the military should serve as a socio-economic militia, that national development should be its central duty, and that its focus should be upon such concerns as housing and road construction.[38] It was felt that this would in effect suspend the military in civil society, limiting its political options, or at least its potential popular support. This policy was enhanced by the traditional lack of barracks housing for military personnel, which placed them physically among civilians. The crimes later committed by soldiers and ex-soldiers living among civilians, especially after the Uganda conflict, even contributed to this socio-economic and political suspension: they further undercut the ability of the military to claim some sort of "purification" or redemptory political role with the civilian population.[39]

A fourth element of the policy changes after 1964 was both costly and arguably counterproductive, at least in the long run: selected demands of the soldiers, such as immediate *Africanization* of the officer corps, and, perhaps more significant in the long term, major pay increases, were (and continued to be) promptly met.[40] In fact, meeting military pay demands remains a central government priority, in spite of the fact that the peacetime military -- with virtually no international conflict in sight -- lays claim to about fourteen percent of the national budget.

A fifth policy geared to ensure the maintenance of civilian rule centered on recruitment and balance of ethnic representation within the military. Prior to the 1964 mutiny, most of the Tanganyikan army personnel had been drawn from several warlike tribes, including the Hehe and the Kuria.[41] After 1964, a strict formula of balanced recruitment and promotion further *nationalized* the military, while purging potentially adventuristic cultural cohorts.[42]

A sixth major policy after 1964 involved the creation of a military mission abroad through the militarization of Tanzanian foreign policy. The establishment of the Pan African Freedom Movement of East, Central and Southern Africa (PAFMECSA), and the growth of Tanzania's role in providing training and asylum to African liberation movements, derived from Nyerere's commitment to the struggles to end colonialism. As these became increasingly militarized, the Tanzanian Peoples' Defence Force (TPDF) evolved to meet its structured, professional military mission.[43] This was the second of what Mazrui called the *two themes* regarding military behavior in Tanzania: "the marked distrust of men under arms at home combined with a faith in military or quasi-military solutions to some of the remaining colonial problems in Africa."[44] Such a broadly defined foreign mission added to overall military expertise and political integration of the officer corps. This was particularly evident between 1969 and 1975, when Tanzanian forces were said to have participated directly in FRELIMO's struggle for the independence of Mozambique.[45]

While these policies have generally accomplished the difficult task of mitigating the threat of a military coup in Tanzania, the tactic of "civilianizing" the military, while simultaneously increasing the influence of the military in civil society, has apparently had its costs, as the invasion of Uganda in 1979 graphically demonstrated. Bienen argues that the invasion force that responded to Idi Amin's quixotic attack on Tanzania in late 1978 was "not a disciplined and professional organization."[46] While Avirgan and Honey's first-hand journalistic account[47] disputes this contention to some extent, it concurs that the invasion represented a militarization of political priorities, along the lines that Mazrui had predicted a decade earlier, rather than a professional exercise in legitimate national defense.[48] The overthrow of Amin had essentially become a national political priority in Tanzania, with the military serving as the instrument of that priority.

The war and invasion of Uganda undercut the Tanzanian political system's control over potentially threatening military behavior in at least two ways, while being proclaimed in the world press as "the first time in Africa's post-colonial history that one country ha[d] successfully invaded another, occupied its capital and overthrown its ruler."[49] In the first place, officers and enlisted men in the TPDF gained practical experience in a dangerous art: the direct military intervention in national (Uganda's) political processes, coupled with the institutionally dispersed gratification of looting and revenge-taking.[50] Also, the costs of the war, estimated at US$ 1 million per day at its height,[51] impacted Tanzania's struggling economy and arguably caused years of economic depression.[52] Moreover, it resulted in political activism by soldiers over consequent shortfalls in military funding. In 1980, for example, as many as 1,000 soldiers, including thirty officers, were said to have been arrested and held after demonstrating in Dar es Salaam over a war-related pay dispute.[53] With the deterioration of the economy, dissent within the military continued to grow, and this in turn likely led to subsequent (and costly) political promotions of senior commanders who had been associated with the war.[54]

In December and January, 1982-83, a serious military conspiracy was uncovered and crushed. Although some descriptions of the event have stressed its seriousness, and one account described a confrontation in which Nyerere faced would-be assassins at the State House in Dar es Salaam and convinced them to surrender,[55] other sources contend that the *plot* was so thoroughly infiltrated by security agents that it was paralyzed from its inception.[56] The character of the official press coverage reinforces the gravity of the event delays, inconsistencies and confusion predominated.[57] Its first mention within Tanzania was on January 21, 1983, when Shihata, the official Tanzanian news agency, announced that the TPDF had "uncovered a plot" to "cause disturbance and embarrass" the country earlier in the month. This report noted dryly that although the TPDF had uncovered the plot, and soldiers and civilians were involved, the TPDF "was in no way involved in the conspiracy."[58] More than a month later, and following an unusual and ostensibly unrelated rebuke of "some soldiers" by Defence Minister Twalipo for their failure "to maintain discipline in the army and follow laid down procedures,"[59] Shihata announced, as if the event was by now familiar to the public, that 28 people had been charged in *the Treason Case.* Twenty of the names listed were of soldiers, and all but one of these were officers, and their addresses showed a wide geographical distribution, with emphasis upon the Kagera Region, Dar es Salaam, and TPDF Headquarters. One of the alleged civilian conspirators was the personal assistant to the president for the Kagera Region Development Project. The defendants were now described as being held "in connection with plotting to overthrow the Government."[60] Three weeks later, in the next mention of the case, specific charges of "conspiring to cause the death of the President of Tanzania," conspiring to depose the President, and plotting to overthrow the government were announced.[61] One observer noted that the plot, which appears to have been organized by Tanzanians living abroad, involved promises of *economic liberalization* if the coup succeeded.[62]

Three central foci appear to have emerged in the efforts to control the threat of military intervention in Tanzania after 1983: first, there was a profound reinforcement of what has been called the mutual "politicization of the military and the militarization of civil society."[63] Extended training in ideology and the creation of formal party and government positions for military officers was balanced against an extensive program in military training and service for civilians. It was expected that civil society, infused with a new emphasis upon people's militias and participation in national military service, constituted a greater balance to professional military power. Second, Tanzanian foreign policy continued to provide the military with a legitimate and patriotic foreign mission that was associated with the Southern African liberation struggles; the momentum of this foreign policy preference, while clearly not formulated solely for that express purpose, was enhanced by its obviously salutary domestic effects: such endeavors occupied the military in a non-threatening and even diplomatically desirable activity. While there is little research into the precise nature of the foreign military mission, given its highly secretive character, it appears that consequent improvements in professional military *esprit d'corps*, especially among the officer corps, contributed significantly to their ready willingness to engage in domestic civic action projects. Third, continually high (and rising) military budgets, especially in recent years,[64] coupled with the special political perquisites of senior military officers, appear to represent a systematic strategy of cooptation. In the eyes of senior officers, at least, civilian single-party government in Tanzania may well be seen as the best possible bargaining agent for their individual interests.[65]

Several broad policies, then, can be interpreted together as having represented an effective and protracted campaign by the Tanzanian polity to control independent military behavior after 1964. These policies, or general policy areas, encompassed the cultural, sociological, political and economic spheres, and included the careful balance of ethnic representation within the military, ultimately incorporating the military, ideologically and politically, into the single party state and society. This policy of enhancing the political influence of the military in of civil society included a continual purging of charismatic officers from key command positions. Soldiers were, during much of the post-Independence period, rewarded economically, at least in a relative sense. Potential and actual military conspiracies were effectively infiltrated and crushed.

The central political factor that made most of these policies possible over the years was indisputably the single-party state, with its monopoly over rewards and sanctions. It is also important to underscore the typically Tanzanian proclivity for peaceful political compromise, and a deep cultural suspicion of military intentions, both of which were elegantly intertwined in the leadership of President Nyerere.[66] A burgeoning discussion of multipartyism, which has proceeded with Nyerere's blessing in early 1990, and the ex-president's formal retirement form national politics in August of 1990, may also spell the end of this integrated complex of policies that have protected Tanzania, perhaps more than any other African country, from the threat of military intervention.

Tanzania in the 1990s

The end of the Cold War, and particularly the years 1989 and 1990, have had a profound influence on African politics, perhaps the most profound single effect since the independence era of 1957 to 1964. Tanzania witnessed the unequivocal retirement of Julius K. Nyerere from his last formal position in national politics, the Chair of the CCM, in August, 1990. In the Tanzanian context, it is critical that the retirement of Nyerere *and* the relaxation of the East-West struggle took place simultaneously. The imminent end of the single-party state, with its capacity to coopt and diffuse political threats, and the loss of Nyerere's unique emphasis upon Tanzanian nationalism, underscore the likelihood that Tanzania will experience profound political changes during the next several years. In particular, the African *perestroika* and Nyerere's retirement both appear to threaten the future capacity of the Tanzanian state to control military intervention.

What is arguably the greatest single political achievement in the politics of East Africa, Tanzania's creation of a unified national culture, a virtual transcendence of ethnic (tribal) divisions, has been effectively replicated within the professional military. The relative failure of the neighboring countries of Kenya and Uganda to create a national identity has meant that they have had to contend with the predominance of certain large subnational ethnic groups, which have continually proven their willingness to use the military in their struggle for national supremacy. Nyerere consistently emphasized a common national language, Kiswahili, religious tolerance, and the celebration of Tanzania's natural ethnic mozaic, where the largest single ethnic group encompasses only eleven percent of the population, and where most of the other hundred or so groups are under five percent, in the creation of this single, national identity. The current African *perestroika*, however, has stridently reinforced localism, and when this tendency is coupled with the loss of Nyerere's adroit nationalistic leadership, the unavoidable conclusion is that the delicate balance of ethnic groups in Tanzania will soon be at risk. A change in the ethnic balance in civil society has direct implications for the professional military establishment.

Another concern, suggested by some observers after the accession to the presidency of a Zanzibari Moslem, Ali Hassan Mwinyi, in 1985, is that religion could come to play a greater role in *ethnic identity* in the future. Roughly thirty-five percent of Tanzanians are Islamic, the largest single religious grouping. Certain elements in the Islamic community in Tanzania have been said to have adopted the slogan, "we are in power and we want 40 years in power."[67] While they are generally thought to be largely passive as a political interest group, and to suffer from chronic and politically debilitating internal conflicts,[68] they nevertheless remain a concern if only because of their size relative to the multiplicity of other, much smaller groups.

The advent of multipartyism in Eastern Europe in 1989 and 1990, which appears to have affected Tanzania's current reassessment of its single-party state (especially following a series of interviews by Nyerere in the national media in early 1990), poses a far greater threat to the preservation of civilian rule in Tanzania. After February 1990, when Nyerere announced that a national debate concerning multipartyism in Tanzania would be unhealthy,[69] a political transformation appears to have been gaining momentum. On June 26, 1990, Nyerere announced to the nation that a multiparty democracy in Tanzania was "inevitable."[70] At least some senior military officers are thought to oppose the national adoption of a multiparty system for personal reasons: they would lose their political opportunities and be expected to return to a *purely professional* role, a diminution of social and political (not to mention material) status.[71]

Incidents of student activism have also underscored the fragility of civilian rule in Tanzania. The closure by President Mwinyi of the University of Dar es Salaam in May 1990, after what was essentially a mild student protest which included a brief boycott of classes, seems to have represented a concession to the military. The student protest had been organized around vague and changing concerns, although students consistently objected to the reversal of the percentages of the national budget allocated to the *military* and to *education* between 1970 and 1990 (4 percent and 14 percent, changing to 14 percent and 4 percent, respectively). One student spokesperson stressed that the students saw themselves as *an opposition party*,[72] and consequently felt it to be their duty to protest the high military budget in peacetime. A Political Science undergraduate, who was also a Tanzanian government employee, recounted that during lunch with a friend at the Officers' Mess in Dar es Salaam, he had heard *very senior* officers angrily discussing the need to "shoot some students" because of their blatant attack on *military rights*.[73] Shortly after the closure of the university, a local military barracks held a noisy rally in support of the measure which was witnessed by many people and could be heard on the university campus nearby. Although it was widely discussed on campus, it was not mentioned in the government-controlled media. Meanwhile, official civilian rallies in support of the university's closure were prominently featured in the media.[74] Suppression of media coverage of vehement military reactions to the political challenge posed by the students suggests that increased political pluralism already threatens the preservation of civilian rule in Tanzania. The expense of an inflated military budget in peacetime is likely to become the target of an opposition party as soon as multipartyism is adopted.

The assignment of a *new role* to the professional army, including a progressive erosion of its foreign mission, and a growing political emphasis upon such *internal* functions as civic action and police work, also reflect the growing influences of the African *perestroika* and the retirement of Nyerere. The rapid diminution of Tanzania's participation in the liberation struggles in Southern Africa is the product of the end of the Cold War, the peaceful resolution of some of the African liberation struggles, and a general ideological relaxation following Nyerere's retirement from the presidency. In November, 1989, for example, President Mwinyi reminded the TPDF publicly that "you are not mercenaries, but patriotic soldiers who swing into action when national sovereignty is threatened, but in peacetime, you are obliged, like all other patriots, to engage in nation-building activities."[75] He warned against *agitators* within the military.

Mwinyi announced, in January 1990, that Tanzania had fulfilled its foreign commitments, and that "this climate allows us to shift most of our attention to the internal front."[76] Interestingly, he rated the building of barracks as the highest priority because, as he told members of the Armed Forces Regional Party Executive Committee meeting in Dar es Salaam, "some of the people you live with [out of barracks] are bandits, who may influence you." He also suggested the formation of army manpower brigades for food production, commended army fire fighters for successfully extinguishing an oil tank blaze, asked why it was that no army personnel had participated in repairing schools and dispensaries after a December 1989 cyclone hit Dar es Salaam, and added that the army could be used to repair roads.[77] Nevertheless, the highest priority appears to have been the building of barracks, and frequent references to this subsequently appeared in the government-controlled media. The geographical and physical positioning of the professional military may, in fact, be emerging as one aspect of a more extensive program to preserve civilian rule in Tanzania.

The preservation of a politically integrated and responsible military establishment in Tanzania has apparently necessitated a consistent "politicization of the military and . . . militarization of civil society." This has rested upon a fortuitous blend of sociopolitical circumstances and consistent efforts on the part of key political figures, particularly Nyerere. With the beginning of the 1990s, it no longer appears likely that these conditions will persist. The political and ideological bases of the single-party state in Tanzania have rapidly eroded, Southern African liberation struggles -- and Tanzania's related foreign military mission -- appear to be ending.

The need to reevaluate the preservation of civilian rule in Tanzania is further underscored by the growing challenges to the military budget in a new and, perhaps, multiparty political system, and a possible weakening of egalitarian multiculturalism within Tanzania. M. J. V. Bell argued in 1968 that the two civilian governments in Africa which were "most likely to survive" were Guinea and Tanzania.[78] A successful military coup in Guinea in 1984, and in many other African countries during the past two decades, further suggest the uniqueness of Tanzania as a case study of non-intervention, and its utility as a model of the successful preservation of civilian rule in Africa.

Notes

1. Roberta E. McKown, "Domestic Correlates of Military Intervention in African Politics," in G. A. Kourvetaris and B. A. Dobratz, eds., *World Perspectives in the Sociology of the Military* (New Jersey: Transaction Books, 1976), pp. 191-206.

2. Eric A. Nordlinger, *Soldiers in Politics: Military Coups and Governments* (Englewood Cliffs, New Jersey: Prentice-Hall, 1977).

3. James M. Lutz, "The Diffusion of Political Phenomena in Sub-Saharan Africa," *Journal of Political and Military Sociology*, 17 (1989), pp. 93-114.

4. Frederic S. Pearson and Robert A. Baumann, "International Military Intervention in Sub-Saharan African Subsystems," *Journal of Political and Military Sociology*, 17 (1989), pp. 115-150; Ali A. Mazrui, "The Lumpen Proletariat and the Lumpen Militariat: African Soldiers as a New Political Class," *Political Studies*, 21 (1973), p. 4.

5. Claude E. Welch, Jr., "Personalism and Corporatism in African Armies," in Catherine McArdle Kelleher, ed., *Political-Military Systems: Comparative Perspectives* (Beverly Hills: Sage Publications, 1974), pp. 125-145.

6. William Tordoff, *Government and Politics in Africa* (Bloomington: Indiana University Press, 1984), p. 156.

7. Douglas G. Anglin, "Southern African Responses to Eastern European Developments," *Journal of Modern African Studies*, 28 (1990), pp. 431-455.

8. Paper presented at University of Dar es Salaam, Tanzania, June 4, 1990.

9. The latter position was argued by Julius Nyerere's brother, Joseph.

10. Ali A. Mazrui, "Anti-Militarism and Political Militancy in Tanzania," in Jacques Van Doorn, ed., *Military Profession and Military Regimes* (The Hague: Mouton, 1969).

11. M. J. V. Bell, "The Military in the New States of Africa," in Jacques Van Doorn, ed., *Armed Forces and Society: Sociological Essays* (The Hague: Mouton, 1968), p. 273.

12. John Lonsdale, "Some Origins of Nationalism in Tanzania," in Lionel Cliffe and John S. Saul, eds., *Socialism in Tanzania*, Vol. 1 (Nairobi: East African Publishing House, 1972), p. 25.

13. Ibid., pp. 26-28.

14. Robert W. Jackman, "The Predictability of Coups d'Etat: A Model with African Data," *American Political Science Review* 72 (1978), pp. 1262-1275.

15. Ibid., p. 1273.

16. Roberta E. McKown and Robert E. Kauffman, "Party System as a Comparative Analytical Concept in African Politics," *Comparative Politics* (1973), pp. 47-72.

17. Jackman, "The Predictability of Coups d'Etat," p. 1273. *Emphasis added.*

18. Ibid., p. 1274. *Emphasis added.*

19. E.g., David L. Horne, "Passing the Baton: The Presidential Legacy of Julius K. Nyerere," *Journal of African Studies* 14 (1987), p. 93.

20. The author conducted doctoral dissertation research on the military and development in Brazil during 1980 and 1981 when the dictatorship, in self-defense, was lashing out at its critics; far less anxiety on the part of interviewees was encountered than in Tanzania in 1990, on roughly the same topic.

21. Personal interview, March 15, 1990, Dar es Salaam.

22.. Ruth First, *The Barrel of a Gun: Political Power in Africa and the Coup d'Etat* (London: Allen Lane The Penguin Press, 1970), p. 20; Nordlinger, *Soldiers in Politics*, p. 138.

23. Mazrui commented in 1969 on "the essentially pacific record of the people of Tanganyika as compared with some of their neighbors. The people that had sacrificed 120,000 lives in the Maji Maji rebellion against the Germans in 1905-6 came to develop a form of nationalism that was at once shrewd and placid." "Anti-Militarism and Political Militancy in Tanzania," p. 220.

24. Henry S. Bienen, "National Security in Tanganyika after the Mutiny," in Lionel Cliff and John S. Saul, eds., *Socialism in Tanzania* (Nairobi: East African Publishing House, 1972), pp. 216-225; First, *The Barrel of a Gun*; Mazrui, "Anti-Militarism and Political Militancy in Tanzania."

25. Bienen, "National Security in Tanganyika," p. 218; First, *The Barrel of a Gun*, pp. 205-6.

26. Mazrui, "The Lumpen Proletariat and the Lumpen Militariat," p. 8. First noted in 1970 that early interventions in systems that later became prone to coups often involved pay disputes. *The Barrel of a Gun*, p. 21.

27. Bienen, "National Security in Tanganyika," p. 217.

28. His foreign and Defense Minister, Oscar Kambona, remained visible, negotiating with the mutineers with "courage and loyalty." Ibid., p. 220.

29. Ibid., p. 220.

30. Quoted in : Mazrui, "Anti-Militarism and Political Militancy in Tanzania," p. 225.

31. Ibid., p. 226. Tanganyika had to rely on borrowed Nigerian troops for awhile after the British troops had withdrawn.

32. Personal interview with a Tanzanian Member of Parliament, June 27, 1990, Dar es Salaam.

33. TANU and the Afro-Shirzi Party of Zanzibar were joined in the single Chama cha Mapinduzi (CCM, or Revolutionary Party) in 1977.

34. First, *The Barrel of a Gun*, p. 205; Bienen, "National Security in Tanganyika," p. 220.

35. Ibid., p. 222.

36. Mazrui, "Anti-Militarism and Political Militancy in Tanzania," p. 227.

37. Ibid., p. 227.

38. Ibid., p. 226.

39. Personal interview with a Tanzanian Member of Parliament, June 27, 1990, Dar es Salaam.

40. Bienen, *Armed Forces, Conflict and Change in Africa* (Boulder: Westview Press, 1989), p. 25.

41. First, *The Barrel of a Gun*, p. 78

42. Many members of these warlike ethnic groups later enlisted during the war with Uganda, often moving to distant recruiting stations before being admitted. Personal interview with a Tanzanian Member of Parliament, June 27, 1990, Dar es Salaam.

43. One observer suggests that it is this role (and its frequently covert character), and *not* the danger of a coup, which explains Tanzanian's caution about discussing the military and politics. Personal interview with a Tanzanian Member of Parliament, June 27, 1990, Dar es Salaam.

44. Mazrui, "Anti-Militarism and Political Militancy in Tanzania," p. 234.

45. Horace Campbell, "Tanzania and the Liberation Process in Southern Africa," *The African Review* 14 (1987), pp. 18-19.

46. Bienen, *Armed Forces, Conflict and Change in Africa*, p. 25.

47. Tony Avirgan and Martha Honey, *War in Uganda: The Legacy of Idi Amin* , Dar es Salaam (Tanzania Publishing House, 1982).

48. Avirgan and Honey discuss Amin's alleged plan to seize a band of territory across Northern Tanzania, through Tanga to the Indian Ocean, but few observers would credit this as more than a demented fantasy. A Ugandan academic later argued that there were "ulterior motives, linked perhaps to "international imperialism," that explained Tanzania's invasion (Okoth, 1987: 159), and the Soviet Union, which had been supplying Amin with arms, turned down a Tanzanian delegation to Moscow that appealed for help after Amin's overthrow. China had been Tanzania's chief supplier. *Africa Research Bulletin* 16 (April 15, 1979), p. 5186.

49. *Newsweek* (April 23, 1979), p. 9.

50. Avirgan and Honey, *War in Uganda*, p. 148 and pp. 211-212; Campbell, "Tanzania and the Liberation Process in Southern Africa," p. 21. Violent crime became increasingly common in Dar es Salaam and other major Tanzanian towns, and within two years "Tanzanian police found that more than 60 percent of the people they arrested were militia members demobilized after the war." Avirgan and Honey, p. 236.

51. *Africa Report* (March-April, 1979), p. 28.

52. Peter Calvocoressi, *Independent Africa and the World* (London: Longman, 1985), p. 48. The war alone crippled government development efforts. *Africa Report* noted that "the invasion forced Tanzania to buy heavy arms abroad, divert funds from other ministries to defence, and commandeer many trucks normally used to transport produce and export crops. Ministries other than Defence have been ordered to suspend new projects, not to fill vacancies, and cut back spending." March-April, 1979, p. 28.

53. *Africa Report* (July-August, 1980), p. 25.

54. Lieutenant General Abdullah Twalipo was appointed Defence Minister in November, 1980, for example. *Africa Report* (January-February, 1981), p. 32.

55. *Africa Confidential* 24, No. 6 (1983), p. 1.

56. Personal interview with a Tanzanian Member of Parliament, June 27, 1990, Dar es Salaam.

57. Press accounts in official media in Tanzania are problematic, as a number of sources have noted, e.g., Ndimara Tegambwage, *Who Tells the Truth in Tanzania?* (Dar es Salaam: Tansi Publishers Limited, 1990); Hadji S. Konde, *Press Freedom in Tanzania* (Arusha: East Africa Publications, Limited, 1984), although Avirgan and Honey, who covered the war in Aganda, stressed that "never once did [Nyerere] or any Tanzanian military official restrict our access to information or try to censor our writing." p. xiii.

58. *Daily News* (January 22, 1983), p. 1.

59. *Daily News* (February 16, 1983), p. 1. The minister blamed the problems on inadequate barracks housing, which resulted in most soldiers living outside the barracks. In a policy pronouncement that may have had some relation to the coup plot, he promised that more housing would be provided "to ensure that all soldiers live[d] in the barracks." He also urged soldiers to understand that Tanzania's problems stemmed from the world economic recession. *Daily News* (February 16, 1983), p. 1.

60. *Daily News* (February 26, 1983), p. 1.

61. *Daily News* (March 12, 1983), p. 1.

62. Personal interview with a Tanzanian Member of Parliament, June 27, 1990, Dar es Salaam.

63. This is the expression of a Tanzanian colleague in the Department of Political Science and Public Administration, University of Dar es Salaam. Personal interview, June 7, 1990.

64. Bienen, *Armed Forces, Conflict and Change in Africa* (Boulder: Westview Press, 1989), p. 109.

65. Alfred Stepan, in his recent book, *Rethinking Military Politics: Brazil and the Southern Cone* (Princeton, New Jersey: Princeton University Press, 1988), argues that the Brazilian military government ceded power to the civilians precisely *because* the dictatorship, lacking legitimacy, had found it politically

difficult to fund the military. After the advent of civilian government in 1985, military budgets rose significantly.

66. Most observers note, however, that Nyerere was *not* very open to compromise on some questions, such as "economic liberalization" and the qualification of the basic principles of Ujamaa.

67. Personal interview with faculty member, Department of Political Science and Public Administration, University of Dar es Salaam, May 8, 1990. Personal interview with a Tanzanian Member of Parliament, June 27, 1990, Dar es Salaam.

68. Personal interview with a Tanzanian Member of Parliament, June 27, 1990, Dar es Salaam. The M.P. stressed that there nevertheless is *ushabiki* (overenthusiasm) among Islamics in Tanzania, and if the religious leadership ever succumbed to this, it could be "very dangerous."

69. *Daily News* (February 22, 1990), p. 1.

70. *Daily News* (June 27, 1990), p. 1.

71. Personal interview with a Tanzanian Member of Parliament, June 27, 1990,

72. Personal interview, student spokesperson, University of Dar es Salaam, May 2, 1990.

73. University of Dar es Salaam, April 19, 1990.

74. E.g., *Sunday News* (May 20, 1990), p. 1; *Daily News* (May 25, 1990), p. 3.

75. *Daily News* (November 16, 1989), p. 1.

76. *Daily News* (January 17, 1990), p. 1. Prime Minister Joseph Warioba has stressed the critical role of the navy in protecting Tanzania from seaborn "enemies" *(Sunday News* [September 3, 1989], p. 1), although few observers believe this to be a high budgetary priority.

77. *Daily News* (January 17, 1990), p. 1. In May, 1990, the military was loudly praised in the government press for its help in reconstruction efforts following massive flooding. *Daily News* (May 2, 1990), p. 1. This was an assignment which had been given to it in a presidential message two weeks earlier. *Daily News* (April 15, 1990), p. 1.

78. Bell, "The Military in the New States of Africa," p. 273.

7

The Persistence and Fragility of Civilian Rule in Kenya

Cobie Harris

Decolonization is the meeting of two forces, opposed to each other by
their very nature, which in fact owe their originality to the sort of
substantification which results from and is nourished by the situation
in the colonies. Their first encounter was marked by violence and
their existence together - that is to say the exploitation of the native
by the settler - was carried on by the dint of a great array of bayonets
and cannons.

- Frantz Fanon

This chapter is an analysis of the socio-political forces that have effectively
blocked military intervention in Kenya from independence to the present. The
analysis suggests that the capacity for Kenya to block military interventions is
based on the extent to which Kenya has transcended the colonial model of using
the armed forces to maintain internal law and order. However, unless the Kenyan
state becomes more constitutionally autochthonous it can not survive as a stable
polity.

Historically, discussions about civilian military rule in Saharan African
states have been silent on the functional continuity between the colonial and
post-colonial military.[1] The omission of any discussion about professional
European armed forces in the colonial context, which were directly responsible
for the repression of African dissent and opposition, armed or otherwise, reifies
the Euro-centric model of military professionalism as the paradigm of civil-
military relations. The Euro-centric myth and standard of a professional army as

being neutral and impersonal is reinforced by the scholarly literature's exclusive focus on structure rather than function of the European colonial armies. Moreover, the scholarly focus on the formal structural characteristics transferred by the colonizer to the colonized avoids the fundamental issue of values and the socialization of the colonial army. The presupposition is that the professional military (a code word for European) derives its ethos from civil society. However, such assumptions are inoperative in the colonial context because civil society was illegitimate and the military was basically mercenary. The Euro-centric paradigm of civil society is characterized by Parsons' pattern variables where modern society is defined in the following terms: impersonal bureaucratic organization, instrumental rationality, individualism/liberty.[2]

The simple fact is that colonization was predicated on the arbitrary use of force to create and maintain the illegitimate usurpation of African sovereignty and liberty by Europeans. Thus, ideas advanced by Carl Rosberg and Robert Jackson about "princely rule" more aptly characterize the colonial interlude because it was colonization that usurped power from legitimate African rulers and thereby corrupted or destroyed African indigenous institutions. For instance, the colonizer destroyed the African institution of executive leadership, referred to in the literature as chieftancy, by eliminating leaders who resisted European domination.[3] Such leaders were replaced with more pliable ones who were more prepared to accept European domination. The purpose of this European policy was to effectively destroy the credibility and legitimacy of indigenous institutions, without providing a suitable legitimate alternative. Donald Cruise O'Brien expressed a similar sentiment when he wrote the following:

> The tendency to moral anarchy in underdevelopment is now widely seen as a consequence of the fact that the intrusion of the colonial system in traditional societies has proved effective in undermining established normative patterns but has left little basis for the construction of a new moral system.[4]

The point is that the African polity was destroyed for purely strategic and economic reasons and not for the development of African people. Although colonization bequeathed institutional structures, such as the nation-state, different forms of bureaucracy, and a standing army, it neither created nor engendered "civic culture" to sustain or operate these new governmental forms. Similarly, although the colonial regime nurtured the "civic culture" of European settlers in Kenya, by allowing them to elect representatives on the Colonial Legislative Council, it still maintained a totalitarian relationship with the overwhelming African majority. In Kenya, the indigenous African majority did not possess any rights respected by the colonial regime. The most stark examples of the disenfranchisement of Africans were in the areas of taxation and land policy. European settlers taxed Africans without representation and stole their land with impunity. Even though the colonial regime assigned one missionary to represent the diversity and complexity of the overwhelming African majority on the council, the autocratic colonial regime effectively precluded African representation on the Colonial Legislative Council. Such gross violations of African human rights by the autocratic colonial system were both created and maintained by the colonial army.

Colonization opened a pandora's box in Africa because it proved that military power rather than authority based on shared values was the cornerstone of modern polity or the nation-state. Thus contemporary "princely rule" is really the continuation of colonial rule based upon military power rather than on the consent of the people.

Moreover, any model that purports to explain coups or the lack of coups should not treat the colonial period as the golden age and independence as the dark age. This implied periodization of African politics not only suggests lingering scholarly ethnocentrism but also creates categories which are artificial polarities. This does not suggest, however, that contemporary African politicians and intellectuals can abdicate their responsibility for autocratic rule during the independence era by focusing only on the indelible structural effects of colonization in the postcolonial period. Rather the colonial period's negative socializing effects on the military, public officials, and politicians should be integrated into any analysis which discusses the performance of major post-colonial political institutions such as the military or the civil service.

My approach to the problem of military-civil relations in black Africa is based on the premise that the current volatility of civil-military relations is caused by the failure of the state to legitimate itself to the citizenry. When political scientists speak about crisis they generally refer to the failure of political leadership, i.e., excessive demands upon the system lead to system overload which in turn leads to an inability of political parties to control and manage political conflict.[5] In regard to the the African polity, the crisis is really more the result of European intervention which contributed to the African polity's simultaneous destruction and reconstruction by foreign powers. Although the colonial powers were able to destroy and rebuild the African polity, they could not imbue the new system with legitimacy. In fact the principle which girded the new system was raw power or force of arms.

According to Machiavelli, all new polities or states are intrinsically unstable because they are devoid of generally acceptable rules that govern the exercise of sovereign power. Hence, in order to create new rules all polities must undergo a very dangerous period of political chaos until new rules can be established which are generally acceptable to the people. For Machiavelli the solution to this period, where law is absent, is the interlude of the "Prince" wherein the "Prince" may be forced to use evil means to achieve the end of reconstituting a new polity. For example, Machiavelli believed that ultimately the most significant person contributing to the longevity of the Roman Republic was Numa, since he was the person responsible for creating the laws which girded the governed to governors together, which in turn engendered political stability.

What is instructive about Machiavelli's bold ideas is that they suggest that the crisis of legitimacy is not due to a development stage in a particular country but to whether or not the historic principles sanctioning the exercise of power have been destroyed. For example, the central battle of our democratic epoch has been the struggle to change the heretofore reigning principle of monarchy to democracy which has generated intense political conflict and deep political cleavages lasting from the American Revolution to the present.[6] One of the great barometers of this transformation has been the organization of the armed forces and their legitimate function in the new polity. In addition, the transition from monarchy to democracy also facilitated the rise of capitalism and the *bourgeoisie*, that in turn, divided power into three spheres political, economic and military. The intrinsic impersonality of a system driven by the impersonal market has in turn facilitated the creation and rise of a "professional military" noted for its neutrality and isolation from political power.[7] This Euro-centric model, however, only holds true for countries like the United States, Britain, and Holland which have completed the transition from feudalism to capitalism to democracy without external intervention and relative ease. In the case of Germany, the functional role of the military was not solved until the allies crushed the military during the Second World War.

In Africa, the imposition of foreign rule was only maintained by the colonial army's repeated interventions to sustain civil order; a model inconsistent for the military of an imperial country. This intervention sent signals to the Africans that armed intervention in the polity was justified as long as the security of state was in question. In Africa, on the other hand, the illegitimacy of the state created a condition where state security would always be in danger, therefore rulers could always justify military intervention in the name of national security.

In this context, the Greek and Hegelian notion of crisis as interpreted by Habermas provides a more analytical insight into the problems of civil military relations in Africa, in general, and Kenya, in particular, because it allows for the dynamic interplay and tension between historical, external constraints and the efficacy of individual political action to alter or transform external constraints. These ideas are found in the following extract from Habermas' work on the legitimation problems of modern society.

> Crisis signifies the turning point in a fateful process that, despite all objectivity, does not simply impose itself from outside and does not remain external to the identity of the persons up in it. The contradiction, expressed in the catastrophic culmination of conflict, is inherent in the structure of the action system and in the personality systems of the principal characters. Fate is fulfilled in the revelation of conflicting norms against which the identities of the participants shatter, unless they are able to summon up the strength to win back their freedom by shattering the mythical power of their fate through the formation of new identities.[8]

In this regard, my analysis of civilian-military relations in Kenya focuses on how Kenya's political regime kept the military at bay. In spite of Kenya's inheritance of an artificial and illegitimate polity imposed on the peoples of Kenya and exclusively maintained by the power of British armed forces, the government of Kenya still managed to break the precedent of armed intervention and maintain a civilian government established by colonial rule.

The remainder of this essay will analyze the social forces in Kenya which facilitated the historical break between the military and political organization of the colonial and post-colonial state. In this regard, the study will focus on three major areas of Kenya's political development that have effectively blocked military intervention: the organization of the armed forces in the society, the role of a vibrant commercialized agricultural sector coupled with an urbanized commercialized sector, and corporatist political arrangements.

Armed Forces and Society

The history of Kenyan armed forces began with the creation of the colonial state; the first instance of military intervention in Kenya was the conquest and defeat of the African nations by the British army which permanently changed their civilian life style. However, from the moment Britain unilaterally declared Kenya a British protectorate, African people continually resisted the imposition of foreign rule from 1895 until independence. In 1895, the Mazuri Rebellion occurred as soon as the Swahili people realized the true implications of colonization. Similarly, the Nandi, Abagusii, and Aembu people resisted British rule until the early 1920's. In 1922, the Kikuyu people. under the leadership of Harry Thuku, also resisted colonial rule. Finally, the "Mau Mau" war from 1952 to 1956 resulted in a state of emergency for all of Kenya until independence was declared.

The significance of African resistance to colonial domination was that it necessitated regular military intervention in order for the colonial regime to maintain social order and control. However, the repeated use of military power violated the idea of a professional military designed primarily to deter foreign aggression. Instead the illegitimacy of the colonial state necessitated that the British military control the state through violence and force. Hence, it was a small step to utilize such force to undermine illegitimate civilian authority in the post-colonial period.

In Kenya, due to the recurrent theme of resistance to colonial subjugation, coupled with an inadequate demographic base, the British used the tactic of dividing Africans into "good Africans" and "bad Africans" to maintain order and control. Given the uneven development of Kenya and the penetration of colonization from the World War II period, the Kikuyus were considered "bad" because they were the most difficult Africans to incorporate into the colonial regime. Kikuyus tended to be more revolutionary that other groups because white settlers stole most of their fertile land which was the essence of their civilization and culture.[9] The very foundation of white settlement in Kenya was predicated on the alienation of African land and most of the stolen land happened to be in the Kikuyu area. Hence, in order to protect their land-based civilization, the Kikuyus started a war of national liberation called the "Mau Mau war" to oust the white settlers and regain their legitimate lands. This "Mau Mau" war, which lasted form 1952-1956, eventually ended with the defeat of the Kikuyu national liberation movement by the British.

As a result of the opposition of the Kikuyu to colonial rule, the British banned them from joining the armed forces. Ironically, as the British were preparing Kenya for independence and dividing Africans into "good" and "bad," those Africans fighting for liberty and justice were excluded from the British military. The obvious reason for their exclusion can be attributed to the Kikuyu's legacy of struggle and resistance to colonial rule. Consequently, from independence to the present, the majority of the armed forces personnel, including officers, were non-Kikuyu even though the Kikuyus were the largest sub-national group in Kenya.

As mentioned earlier the armed forces of Kenya were a colonial creation. The structure and composition of the armed forces were derived form the Kings

African Rifles created by the British in 1902. Essentially, the Kings Africans Rifles (white officered, and black mercenary foot soldiers) primary function was to defend the British Empire's interests whenever and wherever in East and Central Africa its interests were defined.[10] The Kings African Rifles were never a neutral force in Kenyan history. Historically, their function was to suppress internal political opposition. In fact, after the "Mau Mau" national liberation war failed, the Kings African Rifles were integrated into the police forces to maintain order. Yet, in spite of over fifty years of dying in defense of the British empire, there were no black officers in the Kings African Rifles. The absence of African officers was directly related to the white settlers' fear of Africans and the political origin of armed forces in Kenya; that is, their specific function was to defend dominant interests, i.e., the white settler interests, rather than protecting the state from external interests and neutrality in domestic internal affairs.

Under these circumstances the underrepresentation of Africans in the officer corps created a political problem for the British because the Mau Mau war had greatly accelerated the timetable for independence. To create an effective army against the Mau Mau, Britain was compelled to create an affirmative action plan to increase the representation of Africans in the officer corp. Thus in 1956 a new category called the *effendi* was created to accelerate the promotion and development of African officers. In 1958, a special officer school was also opened in Nairobi to produce regular officers. It was only in 1959 that the first East Africans were admitted into Sandhurst, the leading British military academy.

The paucity of African officers was an ominous sign because Kenya was granted independence in 1963 without having developed a professional impersonal bureaucratic military. A period or interlude never existed where Africans served as officers or in any position of power in the colonial armed forces. The only socialization that Africans received on the professional role of armed forces in a political community was six years at best and two years at worst. In this context, it seems inappropriate to delink the performance of the Kenyan military from their colonial socialization and experience or to measure the performance of the African military to the western ideal type of military performance. In this regard, the colonial army's mercenary character, coupled with the second class status of Africans within this force, retarded the development of a positive attitude towards civilian authority.

As a result of colonial domination, Kenya did not possess a national army on the eve of independence and was confronted with the challenge of constructing a national army from various colonial armed forces. The white settlers' fear of African domination led to the development of different military groups in Kenya. White potential power created the following groups: the Kings African Rifles, the Kenyan Regiment (composed exclusively of white settlers), and the Kikuyu Guard (was created as an antidote to the "Mau Mau" in the 1950's). The independence leaders created the national army by combining three battalions from the Kings African Rifles, the 3rd and 5th and by fusing the 11th with the Kenyan Regiment.[11] The leadership of this motley national army fell to British expatriate officers.

Six months after independence, in January 1964, the African component of the Kenya army, composed mostly of junior officers because of years of racial discrimination, revolted against the colonial armed forces. A central issue of the revolt was African resentment to their inferior status and unequal pay compared with their expatriate European counterparts within Kenya's national army.[12] However, lacking the support of the African armed forces and fearing the loss of his power, Jomo Kenyatta motioned that the remaining British troops suppress the revolt.

Although the first revolt in Kenya was swiftly repressed by the British troops, the issue of Africanizing the armed forces remained a very contentious one for more than a decade after independence. It was not until 1973 that an African commanded the Kenyan air force.

Another major issue confronting the management of the armed forces in Kenya was how to decolonize the army by incorporating a greater level of ethnic diversity. As mentioned earlier, the policy of recruiting either mercenaries or pliable Africans to divide and rule the society resulted in a tremendous ethnic imbalance in the armed forces. Such a policy led to the virtual exclusion of Kikuyus from the colonial army, since they had consistently fought colonial subjugation. Yet if the military was to be considered a legitimate national army it could not be perceived as the exclusive domain of one particular ethnic group. Essentially, if one ethnic group were allowed to dominate the national army, the colonial army model would perpetuate. Due to these factors, the ethnic composition of the national army was as follows:

> The Kamba had provided a disproportionate number of recruits...They were still the largest single tribe represented in the officer corps in 1966, with 28 percent of the total compared to their population of 11 percent. The Kikuyu had 22.7 percent of the officers and 19.2 percent, and the Luo component was 10.3 percent, although Luos made up 13.9 percent of the total population.[13]

After the mutiny of African soldiers in the early period of independence, the Kenyan military was restructured and its importance reduced. President Kenyatta addressed the African soldiers' discontent by accelerating the Africanization of all levels of the military and increasing the pay of the soldiers. In implementing these political measures, Kenyatta effectively reduced the autonomy of the armed forces and thereby established the principle that civilian rule was primary. Such measures also reinforced the Kenyan constitutional principle that the president was the only legitimate authority who could order the armed forces into action and established the principle that the president of the republic was also the commander-in-chief of the armed forces.

From 1964 until 1982, the Kenyan armed forces were subordinate to the civilian government in every major budgetary consideration, including the acquisition of new weapon systems. The armed forces were not allowed to hold the civilian authority hostage either by posing a manifest or latent threat to intervene in the polity, if, for example, they were not granted higher wages or a new weapon system. However, in August 1982, within five years after the death of Jomo Kenyatta and 18 years after the first coup attempt, the armed forces attempted to impose their political will on the civilian regime in a failed coup attempt initiated by the air force. The coup attempt in 1982 failed in the same manner as the one in 1964, the major difference being, that in 1982, the Kenyan President did not have to call on foreign officers to suppress the revolt.

What contributed to the second coup attempt was the death of President Kenyatta, the founding father of the republic, and the influx of university students into the Kenyan Air Force, stimulated by the air force's need for more technical and specialized workers. The army and the specialized para-military General Service Units (GSU), on the other hand, were recruited in the villages.[14] The admission of university students into the air force ranks proved to be problematic, given the historical antagonism between the university and the dominant ideology of the political leadership. Students came to the armed forces not for patriotic reasons but for economic considerations and were socialized by the volatile relationship between the government and the university. In addition, some of these new recruits had become acquainted with Marxist thought and dependency theory which provided an alternative and plausible critique of Kenya's development from independence to the present, especially Kenya's reliance on tourism and toleration of extreme income inequality.

However, the most important radical idea circulating around the universities was the idea that political power was derived from military power. Ironically, the legitimacy of this principle was also reinforced by the colonial legacy because colonial rule was created and sustained by violence. The Maoist idea that political power comes from the barrel of a gun predisposed leftists to go to the mountains or to support military coups against decadent and illegitimate civilian regimes. As a substitute for the creation of national liberation army, revolutionaries instead joined the military ranks to create a revolution from above. The classic case and point was the overthrow of Haile-Selassie in Ethiopia, where radical intellectuals allied themselves with sections of the armed forces in order to push their revolution forward; although radical support was predicated on the belief that once the *ancien regime* was destroyed the radicals would then substitute themselves for the military. The main difference between Kenya and Ethiopia, however, was that the radical elements were not as developed in Kenya as they were in Ethiopia. For instance, movements like Pambana and MwaKenya were not created until the early eighties.

Nonetheless, the demonstration effect of the radical coup in Ethiopia had a latent impact on the progressive elements in the Kenya air force, because some members of the latter attempted to stage a coup. The striking similarity between the Ethiopian coup and the failed Kenyan coup was the attempt by Kenyan soldiers to forge an alliance with the university and other dissident intellectuals.

Around 2:00 a.m. August 1st, 1981, non-commissioned officers (NCOs) in Kenya Air Force mutinied and took over Kenya's main air bases, Nanyuki, Embakasi, and Eastleigh. By 5:00 a.m. Kenya's two major airports, the Central Bank of Kenya and the Voice of Kenya radio station were also overtaken. The rebels then enlisted the support of their natural allies, university students. In fact, some student leaders broadcasted over the national radio a call for support and solidarity with the soldiers' rebellion. However, at day break, when it became clear to the African population that the government was no longer in control, Africans began pillaging Asian and European businesses in the city center.[15] This spontaneous urban insurrection by African people indicated not only the deep divisions within Kenya, but how these young officers had virtually lost control of their own revolution. Coordination and command of the mutinous groups became impossible because the coup was initiated by air force NCOs within the smallest unit of the Kenyan armed forces. Hence, when the army along with units from the paramilitary police force, the GSU took measures to suppress the revolt, the rebels lack of a command and control system made it relatively easy for loyalist troops to end it. The coup was effectively over within twenty-four hours.[16] Under the command of Major General Mohamoud Mohamed the army was rallied and succeeded in defeating the insurgents.[17] In the aftermath of the coup, President Moi immediately disbanded the entire 3,000 airforce personnel while Major General Mohamoud Mohamed was commissioned by Moi to create a new air force. President Moi also closed Nairobi and Kenyatta universities because of the threatening alliance between rebels and students. Moi also made it mandatory for students to take a loyalty oath in order to regain admission in the university when they reopened.[18]

The Charismatic Leadership of Jomo Kenyatta

The persistance of civilian rule or democracy in Kenya is inextricably linked to Jomo Kenyatta and the Mau Mau revolt. The rise of Kenyatta and the Mau Mau were indispensable for the creation and maintenance of political stability because he was able to infuse his tremendous amount of personal credibility into the office of the executive office.

Charismatic leadership and the failed Kikuyu national liberation struggle are correlated because the violent national liberation struggle in central province was directly responsible for the ascendancy of Jomo Kenyatta as the most important political figure in Kenya after World War II. The British surprised by the African revolt, immediately assigned blame and responsibility incorrectly to Kenyatta. The reason why the British colonial administration held Kenyatta accountable was due to his prominent position as an African nationalist in the central province. In actuality Kenyatta represented the more conservative wing of the nationalist movement.[19] The real leader of the Kikuyu national liberation front was Dedan Kimathi Waciuri, who was eventually captured and executed by the British.

The unintended effect of Kenyatta's imprisonment was that it transformed him into a hero; his name became inseparable from independence. In short, the British colonial administration could not have created a better leader for Kenya's transition from a colony to an independent state. Kenyatta was the ideal leader because his imprisonment by the colonial regime engendered his credibility with the progressive forces in the country as well as with the defeated Mau Mau, while his principled opposition to violence as the means to achieve liberation reassured the colonial administration who worried about the fate of the remaining white settlers. Hence, as the first president of the republic, Kenyatta was able to legitimate the post-colonial state despite the fact that the state was destined to continue along the colonial path of unequal development. Even though Kenyatta's regime did not address in any fundamental way the desire of the Kenyan Land Freedom Army for redistribution of the stolen lands which were still occupied by white settlers.

Notwithstanding Kenyatta's failure to address landlessness, extreme inequality, and social equality, masses of people still considered Kenyatta the founding father of the republic. Kenyatta's charisma allowed him to create a praetorian guard called the General Service Unit (GSU) a paramilitary force designed to deal with internal security. Although compared to the army the GSU was much smaller, it was composed of about 2000 well equipped and mobile units (The army was composed of about 7,500 people).[20]

Kenyatta's credibility also allowed him to effectively deploy these units to quell university disturbances or eliminate challengers such as Tom Mboya or opponents such as J.M. Kariuki.[21] Kenyatta's persona as the founder of the republic allowed him to be exceedingly tolerant of a highly critical parliamentary body and a comparatively free and open press which was not simply the voice of the regime. What was remarkable about Kenyatta's rule was that he was a teflon president in the sense that he was never held personally accountable or responsible for any crimes or injustices committed during his reign. Even Odinga Oginga the first vice president of the republic, who eventually founded the leading opposition party, called the Kenyan People's Union, never held Kenyatta personally responsible for the failure of independence to significantly change the structure of power and privilege and create more social equality.[22]

Agricultural Commercialization and Urbanization

The second major factor contributing to the efficacy of civilian government was the large presence of white settlers who developed a very prosperous cash crop economy coupled with an energetic Asian commercial class whose existence and expansion was inextricably related to expanding white settler agri-business development. The significance of the European and Asian sectors is that their political and socio-economic articulation with the autocratic colonial state was as citizens. British settlers, and to more limited extent, Asians, were granted citizenship rights such as freedom of association, freedom of speech, and representation on the Colonial Legislative Council. In stark contrast, the overwhelming African majority was treated as subjects. Adding insult to injury, Africans were subjected to third class citizenship and even forced to wear an identity badge called *kipande* around their neck like cattle. They were also denied the rights of freedom of association while their political associations and leaders like Harry Thuku were banned or put in preventive detention. Furthermore, the British levied taxes on Africans without equal representation on the Colonial Legislative Council.

The legacy of the colonial state bequeathed two conflicting political traditions, one totalitarian and paternalistic, and another democratic and individualistic to the post-colonial state. The theory of social change expounded by Barrington Moore in his work the *Social Origins of Dictatorship and Democracy* provides an additional framework for analyzing the persistence of democracy in Kenya. The most relevant aspects of Moore's analysis of Kenya is the relationship of the dominant classes, peasants, to the commercialization of agriculture. In Moore's framework, the democratic road is predicated on the emergence of an independent *bourgeoisie* in which the landed upper classes and peasantry are destroyed by the revolution. In Kenya, the destruction of the pre-capitalist social formation, which was equivalent to the European peasantry, was brought about by the British defeat of all the African nations in pre-colonial Kenya. For Moore, another factor which contributed to whether countries chose the democratic capitalist road was the character of the social structure before modernization. Moore suggests that there are three main characteristics for a democratic approach to modernization: the autonomy and immunity of groups from the power of the ruler; the concept of the right to resist unjust authority; the idea of contracts based upon reciprocity and made by free individuals.[23]

Of course, in the colonial context, the ruling class was the colonial administration and Africans were essentially reduced to serfs without rights or immunities from arbitrary colonial rule, coupled with the total suppression of their political autonomy. What made Kenya unique was that the landholding class which initiated commercialization of the agricultural sector and business sectors were foreigners. The existence of a democratic exogenous ruling class based on commercialized agriculture, coupled with an urbanized Euro-Asian sector has served as a major pillar for constitutional rule in Kenya, though necessary, were insufficient to maintain democracy, since they were mainly concerned with protecting civic and property rights, and they did not represent the majority. These two sectors were like air pockets in a totalitarian sea orchestrated and created by colonization. The Euro-Asian's need to secure their political socio-economic interests compelled them to include the overwhelming African majority on the basis of civic equality. However, civic equality was insufficient compensation for the majority of Africans; the egregious crimes of the colonial period required an ambitious land redistribution program. Thus, to legitimate the independent constitutional government, the Kenyan government instituted two programs to bridge the socio-economic gulf between Africans and the Euro-Asian community: Africanization of the civil service, and redistribution of a million acres to African small holder cultivators. Such governmental measures were indispensable for civilian control and political stability in the post-colonial period.

Corporatism

Another factor contributing to Kenya's constitutional stability was the political regime's use of a corporatist strategy to mediate the conflict between labor and capital, as a way to achieve and maintain political solidarity. My notion of corporatism is based on Schmitter's conception.

> Corporatism can be defined as system of interest representation in which the constituent units are organized into a limited number of singular, compulsory, noncompetitive hierarchically ordered and functionally differentiated categories, recognized or licensed...by the state and granted a deliberate representational monopoly within their respective categories in exchange for observing certain controls on their selection of leaders and articulation of demands and supporters.[24]

Since independence there have been three Tripartite Agreements. In Kenya, tripartist agreements were made between the Kenyan government, the Federation of Kenya Employers and Trade Unions (Cotu). The essence of these agreements is summarized in the preamble of the first agreement in the 1964.

> In acceptance of the fact that the unemployment problem has now become so serious as to constitute a national emergency, and while realizing that the ultimate solution lies in the implementation of long term plans to create a developing economy, we have agreed that there is an urgent need for immediate relief measures designed to create breathing space during which such long-term plan can be established.[25]

In the 1964 Agreement, wages were frozen while the public sector agreed to expand employment by 15 percent and the private sector by 10 percent. Under the 1970 Agreement, unions accepted another wage freeze. Government and the private sector also agreed to expand employment by ten percent in 1979. The same was also true for the Agreement signed in (Weekly Review, 1979).[26]

The general consensus within and outside of Kenya was that these Agreements did not improve the economic or employment opportunities.[27] Although these Agreements failed to reach desired economic goals, they did manage to engender political stability and confidence in the government because such policies indicated that the government was at least managing the problem. The civilian regime's ability to create a consensus between labor and business to curb their demands without resorting to repression further insulated the government from depending on the military for its survival. This strategy proved successful because the government was able to incorporate the military, labor and business into the government without the use of force and as autonomous units. The net effect was that the civilian regime to act with a great degree of autonomy and without the threat of military intervention.

Summing Up

In conclusion, the insulation of the Kenya government from military intervention was due to a configuration of social forces ranging from white settlers and the commercialization of agriculture, to the destruction and transformation of pre-capitalist African landholders into market driven small holder cultivators, and to the creation of an urban economy. The constellation of these social forces insulated the constitutional government from cannibalization by the colonial armed forces. Unless the Eurocentric foundation of constitutional government is changed the state will not become legitimate because ultimately the colonial and post-colonial state is based upon force rather than consent. As the post-colonial government loses more credibility and efficacy, liberty and accountability are the only weapons that can keep the military at bay. Presently, the president has been compelled by the international community, coupled with rising internal opposition, to end KANU's monopoly of political power and allow for multiparty competition.

Notes

1. See S. Decalo, *Coups and Army Rule in Africa: Studies in Military Style*, (New Haven: Yale University Press, 1976); H. Bienen, *Armies and Parties in Africa*, (New York: Africana Publishing Company, 1978); W. Gutteridge, *The Military in African Politics*, (London: Methuen & CO LTD, 1969); S. Baynham, ed. *Military Power and Politics in Black Africa*, (London: Croom Helm, 1986).

2. T. Parsons, "Evolutionary Universals in Society," in T. Parsons, *Sociological Theory and Modern Society*, (New York: Free Press, 1967).

3. T. Hodgkin, See *Nationalism in Colonial Africa*, London, 1956.

4. D. Cruise O'Brien "Modernization, Order and Erosion of a Democratic Ideal," *Journal of Development Studies* 8 (4) 1972: 351-378.

5. See S. Huntington, *Political Order in Changing Societies*, (New Haven: Yale University Press, 1968).

6. See R. Bendix, *Kings or People Power and the Mandate to Rule*, (Berkeley: University of California, 1978).

7. M. Mann, *States, War and Capitalism*, (London: Blackwell, 1988). Chapt. 4.

8. J. Habermas, *Legitimation Crisis*, (Boston: Beacon Press, 1975), p. 2.

9. C.G. Rosberg and J. Nottingham, *The Myth of the Mau Mau*, (New York: Praeger, 1966), Chapt. 6.

10. M. Bartlett, *The Kings African Rifles*, (Great Britain: Gale and Polden Limited, 1956).

11. I. Kaplan, *Area Handbook for Kenya*, (Washington, D.C.: U.S. Government Printing Office, 1975), pp. 399-412.

12. Kaplan, *Area Handbook for Kenya*, p. 402.

13. H. Bienen, *Armies and Parties in Africa*, (New York: Africana Publishing Co. 1978), p. 178.

14. K. Currie, "The Pambana of August 1-Kenya's Abortive Coup," *Political Quarterly*, 57 (1), 1986: 47-60. pp. 49-50.

15. *African Confidential Report*, 1975-6, p. B222-3.

16. *African Research Bulletin*, June 1975, p. 3660.

17. Currie, "The Pambena of August 1-Kenya's Abortive Coup," *Political Quarterly*, p. 55.

18. *African Contemporary Record*, 1982, p. 181.

19. Colin Leyes, *Underdevelopment in Kenya* (Berkeley: University of California Press, 1974).

20. *African Confidential Report*, 1975-76, pp. B222-3.

21. *African Research Bulleting*, June 1975, p. 3660.

22. O. Odinga, *Not Yet Uhura*, (New York: Hill & Wang, 1967).

23. B. Moore, *Social Origins of Dictatorship and Democracy*, (Boston: Beacon Press, 1966).

24. P.C. Schmitter, "Still the century of corporatism?" *Review of Politics* 1974 36: 85-131.

25. *Ministry of Labour and Social Sciences, Annual Report*, (Nairobi: Government Printer, 1964.)

26. *Weekly Review*, 1979. Nairobi, Kenya.

27. *Central Organization of Trade Unions, Development and Employment Creation in Kenya*, Nairobi, 1979.

8

Civilian Control of the Military in Africa: The Case of Zambia

Baffour Agyeman-Duah

Nearly two decades ago when Claude E. Welch edited a collection of case studies on *Civilian Control of the Military*, he precluded African countries because, as he put it, "independent African countries [had] yet to establish means of civilian control that [had] stood the test of time."[1] Even though he noted, at the time, five states as having survived the wave of military onslaught on civilian governments in Africa, the number, according to him, was simply a "handful" to merit any serious academic study. Moreover, by 1976 the incessant military *coups d'état* on the continent had shrivelled any confidence about the survivability of these 'exceptional' states. Welch's assertion was, therefore, empirically and theoretically founded.

Indeed, by the early eighties, the role of the "man on horseback" in African politics could hardly be considered transient as military interventions became institutionalized, if not constitutionalized, in many states. According to a study by Pat McGowan and Thomas Johnson, by 1985 no less that 60 successful and 71 attempted *coups d'état* had occurred in 37 states since January 1956.[2] Another study in 1990 of the interrelationships among coups, regime change, and interstate conflicts in West Africa confirmed the escalation of coups in this subregion.[3] Furthermore, the study indicated the contagiousness of coups and the causal relationship between them and interstate conflicts, particularly where the perpetrators had radical perspectives. Through this turbulent period of praetorian ascendency in postcolonial African politics, however, an impressive number of states successfully controlled their military's propensity for

141

intervention and, consequently, maintained civilian rule. In early 1991 one could count among these The Gambia, Senegal, Gabon, Cote d'Ivoire, Cameroon, Cape Verde, Tanzania, Kenya, Zimbabwe, Malawi, Botswana, Djibouti, Swaziland, Lesotho, Mauritius, and Zambia. In fact, three of them -- Senegal (1981), Cameroon (1982), Tanzania (1986) -- managed a peaceful transfer of power from one civilian president to another, while two others, Mauritius (1982) and Cape Verde (1991), changed regimes through the ballot box in multiparty competitive elections.[4] Some others -- Kenya (1978), Botswana (1980), Angola (1979), Swaziland (1982), and Mozambique (1986) -- experienced constitutional top-level leadership succession, mostly following the death of incumbent leaders. Viewed against the background of Welch's litmus test, these states have truly "stood the test of time." Thus, the sustained focus on coups in the literature that helped to fortify the general view that coups have become a norm of modern African political behavior need to be redressed. Instances of civilian rule should no longer be dismissed as simply "exceptions to the rule."

It seems propitious to refocus and reshape the discussion on civil-military relations in Africa. Instead of exploring why coups occur, we should begin to ask why and how some civilian regimes have sustained their control of the military over the years. To borrow from Samuel E. Finer's often-quoted work, "[i]nstead of asking why the military engage in politics, we ought surely to be asking why they ever do otherwise .... Why and how do civilian forms of rule persist?"[5] Considering that all the states listed earlier have experienced at least a rumor of a coup and, in some cases, even attempted coups, such inquiries also ought to highlight reasons for civilian regimes' success in preempting coups.

This chapter will probe civilian control of the military in one African state, namely Zambia, for the primary reason that the country possesses all the major characteristics necessary for a study of this kind. First, Zambia is one of the few that have the longest history of civilian rule. Gaining its independence from British colonial rule in 1964, Zambia has been ruled consistently by one political party under one president, Kenneth Kaunda. Second, although Zambia's postcolonial history has exemplified most of the ills usually prescribed as reasons for military interventions, the country has been able to sustain civilian rule. Third and finally, Zambia has, reportedly, successfully withstood several plots and attempted coups. Hopefully, the discussion would show that the Zambian success in maintaining civilian rule, while not entirely unique, provides insights into how military interventions in African politics might be restrained.

Theoretical Analysis

The inverse of the question as to why do the military intervene in politics could also provide the clue to why they do not and, hence, why civilian regimes prevail. Thus theories of why coups occur provide a valuable basis for the discussion. In 1968 Edward Luttwak theorized that unsophisticated states are more coup-proned than sophisticated ones.[6] According to this theory, a sophisticated state, like a "machine," is one where the security apparatuses are organized, regimented, disciplined and rigid. It is very difficult to execute a coup in such a state, Luttwak contends, especially when the "machine" is sufficiently sophisticated to exercise discretion, according to a given conception of what is "proper and what is not, in the orders that it executes."[7] Differentiating between "sophisticated" and "unsophisticated" states (euphemisms for the strong and well established states of the West and the newly independent states respectively), Luttwak was able to determine conditions that make coups possible in weak states. Among them were the lack of regime legitimacy, absence of adequate dialogue between rulers and ruled, economic crisis and deprivation, and chronic instability.[8]

In his case study of the Ghanaian coup of 1966, Jon Kraus attributed the intervention to two main variables: "the flagrant abuses of power" by the incumbent regime and "the country's desperate economic plight."[9] According to Kraus,

> The abuses of power were marked by Nkrumah's [the president] and the CPP's [ruling party] claim to all power and political choice, arbitrary government, and increasingly repressive laws and actions. The economic deterioration, acutely felt by the Ghanaians, included rampant inflation (with a wage freeze), increasingly widespread unemployment, a drastic shortage of essential goods an spare parts, and serious mismanagement in the distribution of existing goods.[10]

The interaction between these political and economic factors, combined with objective grievances of the armed forces, precipitated the military's disaffection with Kwame Nkrumah. All this bred what Kraus describes as "the *sine qua non*" of military coups: "a significant loss of legitimacy by the existing government."[11]

The themes espoused by Luttwak and Kraus reinforced an earlier proposition by Finer that the military obtained a "disposition to intervene" when the legitimacy of a government was severely strained.[12] Through the years several other scholars have echoed these precursory arguments.[13] While the *sine qua non* suggested by Kraus has run through all subsequent expositions on coups, it is quite evident that the phenomena are caused by a complexity of forces. This reality was stressed by Claude Welch when he cautioned against a "unicausal analysis" of coups. He warned in 1970: "To assume that 'popular discontent' or 'economic stagnation' or 'neocolonialist interference' brought about the *coups d'état* does not do justice to the unique combinations of circumstances."[14] Welch subsequently summarized eight factors he considered significant in analyzing the incidence of coups. Among them are the declining prestige of the major political party, schisms among prominent politicians, lessened likelihood of external intervention, "contagious" effect from other countries, domestic social antagonism, economic malaise, corruption and inefficiency, and heightened political consciousness of the armed forces.

By turning on the head the arguments for why coups occur, we can anchor the case for why they do not. Thus in contradistinction, the foregoing arguments may also explain the circumstances under which military intervention in politics could be restrained. Subjoining these pervasive propositions is David Goldsworthy's contention that "personal rule" is the paramount determinant of successful civilian control of the military.[15] Drawing on an earlier work by Robert H. Jackson an Carl G. Rosberg,[16] Goldsworthy postulates that because of their colonial past and recency, African states lack strong "institutionalized cultural bases" and "there is little evidence of a national consensus expressed in entrenched and legitimate institutions. It follows that political control of the military....cannot rest upon such a base." Furthermore, he argues, as other writers have done, that soldiers are actual or potential players in the political game. Consequently, "civilian control may generally be seen as a function of military loyalty to the person or the ruler rather than to the abstraction of the state."[17] Echoing Niccolo Machiavelli's *Prince*, Goldsworthy suggests that what sustain long-lived civilian as well as military rulers are the political factors of acumen, personal willpower, skill, and luck.[18]

To what extent have these theoretical explications been exemplified by those African states that have successfully restrained the military from political interventions? What accounts for this success? To understand and appreciate civil-military relations in a civilian-ruled state, I will attempt to ferret out an empirical explanation for the theoretical link. For this I turn to evidence from Zambia where civilian control of the military has endured for over 26 years.

The Military in Zambian Society

The state of Zambia emerged in October 1964 when the British colonial administration handed over power to the elected government of Kenneth Kaunda, leader of the victorious United National Independence Party (UNIP). The new government inherited an army of 2,900 from the erstwhile Northern Rhodesia.[19] Like armies in all new states, the Zambian army assumed its role as the custodian of national sovereignty as well as the most visible symbol of governmental power and national legitimacy.

By 1971 the army had grown to 4,000 and an air force with 400 men had been established. The growth in the armed forces continued in ascending order and assumed dramatic proportions between 1984 and 1987. Between 1964 and 1974 there was an annual average growth of 10 percent with the rate increasing to 15 percent during the following ten-year period (1974-1984). While the 1984 figure of 14,400 represented nearly four and a half times that of 1964, the total armed forces of 16,200 in 1987 was over five times the number at the inception of independence.[20]

The growth of the Zambian armed forces could hardly be discounted as part of the normal desire of new African states to assert their sovereignty and territorial integrity through a credible standing army. Barely a year following its independence, Zambia had to confront the military fallout from Ian Smith's "unilateral declaration of independence" (UDI) in southern Rhodesia. The dramatic growth during the second decade of independence, however, appears to have been necessitated by the intensity of threats to national security as a result of the aggravating interstate conflicts and civil wars that engulfed the entire southern African subregion. Landlocked between Angola and Namibia to the west and Rhodesia and Mozambique to the south -- countries where liberation struggles raged against white minority regimes and Portuguese colonialism -- Zambia was, indeed, precariously situated. The country offered sanctuary and support to the liberation fighters, and this put it under direct fire from the forces of Rhodesia and South Africa who supported the regional political status quo.

As early as 1965 rumors were rife that Rhodesia had a plan to blast the hydropower plant at Kariba, the mainstay of Zambia's industrial development. Indeed, the British rejection of Kaunda's request for troops to protect the dam motivated his early decision to "reconsider [Zambia's] entire defense policy."[21] By the mid-1970s, as the military conditions deteriorated in Angola, Rhodesia, and Namibia, and Zambia's territorial integrity was unremittingly violated, Kaunda, at one point, had to invoke emergency powers. As he stated at the time, "There is foreign interference in our country.... We are at war." [22] Thus, as early as 1969, Zambia was already contemplating the need to purchase a missile air defense system.[23]

Under such extreme security pressures from the warring neighbors, Kaunda announced in November 1978 that the country had not "spent enough on building [the] army" and proceeded, two years later, to purchase $845.4 million worth of arms from the Soviet Union; he also sent his soldiers to train there.[24] These external threats were the major factors contributing to the growth of the Zambian armed forces. The small air force of 400 men established in the late sixties doubled by 1974 and quadrupled ten years later with forty-four combat aircrafts.[25] How did such a rapid expansion in the armed forces impact on their relations with the civil authority?

Colonial Influence on the Military

The pattern of civil-military relations prescribed in the colonial era was carried into Zambia's early postcolonial period. This condition was clearly helped by the British officers who continued their command of the armed forces. These officers ensured the inviolate doctrine of political obedience and the separation of the "armed forces from their social contexts -- that is, to ensure the 'integral' boundaries of the military as an institution."[26] Furthermore, because Zambia achieved independence through relatively peaceful means without a revolutionary struggle, the armed forces "remained on the political sidelines" and carried over their "institutional conservatism characteristic of the colonial period."[27] As described elsewhere, this outlook which characterized the military in most of the early postcolonial African states stressed the respect "for the principle of neutrality in political matters."[28]

The early postcolonial leaders fully expected their armed forces to stay apolitical. As reiterated by Ghana's Nkrumah in a larger context, "*Armies had no political mandate*, and if the national interest compelled army intervention it must immediately afterward hand over to a new civil government elected by the people" [emphasis mine].[29] In Zambia this expectation was ensured by the extended command of the armed forces by the British. Indeed, until Kaunda dismissed a large section of the British officers in January 1979, all threats to his government had remained external, with the sole exception of the rumored coup attempt in December 1973. Incidentally, the coup in Ghana occurred only after Nkrumah had indigenized the command of his armed forces; the same has been true for coups in other African states.

The argument for the apolitical character of the military is not to say that members of the institution were completely cut off, insulated, or immuned from the social cleavages and conflicts that afflicted the society at large. To the contrary, even in the colonial era soldiers were an integral part of the wider social system with which they interacted. Rene Lemarchand stressed this point when he cautioned against any assumption that the "military training and indoctrination in the ideals of discipline and obedience [would] take precedence over ethnic, familial, or personal loyalty in situations where soldiers are forced to choose between military duty and personal duty."[30] In this context, therefore, the Zambian armed forces, in spite of their colonial character, were equally susceptible to the same kinds of anxieties as those of the larger population.

Domestic Pressures

The decade of the eighties witnessed a rapid depreciation in the external pressures against Zambia, while domestic challenges to Kaunda and the UNIP government became pronounced. Externally, a condition of peace evolved in the subregion as a result of the diminished intensity in the struggles in Angola and Mozambique where freedom from colonial rule was achieved in 1975, and the attainment of majority rule in Rhodesia (Zimbabwe) in 1980. Domestically, there was a growing restlessness among the population as Zambia's economic crisis came to a head. And, as the people began to express their disenchantment and Kaunda's political opponents became more vocal, the country's domestic politics grew contentious. Thus, for the government, it became extremely necessary to elevate the armed forces' internal security role.

Zambia's internal security problems were exacerbated following the change from a multi-party competitive political system to a single-party system in 1972. The banning of the opposition United Progressive Party (UPP) and the detention of its leader, Simon Kapwepwe and several other officials of the party that year, began to aggravate the crisis in Zambian politics and led to a heightened internal security concern. Even though the UPP's predecessor, the United Party, was banned and its leader, Nalumino Mundia, arrested earlier in 1968 in connection with the political riots in the copper-belt town of Chillialabombwe in August, the demise of the UPP and the legalization of the one-party state effectively shut out organized opposition and, in so doing, sharpened the internal conflict. In fact, the first reported coup attempt occurred in December 1973, a few months following the institutionalization of the one-party system.

The political difficulties were compounded by the accelerating decline in the national economy. With a mono-culture (almost totally dependent on copper) and neocolonial economy, Zambia has historically been extremely vulnerable to the mutations in the international economy. But, as Tony Hodges notes, the "turning point in the Zambia's postcolonial fortunes came in 1973-75. The quadrupling of oil prices and the beginning of the long slump in copper prices plunged Zambia into a crisis form which it has never recovered."[31] Furthermore, the economy was ruined by the prolonged confrontation with Rhodesia during the period of the illegal rule of Ian Smith (1965-1980).

By the early eighties the cumulative impact of the decline in the economy had created severe hardships for the Zambians. The government, subsequently, accepted to implement the International Monetary Fund (IMF) program to restore the shattered economy. The restoration program, however, failed to yield timely results and instead worsened the plight of the masses. For instance, the program required the withdrawal of government subsidies to some basic items of livelihood. The government's attempt to enforce this requirement in relation to maize, the country's staple food, resulted in a price increase of 120% and led to massive violent riots in December 1986. As described by Kaunda in his address jettisoning the IMF program, "income per head of population had fallen from the equivalent of $630 in 1981 to below $200 in 1987; unemployment was rising; and inflation had gone up for 21% in 1985 to 61% in 1986."[32]

Most theorists of political change would argue that the economic condition as it prevailed in Zambia, made the country vulnerable to mass agitation and change. Popular agitation did, indeed, erupt in the country, but, contrary to theoretical assumptions, political change did not follow. In early 1985, a wave of strikes and work stoppages paralyzed the country's hospitals, forcing Kaunda to issue a rarely used presidential decree to ban strikes. Worse strikes and mass unrest were to come a year later. The attempt to raise the price of maize as part of the IMF program sparked unprecedented riots in which 15 people were reportedly killed and over 450 arrested. This four-day riot forced Kaunda to rescind the price increase in what was described as "a devastating blow to his personal esteem."[33] The rioters had singled out houses of UNIP officials for attack. Also, in the October 1987 copperbelt riots, the party's offices were among the targets of mob attacks. The assault on the UNIP indicated a serious erosion of its effectiveness and popularity and, subsequently, its legitimacy and, implicitly, that of the leader.

The Zambian armed forces could not be immune to the mass restiveness. Twice in 1987 reports surfaced of plots to overthrow the government. In April a number of businessmen were accused of plotting with South African agents to instigate a military coup.[34] The following month, the veteran opposition leader, Alfred Chambeshi, was arrested for allegedly conspiring with UNITA forces of Angola to stage a coup. While these incidents were indirectly linked to the armed forces, they, nevertheless, reflected the forces' tenuousness and that of internal security. In fact, in October 1988, six senior officers, including the army commander, Lt. Gen. Christon Tembo, were detained for alleged subversive activities.[35] To contain the increasing threat from the armed forces, Kaunda resorted to his long adopted practice of coopting the service chiefs into his administration. Thus, he reshuffled his cabinet in November and included three generals. Again in July 1990 he added Lt. Gen. Hanniah Lungu to the cabinet as defense minister following an attempted coup in the preceding month.

The outbreak of food riots in June 1990 in which several people were killed by security forces and the forces' invasion of the University of Zambia to arrest anti-government student leaders and close the campus, might have instigated another coup attempt. On June 30, a young officer, Lt. Mwamba Luchembe, seized the Zambian national radio and announced the overthrow of Kaunda. Although this attempt proved to be a careless adventure by one disaffected officer, the spontaneous public support it received testified to the wanning popularity of Kaunda and his government.

Evidently, Zambia portrays most of the factors that theorists prescribe for military interventions in politics. The armed forces were expanded and adequately equipped to withstand external aggression. They possessed, therefore, the wherewithal to execute a *coup d'état* , were they to be so inclined to act. The country's political and economic conditions, particularly during the decade of the eighties, could provide the rationale and the justification for the intervention. Both the president and his ruling party appeared to have sunk in their popularity and, perhaps, in their legitimacy. While the armed forces became visibly restless, no concerted attempt was made to overthrow the civil authority. The question of why the Kaunda government has "stood the test of time" in the face of such immense domestic contradictions is the focus of the following section of the discussion.

Why Kaunda and the UNIP Have Survived

The fact that Kenneth Kaunda and his United National Independence Party have successfully controlled the military in Zambia from political intervention, can be attributed to many and varied factors. Among them are Kaunda's leadership style, the role and function of the party, and Zambia's role in the politics of the subregion.

Kaunda's Style of Governance

First and foremost is Kaunda's style of rule. As described by William Tordoff, "he is a skillful politician who combines a strong moral sense derived from his Christian upbringing with a good deal of pragmatism."[36] Goldsworthy attributes much of the success of civilian control of the military to the "ability and fortune of the individual at the top," and in the case of Zambia, Kaunda appears to vindicate this assumption. His leadership has been remarkable for its frugality, moderation, and pragmatism.

Kaunda has maintained a personal trait that seems to eschew extravagance, corruption, and blatant abuses of power. Setting a high standard for himself, he has been quick to discipline corrupt and fraudulent members of his administration, party functionaries, and those in the civil service. For instance, in November 1970 he suspended a number of cabinet ministers and public officials on charges of tampering with government funds. One minister was put on trial, while the others were reinstated only after the Director of Public Prosecution had certified no evidence of misconduct against them. The following year four party officials were suspended for indiscipline and three ministers were dismissed following the publication of a judicial report on charges of "tribalism" within the government. Again, in May 1987 senior staff members of the Bank of Zambia were fired for alleged irregularities.[37] Such prompt disciplinary measures strongly suggested that Kaunda and his government were above reproach and could not be seen to condone and connive corruption, one of the usual charges to justify military coups.

The political skills of Kaunda have been demonstrated in his ability to rise above factionalism. He has balanced the interests of the three dominant ethnic groups, the Bemba, the Tonga, and the Barotse, and staunchly resisted ethnic identifications in the distribution of national values. Thus, he has successfully presented himself as the "father" of all the people. Within the UNIP, he has stood above factional interests and, on occasion, has threatened to resign out of disgust for party infighting. Kaunda has thus proved to be the unifying force within the party as well as in the nation.

As a political pragmatist and tactician, Kaunda knows when to be obstinate, when to compromise and recompense, and when to coopt. A good example of his acts of pragmatism was when he violently suppressed the mass riots over the price of maize in 1986 and, thereafter, rescinded the decision and railed the IMF recovery program. Again, after berating popular demand in early 1990 for the reinstatement of multiparty system (a subject I will address in the concluding section), he signed a constitutional amendment in December to allow the formation of opposition parties. His periodic reshuffling and coopting of service commanders into civilian positions is an illustration of his strategy to disorient the armed forces and, thereby, make it difficult for them to plot successfully against him. The appointment of Gen. Tembo as high commissioner to Canada in 1987, for example, was widely viewed as designed to forestall a possible military unrest. Again, as mentioned before, Kaunda has always brought his top generals into his cabinet, ostensibly to give the military a stake in the survival of the government.

The UNIP and Morality as Stabilizing Forces

The UNIP has also served as a stabilizing factor by ensuring a horizontal distribution of rewards among the socially significant classes, that is to say, those that could possibly rock the boat. Tordoff has indeed noted that the Zambian political system has brought "material benefits to senior politicians and administrators, business men and small professional elite, *among whom are officers in the defense services*" [emphasis mine].[38] Such an all-inclusive approach has ensured that all the prominent sectors of the society have a vested interest in the political system and, therefore, its survival. The UNIP's strategy makes an interesting comparison with the Convention People's Party (CPP) of Nkrumah's Ghana, another single-party state. Unlike the UNIP, the CPP was a dividing force; built on the support of "veranda boys" (common "uneducated" people), the CPP grew to alienate most of the socially significant classes.[39] Nkrumah particularly alienated the regular armed forces when, to their chagrin, he created and nourished a special Presidential Guard Regiment for his personal protection.

The UNIP has become a veritable instrument of patronage in the Zambian political system for Kaunda to build and maintain support. In a single-party system, the control over and distribution of resources are the domain of the UNIP; allegiance and loyalty to it, therefore, ensures one's access to the state and whatever it dispenses. Tordoff, again, has noted that in the First Republican period the use of patronage was widespread and it determined the award of loans, contracts, and projects in the districts. While the downturn in the economy in the Second Republic may have restricted available resources, it might have created new avenues for the party to use patronage. Tordoff claims that the government maintains tight controls and local administrations are made to be "dependent on centrally allocated funds."[40] To most Zambians, therefore, to be economically and politically upwardly mobile is to join and positively identify with the party. Even though the armed forces are not formally incorporated into the UNIP, officers and men, like other citizens desiring mobility, rely on the party for promotion and material rewards.

To buttress the UNIP's stabilizing role and that of his moral standing, Kaunda has adopted "humanism," an ideology that espouses a human-centered society with traditional communal values, as the cornerstone of his domestic policy. The eclecticism of this ideology (an amalgamation of capitalism, socialism and populism), according to Tordoff, "mirrors the various elements within Zambian society and seeks to accommodate all the interests that go to make up the coalition over which Kaunda presides."[41] Though "humanism" does not appear to have been popularly and successfully inculcated in the people, it has given the president a powerful moral position to draw on their sympathies and reconcile the various elements of the Zambian society. The Zambian armed forces are presumably under the spell of this moral force. While class differentiations exist, they have been less pronounced in terms of their competition over national values; the military class has been no exception.

The Use of Intelligence

Kaunda has also made an effective use of the intelligence and security apparatus in dealing with potential threats to his rule and in quelling mass protests and student unrest. That all the alleged coup plots could not materialize were due in large part to the efficacy of his internal security system. Unlike some African leaders, Kaunda has had no need to enter into military or security assistance relationship with the former metropole or any other external power. Such blatant neocolonial linkages are found in other single-party or one-party dominant states such as Côte d'Ivoire, Djibouti, Gabon and Senegal where internal security has been assured mainly through the stationing of French troops and the assurance of the French government, through word and deed, to support the status quo. The French government has, in fact, intervened directly in several of its client states in Africa. The success of security self-reliance in Zambia may be credited not only to the intelligence and security apparatus, but also to the domestic political environment that seems to be less antagonistic and repressive.

Influence of Regional Politics

Another element that has ensured the survivability of civilian rule is Zambia's international standing relative to the Southern African subregion and its political environment. With its pivotal position as a Frontline State, Zambia played a heroic role in harboring liberation fighters and assisting in the search for a just peace. Consequently, the country gained much international respect and sympathy for the retributions it suffered at the hands of South Africa and Rhodesia. The Zambian people were more sympathetic to their government and they rallied around their leader who was seen as a helpless victim of aggrandizement by his white neighbors. This helped to distract public attention from domestic problems and the government's own inabilities. Thus, Kaunda and his party were less to blame for the mounting economic difficulties of the 1970's. More germane to the present discussion was the preoccupation of the armed forces with the external assaults. In the face of the mounting assaults from without and the conflicts in the subregion, the armed forces were obliged to be more alert to national defense and honor than to attempt to overthrow a popular government.

Civilian rule in Zambia has been bolstered by the subregional political environment. The dearth of coups in the Southern African region has created a political culture that supports civilian control of the military. In West Africa, for instance, *coups d'état* have been endemic; at the last count, 75% of the 16 states of the subregion had experienced successful coups and the contagiousness of this phenomenon was much in evidence. Furthermore, 14 states were under some type of military regime.[42] The picture in southern Africa is different; civilian rule seems to be the norm in spite of the extensive militarization that resulted from the liberation struggles. In the absence of coups, the armed forces of the regional states have been spared the contagious pressures so prevalent in West Africa. In this context, the subregional environment in the south has tended to discourage the Zambian armed forces from seriously considering a coup.

However, as the discussion has shown, the domestic contradictions of the 1980s severely tested the survivability of Kaunda and the UNIP. Even though his leadership and legitimacy as well as that of the party appeared to have been considerably strained toward the end of the decade, the fact that the armed forces remained loyal has vindicated the reasons suggested for Kaunda's continuing leadership. At the same time, the restlessness among the population, including the military, poignantly indicated the necessity for a new approach to Zambian politics and development. As it has been demonstrated by several African states, military loyalty to civil authority becomes suspect when political and economic crises are aggravated. What does the future hold for civilian control of the military in Zambia? Since the survival of civilian rule has so far been ensured in a large measure by Kaunda's personality, what are the prospects for civilian rule in Zambia after his natural demise? The remainder of this chapter will address these questions concerning the likelihood of continuing civilian rule in Zambia.

The Future of Civilian Rule

The continuing survival of civilian rule in Zambia will depend on three important factors, namely, (1) the flexibility and adaptability of Kenneth Kaunda to the changing needs and desires of his people, (2) the continuing acceptance by the armed forces of their stake in maintaining civilian control, and (3) improvement in the economy. Let us dilate on each of these points.

A major desire of the Zambian people, as expressed throughout 1990, is a change in the political status quo, to shift to a multi-party competitive political system where fundamental human rights and liberties would be guaranteed and respected.[43] This desire stems form two major sources: Zambia's economic failure and the UNIP's inability to deal with it, and the increasing recognition of human rights as an important element for development.

The desire for political change is rooted in the abysmal economic inefficiency of the single-party system and the system's inability to be receptive to the marketplace of ideas. The audacity of opponents to publicly and unequivocally demand change was, however, inspired by the Soviet policies of *glasnost* and *perestroika* whose global political implications influenced most other African states during 1990 to initiate reforms.[44] The near-euphoria over the probability of change in Africa was sounded by Colin Legum who declared the continent to be on the threshold of a "second independence," the first from colonialism, and now, in the postcolonial era, from military and single-party dictatorships.[45] Even though the single-party system was introduced and justified in Africa with convincing arguments in the 1960s and early 1970s,[46] by the end of the 1980s, it was evident that the system had lost its luster, utility, credibility, and efficacy for solving national problems. In fact, a veteran observer of African politics, Claude Welch, has already proclaimed the "*requiem in pace*" for the single-party paradigm.[47] The desire and agitation for change in Zambia and, for that matter, other single-party states in Africa, is therefore, an issue which is very high on the national political agenda.

As a political realist and pragmatist, Kenneth Kaunda has understood and appreciated the mood of his people and that of the world at large. He is aging and perhaps self-serving, but he has seemed responsive to new and popular currents. After resisting and berating those calling for a multiparty system, he relented and signed, on 17 December 1990, a constitutional amendment that permits political pluralism in Zambia.

It is certainly too early to assess and predict the outcome of the new politics in Zambia, but I would be remiss if I failed to point out that multipartyism, by itself, would not solve the multi-faceted problems of the country, no more than it would solve the problems of any other country. The potency of the multiparty system lies in its ability to release the creative energies of people and allowing them to utilize such energies in the pursuit of individual and societal goals. Inherently democratic, the multiparty system could also restrain the overextension of the state and its repressive character. Contrary to liberal notions, democracy ought to be popular and ensure equal access to and equitable distribution of society's goods. And, finally, the system provides for choice in leadership and popular input in the making of laws that govern people's lives. If Kaunda has the ability and the willingness to nurture the multiparty system in these directions, then he will just not be ensuring his own rule and, of course, the inevitability of losing power, albeit peacefully, but also history would credit him for bequeathing an enduring political system to his country.

As Zambia moves toward a new political order, it would be crucial to bring along the armed forces to accept that they have a stake in maintaining the new political arrangement under civilian control. Such an acceptance may be achieved through a systematic training (indoctrination?) of the military personnel in patriotism that would enhance the respect for constitutional rule. Beyond that, the tried strategy to coopt officers and include the military class in the horizontal distribution of national values ought to continue. As Zambia's own experience shows, the safest strategy to blunt the military appetite for political intervention is not to alienate it, but to make it responsible for and have a stake in the survival of the political system. This is, in fact, the case in the so-called developed political systems that Luttwak termed "sophisticated" states, where military subservience to civil authority is the norm.

The continuing survival of civilian control of the military in Zambia will depend on the government's ability to improve the general economic condition and the well-being of the people. While this factor is important, it is not as critical as those of elite flexibility and military acceptance of civilian rule whose success may, in turn, facilitate an environment conducive to sustainable economic development. Nonetheless, since economic decline and a leader's inability to overcome it has been one of the perennial reasons for military *coups d'état* in Africa, it behooves governments to assiduously pursue the improvement of a nation's economy.

In conclusion, the prospects for a quick turnabout in the Zambian economy seems stark owing to the country's historic development. However, understanding and appreciating this fact, the armed forces could be more sympathetic and willing to support the civilian government in finding solutions than overthrowing it. After those incessant interventions, it must be clear by now to the African "man on horseback" that he has not proven himself to be qualitatively any different from and superior to the civilian in terms of leadership and ethics in politics. Perhaps, this could be the most single deterring factor for a military coup in Zambia today and, inversely, the guarantee for a continued civilian control of the military in that country and, happily, elsewhere in Africa.

Postscript

In line with the December 1990 decision to allow multiparty politics in Zambia, the first competitive national elections in nearly a quarter-century were held on 31 October, 1991. A trade unionist, Frederick Chibula, was overwhelmingly elected to replace Kenneth Kaunda as president. Kaunda's crushing defeat--Chibula captured 80 per cent of the votes -- dramatized the Zambian people's extreme disenchantment with his 27-year rule. Nevertheless, by conceding power in a relatively peaceful election, Kaunda reified the growing expectation for democratic practice in Africa and assured the continuity of a legitimate civilian rule in Zambia.

Chibula's ability to sustain the mantle of civilian control of the military in Zambia would depend largely on the continued perception that the armed forces have a vested interest in the political status quo. Also germane to the success of civilian rule would be the new president's style of governance. Though a different personality, Chibula would have to unify the nation and display the political flexibility, adaptability, and realism that were the major traits of his predecessor.

Chibula has received a popular mandate to rule Zambia and address the mammoth socioeconomic problems he has inherited. His capacity to handle the trauma of development and neutralize political lability will be decisive in maintaining civilian control and denying the military any pretext for adventurism. To achieve this, the improvement in the material conditions of the people should be high on the agenda of the new ruling *élite* in Zambia.

Notes

I am grateful to Albert Owusu-Sarpong and Patrick Idoye for their helpful comments on an earlier draft of this paper.

1. Claude E. Welch, Jr., ed., *Civilian Control of the Military: Theories and Cases from Developing Countries* (Albany, NY: Suny Press, 1976), xi.
2. Pat McGowan and Thomas Johnston, "African Military Coups d'Etat and Underdevelopment: a quantitative historical analysis," *Journal of Modern African Studies* 22: 4 (December 1984), pp. 633-66.
3. Baffour Agyeman-Duah, "Military Coups, Regime Change, and Interstate Conflicts in West Africa," *Armed Forces & Society* 16: 4 (Summer 1990), pp. 547-70.
4. In a multiparty election on 18 February, 1991, Antonio Monteiro ended 15 years of one-party rule in Cape Verde by defeating Pereira who had ruled Cape Verde since the country's independence in 1975. See: *Greensboro News & Record*, 19 February, 1991, p. A4; "Pereira Ousted," *West Africa* (London) 25 February-3 March, 1991, p. 277.
5. Samuel E. Finer, *The Man on Horseback: The Role of the Military in Politics* (London: Pall Mall Press, 1962), pp. 5, 12.
6. Edward Luttwak, *Coup d'Etat: A Practical Handbook* (New York: Alfred Knopf, 1968), p. 6.
7. *Ibid.*
8. *Ibid.*, particularly Chapter 2.
9. Jon Kraus, "Ghana 1966." In William G. Andrews and Uri Ra'anan, eds., *The Politics of the Coup d'Etat: Five Case Studies* (New York: Van Nostrand Reinhold Co., 1969), pp. 89-131.
10. *Ibid.*, pp. 89-90.
11. *Ibid.*, p. 100.
12. Finer, *The Man on Horseback*, pp. 23-71.
13. Relevant and useful publications include Henry Bienen, "Civil-Military Relations in the Third World," *International Political Science Review* 2: 3 (1981), pp. 363-70; T. Johnson, R. Slater, and P. McGowan, "Explaining African Military Coups d'Etat, 1960-82," *American Political Science Review* 78: 2 (September 1984), pp. 622-40; Samuel Decalo, *Coups and Army Rule in Africa: Studies in Military Style* (New Haven: Yale University Press, 1976).
14. Claude Welch, Jr., "The Roots and Implications of Military Interventions." In Claude Welch, ed., *Soldiers and State in Africa* (Evanston, IL: Northwestern University Press, 1970), p. 17.

158

15. David Goldsworthy, "Armies and Politics in Civilian Regimes." In Simon Baynham, ed., *Military Power and Politics in Black Africa* (New York: St. Martin's Press, 1986), pp. 97-129.

16. Robert A. Jackson and Carl G. Rosbert, *Personal Rule in Black Africa: Prince, Autocrat, Prophet, Tyrant* (Berkeley and Los Angeles: California University Press, 1982).

17. Goldsworthy, "Armies and Politics...," pp. 105 and 106.

18. Machiavelli is more blatant on this point. He considered "a complex endowment comprising skill, courage, decisiveness, adaptability, and ruthlessness. It is above all, the ability and resolution to pursue whatever course of action is expedient to achieve precise political objectives." See: Sydney Anglo, "Nicco Machiavelli: The Anatomy of Political and Military Decadence," in Brian Redhead, ed., *Political Thought from Plato to NATO* (Chicago: The Dorsey Press, 1988), p. 79.

19. See "The Armies of Africa," *Africa Report* 9: 1 (January 1964), p. 16. Northern Rhodesia became Zambia at independence.

20. Figures on the armed forces were compiled and analyzed from Colin Legum, ed., *Africa Contemporary Record* 4: B263; 7: B330; 14: B877-878; 17: B856. (New York: Africana Publications).

21. See: *Facts on File*, XXV, 1310, 2-8 December, 1965: 444A2.

22. *Ibid.*, 31 January, 1976: 77E3.

23. See: *The Washington Post* 26 March, 1969.

24. *Facts on File*, 15 February, 1980: 119E1.

25. Legum, *African Contemporary Record* 4: B263; 17: B856.

26. Robin Lockham, "A Comparative Typology of Civil-Military Relations," quoted in Claude Welch, Jr., "Emerging Patterns of Civil-Military Relations in Africa," in Bruce Arlinghaus, ed., *Africa Security Issues* (Boulder, CO: Westview, 1984), pp. 126-39.

27. Welch, "Emerging Patterns.."

28. Agyeman-Duah, "Military Coups, Regime Change."

29. Address by Nkrumah at the budget session of Parliament in January 1966, reported in *West Africa* (London), 5 February, 1966. Ironically, he was overthrown a few weeks later on 24 February.

30. Rene Lemarchand, "African Armies in Colonial and Contemporary Perspective: the search for connections," *Journal of Political & Military Sociology* 4: 2 Fall 1976), p. 263.

31. See: Tony Hodges, "Zambia's Autonomous Adjustment," *Africa Rocovery* (December 1988).

32. Legum, *Africa Contemporary Record* (1988): B870.

33. See: *Africa Research Bulletin* 23, 12 (January 15, 1987): 8347C-8348ABC.

34. *Ibid.*, 24, 4 (May 15, 1987): 8482ABC.

35. See: *Keesings Record of World Events* XXXIV (November 1988); p. 36264.

36. William Tordoff, "Political Parties in Zambia," In Vicky Randall, ed., *Political Parties in the Third World* (London: Sage, 1988), p. 17.

37. See: *Facts on File* 3-9 June, 1971: 433E2; *Keesings Record* XXXIV (June 1988); p. 35944.

38. Tordoff, "Political Parties in Zambia," p. 28.

39. See: Robert Pinkney, "Ghana: An Alternating Military/Party System," in Randall, ed., *Political Parties in the Third World*, pp. 33-57.

40. *Ibid.*, p. 23.

41. Tordoff, "Political Parties in Zambia," p. 16.

42. Agyeman-Duah, "Military Coups, Regime Change."

43. Zambian Humanism places humankind at the center of all political and economic activities and theoretically guarantees the rights and liberties of the individual even in the single-party system. In practice, however, these lofty ideals could not be realized as evidenced by popular restlessness among the population. For a detailed treatment of "humanism" see: Kenneth Kaunda, *Humanism in Zambia* (Lusaka: Zambia Information Service, 1967). Also, Emeka Patrick Idoye, *Popular Theatre and Politics in Zambia: A Case Study of the University of Zambia Theatre*, doctoral diss., University of Florida, 1981, Chapter 2.

44. Baffour Agyeman-Duah, "Gorbachevism, The New World Political Order, and the African Condition," *TransAfrica Forum* (Washington, D.C.), forthcoming.

45. Colin Legum, "The Coming of Africa's Second Independence," *The Washington Quearterly* XX:XX (Winter 1990), pp. 120-40.

46. See, for instance, James S. Coleman and Carl G. Rosberg, *Political Parties and National Integration in Tropical Africa* (Berkeley and Los Angeles: University of California, 1964) and Aristide Zolberg, *Creating Political Order: The Party States of West Africa* (Chicago: Rand McNally, 1967).

47. Claude Welch, Jr., "The Single Party Paradigm: De Mortuis?" a paper presented at the 1990 meeting of the African Studies Association, Baltimore, MD.

9

Constitutional Government in Jamaica: The Historical and Political Underpinnings

Carl Stone

Introduction

Most developing countries have at some time attempted to develop civilian rule based on a written constitution that defines the rules of political succession, the limits to governmental authority and the rights of citizens. In most such developing countries, however, civilian rule based on constitutional government in which the power of the state is regulated by the ground rules of a written constitution has not survived or has survived for only short periods. These developing country initiatives toward constitutionally based civilian rule have usually broken down and have been replaced by one party states, military rule, and other varieties of unconstitutional authoritarian regimes based on political monopolies preserved by coercion and lacking in genuine legitimacy.

In the period between 1960 and 1990, only 24 states among the 128 non-communist independent developing countries have shown consistency and continuity in developing and preserving civilian rule based on constitutional government. Civilian rule has been preserved in other developing countries where political monopolies suppress opposition and competitive politics (Kenya, Malawi, Zambia and Ivory Coast). But such regimes by their very nature manipulate, override and render impotent constitutional regulation of the power and authority of the state. These political monopolies undermine the rule of law, erode the civic and political rights of citizens and constrain the level of accountability civil society can exercise over those who govern. Indeed, coercion and force rather than legitimacy invariably become, in the long run, the main basis for citizens compliance in such states.

The English speaking Caribbean[1] is the only region in the Third World in which civilian rule based on constitutional government has been developed and preserved in a majority of independent states.[2] In this region nine of the twelve independent states (or 75%) have preserved constitutional government combined with civilian rule on an uninterrupted basis between 1960 and 1990. In the other three independent states (Guyana, Suriname and Grenada) constitutional government combined with civilian rule has broken down.

As an English speaking Caribbean country, therefore, Jamaica represents a relatively atypical case in the development and survival of civilian rule and constitutional government. To analyze the Jamaican case, it is necessary to focus on both the factors that make the English speaking Caribbean states unique among developing countries as regards civilian and constitutional rule as well as to focus on factors specific to Jamaica which have aided the preservation so far of civilian led constitutional government.

Theories on Constitutional Collapse

The large scale demise and widespread collapse of constitutionally based civilian regimes in developing countries in the post war years have led to a wide variety of theories and explanations of this phenomenon in Asia, Africa and Latin America.[3] Some of these theories are not relevant but others offer some insights into both the Caribbean and Jamaican patterns of stable civilian rule. The main explanations include the following:

Theories of uneven modernization which suggest that rapid urbanization and social change accompanied by weak economies and failure to industrialize create a huge expectations gap between the social demands of citizens and the capacity of these polities to fulfill these demands. The result is violence from below, political instability and constitutional collapse;

Class theories based on the functional role of authoritarian regimes to protect and support capital. Civilian led constitutional regimes collapse under stress and become victims of military coups when they throw up radical or populist leaders who threaten bourgeois interests;

Historical and political-cultural explanations of the entrenched values or historical experiences which reinforce militarism and define a large traditional role for the military in political life. The effect is that civilian led regimes become very vulnerable to attacks by the military;

Theories of weak and fragmented societies too divided by tribalisms, cultural pluralism and contending ethnic groups to sustain stable constitutional government, leading to struggles for power using military intervention as the ultimate means of political control;

Ideas suggesting the importance of European colonial contacts which socialized colonized societies into the political culture of the European Metropolis, with the result that divergent colonial experiences lead to differential propensities by various ex-colonies to sustain constitutional government based on civilian rule;

Theories of the benign influences of rapid social modernization (urbanization, literacy, larger middle class, and more exposure to mass media) which it is suggested increase demands for more democratic politics and strengthen the support base for constitutionally based civilian rule;

Theories about the political socialization and ideology of the military which predispose them to intervene in politics based on highly politicized self-concepts that project the military as guardians of national interest or as the only effective modernizing force in the society; and

Cycles of change in which forms of managing state power come into question or are abandoned due to their perceived failure to provide fulfillment of citizens' expectations and willingness to try alternative. Constitutional rule and authoritarian rule will, therefore, alternate over time as each in turn is deemed as a failure and as preferences shift from one to the other as judgements of their efficacy change over time.

To what extent have these causal factors operated in the English speaking Caribbean? Commitment to stable civilian led constitutional rule has been due to a combination of factors,. Like India and Sri Lanka which have preserved this form of state system, the states in this region experienced very long periods of exposure to British constitutionalist political values. Both the élite and the mass in these countries internalized a deep respect for competitive parties, constitutional rule, civilian led regimes, the rule of law, and political rights. As a result civilian led and constitutionally grounded parliamentary government is deeply rooted in this region's political culture.

Caribbean society, with the sole exception of Jamaica, has been relatively free from the deep class antagonisms which have polarized political life in Latin

America and generated a high propensity in that region for constitutional governments to collapse under the stress of class polarization. Racial and class inequalities are very pronounced in the Caribbean region, with racial minorities (mainly local and foreign whites) enjoying a concentration of ownership over productive assets and a pre-eminence of social influence. In spite of this, there is a core of consensual values which integrates these societies and provides a foundation of acceptance by the subordinate class and racial groups of the social hierarchies and power structures in Caribbean countries. Contrary to theorists who suggest otherwise, in this respect, Caribbean society is as socially integrated as North America or Western European societies.

Most Caribbean societies are racially and culturally homogeneous with the majority of the populations consisting of Blacks of African origin who share a common core of social values with the ethnic minorities. A minority of independent Caribbean countries are, however, victims of ethnic fragmentation and cultural divisions. These countries include Trinidad and Tobago which is polarized between large Black (43%) and large East Indian (40%) ethnic segments which distrust each other, fear domination by the rival ethnic formation and vote along lines of ethnic loyalties. Guyana which is similarly polarized between Blacks and Indians who distrust each other resulting in the seizure and monopoly of power by Blacks utilizing their monopoly control of the state to hijack the constitution and install a corrupt one-party state.

Suriname is also fragmented into a multiplicity of ethnic groups (Indian 35%, Creoles 31%, and Japanese, Chinese, Blacks and Amerindians 25%). In both Trinidad and Suriname militarism has threatened civilian rule. In these two countries, deep distrust and weak legitimacy of the political systems led to a military takeover of civilian rule in the case of Suriname and an unsuccessful attempt at a military take over in Trinidad and Tobago in 1970. The high level of racial, cultural and ethnic homogeneity in most of the region (in contrast to Africa and Asia) has meant that ethnic and cultural fragmentation has not been a significant factor undermining stable constitutional government in the region as a whole.

The military in this region, like other segments of Caribbean society, has itself been socialized with a deep respect for constitutional government and civilian rule, and this has inhibited military intervention in political life. The army officers in the region are recruited from the large Caribbean middle class representing 25 percent to 30 percent of Caribbean societies. The officers in the Caribbean military tend to reflect the political attitudes of this class which are very supportive of constitutional government and civilian rule which place power in the hands of leadership elements dominated by that class.

The middle income societies of the Caribbean are similar in economic and social profile to countries whose political instability has been explained in terms of uneven modernization.[4] The region has experienced rapid postwar increases in mass literacy, urbanization, and communications, accompanied by high expectations for social and economic advancement. This rapid modernization has been accompanied by high unemployment, increased inequality and the growth of radical and populist social ideologies which have questioned the status quo. Black Power movements in the 1960s, and Marxist and socialist currents of ideological thinking in the 1970s in the region both reflected the radicalization of mass politics due to social stresses and increased relative deprivation caused by uneven modernization. The effects of these social tensions have also been expressed in the form of increased violent crimes. These social tensions and stresses, however, have not had any significant impact so far on the stability and continuity of constitutionally grounded civilian rule.

Caribbean social science analysts have, however, been inclined to interpret these social tensions and stresses as signs of a weak society with a high propensity to disintegrate and fall apart.[5] Much of this analysis has been constantly predicting social upheavals, political collapse and disintegration, neither of which has materialized on any significant scales, except in a few countries where political mismanagement and factors other than social deprivation have been the root cause.

Civilian led constitutional government benefitted from the circumstances surrounding its emergence in the Caribbean region in the post war period. A combination of economic depression and extreme social hardships in the 1930's and new waves of political consciousness and aspirations for power by locals pressured the British colonial regime to install representative government and social reforms.[6] The emergent local political parties which gradually took over state power in a slow process of decolonization presided over a post war period in the region characterized by major improvements in social policy (expanded health and educational services) and rapid economic advances due to foreign investment, favorable world markets, economic modernization away from plantation economies and toward tourist-service-mining-manufacturing economies--all accompanied by a massive growth of public sector jobs and improved living standards.

Civilian led constitutional government operated by competing political parties in the Caribbean were, therefore, seen in the region as agents of positive economic and social change, bringing widespread benefits to the majority classes. This perception helped to entrench and reinforce the legitimacy of civilian led constitutional rule governed by political parties, with policy and ideological commitments to uplifting the condition of the poorer classes and to advancing the modernization of these economies.

Economic dislocations in the region after the oil crisis of the 1970s and the adverse world market conditions in the 1980s (high interest rates, low commodity prices, reduced demand for exports and trade protectionism) in a highly trade dependent region have served to tarnish the image of elected civilian rulers as being able and effective managers of the region's economies. As a result, there is an increasing opposition tendency throughout the region which is beginning to question the efficiency of the region's present political leaders and political systems and their collective capacities to solve the country's' economic and social problems. While the stock of legitimacy of Caribbean democratic governments has declined since the 1970s due to this factor, no alternative ideology or political management system is being promoted on a significant scale to replace the present system. Where pressures for change are being generated, they concentrate mainly on how to reform the unsatisfactory features of the Westminster/Whitehall system of parliamentary government.

Caribbean society has been undergoing some fundamental patterns of change in the post war period where we can identify the forces of social modernization as having created a climate that is more accommodating to civilian led democratic politics. The traditional plantation society with its rigid social hierarchy dominated by a small handful of white landowners has been modified over the past five decades. More open urban based societies have developed in the region with extensive opportunities for upward social mobility, larger middle classes, declining peasantries and expanding urban working class formations and lower concentrations of class power. The classes inheriting property have had to share power with the emergent middle class professionals and political leaders. The working class has been able to obtain political rights and political self-expression and that class is now more educated and more politically aware. All of these changes have facilitated greater support for political democracy.

As the largest of the English speaking Caribbean democratic states, Jamaica represents an interesting case study in the development and consolidation of political democracy in a small developing country and in a social environment that appears to be hostile to the survival of stable democratic politics. Jamaica since the 1960s has exhibited many of the features associated with constitutional breakdown in South America. These include class polarization, militant and radical lower class political tendencies confronting conservative middle class and *bourgeois* reactions, ideological antagonisms between right and left, penetration by antagonistic regional ideological interests (Cuba and the USA) and extreme levels of political violence and social instability. The fact is that civilian rule based on constitutional government has remained intact in Jamaica in contrast to Chile and Uruguay where similar factors dismembered long standing constitutional rule and ushered in periods of direct military rule in these two countries.

The two interesting questions to be answered. First of all why Jamaica's political institutions have survived intact so far and avoided efforts by the military to intervene in politics? Second, we need to analyze what are the prospects for continued political stability and institutionalized civilian rule based on parliamentary government. As the country enters into a new phase of its political development in which the legitimacy established in the early post war years is wearing thin and a new crisis of confidence in governing political institutions has developed in the late 1980s and early 1990s.

The Jamaican Case

Since the 1960s Jamaica has been considered by both journalists and academic social science analysts as a prime target for political instability.[7] In the 1960's new political trends in the country's inner city ghetto areas among unemployed youth seemed to be the beginnings of a drift toward violence and instability. These new trends included the following:

Escalating violent crimes against the wealthy and the middle class in the second half of the decade in which a relatively crime free society was transformed by the end of the decade into the region's crime capital;

Militant class and racial consciousness among segments of the *lumpen* youth in the inner city ghetto areas of the capital city and hostility among these strata toward the affluent ethnic minorities, all inspired by a radical Black Power movement representing an alliance between the black university intelligentsia and ghetto *lumpen* elements;

The growth of significant disaffection toward the political and party leaders among the urban unemployed youth who increasingly saw themselves as victims of class and racial oppression;

A succession of three urban riots in 1965, 1968 and 1971 which paralyzed the capital city and dramatized the alienation of sections of the dispossessed urban *lumpen* elements toward the political system;

The arming of ghetto youth loyal to the two competing political parties (the Jamaica Labour Party and the Peoples National party) in what emerged as the beginning of a tradition of political gangs and political violence in confrontations by the parties over control of neighborhoods and territory in inner city ghetto areas in the capital.

Increasingly, as these signs of social and political violence and instability developed over the 1960s to 1970s period, the political leaders who managed the state had to increase both the size of the army and police force as well as engage them separately and jointly in counter-insurgency activity that directly brought both army and police into the management of the political system, with the danger of these institutions could develop a taste for political power and political intervention.

In the 1970s, the stresses and pressures on the Jamaican political system intensified.[8] The People's National Party (PNP) led by popular trade unionist Michael Manley shifted to the left and absorbed the radical anti-system elements from both the intelligentsia and the inner city urban ghetto areas. The new radicalized PNP advocated antagonism toward both foreign and local *bourgeois* classes, embraced and formed links with local and regional communist groups and drifted toward an anti-U.S. foreign policy. It declared itself in support of an uncompromising radical Third World stance on world issues and as being in an alliance of socialist and Third World brotherhood with Communist Cuba.

The challenging Jamaica Labour Party (JLP), led by highly respected businessmen Edward Seaga, shifted to the right, allied itself with the frightened middle class and the affluent ethnic minorities, the United States, militant anti-socialist and pro-capitalist groupings and interests both in Jamaica and in the region, and engaged in an emotional and violent anti-leftist ideological crusade to counter the equally violent leftist crusade by the People's National Party.

The Jamaican private sector was convinced that property rights and the security of capital and investments were at great risk under the PNP socialist government. Many exported their capital and assets, some migrated and others ran down their businesses refusing to reinvest profits earned. The population became terrified of random violence by criminals and political gunmen employing high powered weapons that often possessed greater fire power than the police had. The whole rhythm of social life was dislocated by fear of violence and stories of brutal murders.

Intense political violence culminating in some 500 political killings in 1980, 889 reported murders and 200 killings by the police in that year reduced the society to a state of anarchy and lawlessness. The military and the police both came under political attack by the People's National Party leadership who accused the security forces of plotting to overthrow and undermine PNP socialism. The situation with the army was especially tense because most of the army's officers supported the middle class's antagonism toward the PNP's radical class and socialist position and ideology. Both the army and the police were intimidated by the close connection between Castro's Cuba and the PNP government of the 1970s. These fears were increased as large numbers of Cubans came into the country to assist the PNP government with construction of public buildings and various social projects, including the manning of hospitals and health services.

The security forces became covert allies of the opposition anti-socialist tendencies leading to a sharp break in confidence between the police and army, on the one hand, and the PNP government, on the other. A PNP Junior minister was shot and killed by the police during an election campaign incident. A PNP public meeting was allegedly shot up by the army and the police. An army officer in the National Reserve pointed a gun at the Prime Minister in a tense political incident in which another army officer punched the PNP General Secretary who was also a minister of government. These developments were used to portray the security forces as bent on the overthrow of the PNP government.

As this break with the security forces became more problematic, the governing PNP stepped up the arming of its party gangs in the interest of self-defense. The escalating tensions, distrust and violence seemed heading toward the type of political collapse that occurred in Chile and Uruguay in the 1970s when the army intervened to put an end to ideological polarization, instability, class warfare between leftists and rightists, and the impotence and paralysis of constitutional governments in these two South American democracies.

The entire situation was explosive and potentially destabilizing. The security forces and especially the politically conservative army officers who reflected intense middle class anti-socialist political orientations were provided with motivation to challenge the socialist government, led by Michael Manley. Rumors were circulating in *bourgeois* and middle class circles that the PNP intended to rig the forthcoming elections and to cease having any further free elections thereafter, as occurred in Grenada after the 1979 leftist coup. The probability of a military coup was high over this period. Indeed, during 1980 the PNP government claimed to have discovered an alleged coup plot between a minor party leader and army officers but no firm or reliable evidence was forthcoming to substantiate the claim and the army denied any involvement in the plot.

Rival Cuban and U.S. interests intervened in Jamaican politics supporting the socialist and anti-socialist parties and bringing in resources to assist their Jamaican client interests (both JLP and PNP). The Americans assisted the anti-socialist opposition with generous financial help and promises to give massive aid to the anti-socialist JLP if the party won the 1980 elections. The U.S. government also cut back economic aid to the socialist PNP government and promoted (with the help of the U.S. based international media) a powerful campaign against Manley and the PNP designed to discourage foreign investments in Jamaica and to promote capital flight. The Cubans trained PNP activists in terrorism and guerrilla warfare, supplied technicians to help run social services and brought in high powered weapons for the PNP political gangs. Cubans also got involved in the regionwide propaganda war between socialists and anti-socialists in Jamaica.

The buildup toward instability disintegrated in Jamaica after the opposition JLP supported by strong anti-socialist tendencies decisively won the national elections in October 1980 in the largest seat and popular vote victory in the history of past war elections in Jamaica.[9] In that election a multi-class alliance of voters made up of majorities from the *bourgeoisie*, the middle class, the working class, the unemployed youth, and the peasantry voted out the socialist PNP government for a variety of reasons, some ideological, some having to do with economic mismanagement, and some having to do with violence and instability. Both the army and the police voted with the rest of the population against the socialists.

After the election defeat, the PNP, shocked by the humiliating election loss, shifted its ideological position back to the center, thereby ending the ideological polarization which was the source of much of the tensions in the political system. The party thereafter renewed friendship both with the USA and with the *bourgeois* interests in the economy. Under public opinion pressures both parties organized a political truce in which the violent party gangs were disengaged. Divisive ideological issues have disappeared from the Jamaican political agenda. Confidence in the political system has increased due to a bi-partisan structure of managing the electoral process. Heavy policy pressures from the World Bank and the IMF have pushed the new PNP government elected in 1989 toward continuing most of the economic and social policies of the conservative JLP government of the 1980s.

These austerity World Bank and IMF stabilization and structural adjustment policies have created a new agenda of problems and tensions. By imposing harsh and heavy burdens on the poor and the working class in carrying out these rigid economic policy adjustments, both the JLP in the 1980s and the PNP in the

1990s are seen as having sold out the interests of the poorer classes and as governing on behalf of the rich and in the interests of capital against those of labor and the poor. These harsh adjustment measures include wage controls, devaluations, deregulation of price controls, removal of price subsidies, reductions in health and educational expenditure, tight fiscal management, high interest rates, increased taxation and overall reductions in social expenditure in the budget. A crisis of confidence has developed toward the parties and their leaders as political distrust and cynicism has grown from 12 percent in 1980 to 40 percent by 1990. The party leaders are seen by this large body of politically disaffected as failing to deliver real concrete economic and social benefits to the lower classes.

The majority of this 40 percent of the electorate have become very hostile toward political parties and party leaders and wish to see the power of politicians severely reduced and circumscribed, in contrast to the early post-war years when the consensus was to promote big government to provide more people benefits. Indeed, vocal opinion within this political tendency portrays the politicians as being self-seeking, corrupt and incompetent in public management. Should this tendency increase in both size and intensity its impact could severely weaken the stability of constitutional government and increase the motivation for business and military elites to join forces and seize power if political leaders become committed to policy directions which are seen as threatening either to *bourgeois* or middle class interests.

The anti-system tendencies of the 1960s have, therefore, returned but with a different content. Instead of leftist militancy supporting alternative radical directions for change, the content has been political cynicism, antipolitics, political apathy and disinterest.

What are the major features of crisis management which have permitted the Jamaican political system to overcome these destabilizing tendencies, restore political stability and avoid military intervention in political life? Existing theories of constitutional and regime breakdown are inadequate because they treat politics as being a mere dependent variable being shaped by underlying economic and social causes. These theories all fail to take into account the factor of political management of stress which gives political systems high, medium, or low levels of resilience from such pressures and tensions. Jamaica is clearly an example of a political system which has so far exhibited high levels of political stress management. This high level of management of political stress goes a far way toward explaining the continuity, survival, and persistence of constitutionally based government led by civilians and organized around a highly competitive party system. This critical ingredient of political capability in stress management is perhaps the most important factor which accounts for the continued stability of constitutionally based civilian rule in Jamaica.

A number of factors have contributed to this high level of political stress management in the Jamaican political system. First of all, there is the pragmatic character of the political culture which motivates voters, interest groups, political parties and party leaders to abandon strategies and ideologies which demonstrate no capacity to solve problems or provide fulfillment of aspirations of the people. Flirtation with socialism and big government in the 1970's produced a drastic 30 percent decline in living standards and unprecedented negative economic growth. Enthusiasm for socialism which formed the basis of the 56 percent popular vote "majority for the PNP in the 1976 election evaporated by 1980 and produced a 59% popular vote" victory by an anti-socialist coalition of forces in the 1980 national elections. The working class, the unemployed and the poor who saw socialist policies as offering them hope for upliftment between 1964 and 1976, changed their minds by 1980 based on the hardships experienced as a consequence of the failure of these policies.

Second, the evenly balanced two-party system in which power has been shared by both parties at two term intervals, has helped to stabilize the political system by providing a ballot box solution when the country becomes dissatisfied with a governing party. The frequency with which governments are removed from power via the ballot box discourages designs to seize power by force. As is shown in table 9:1, political parties in opposition have won 5 of the 11 national elections held since 1944 on the basis of universal adult elections over the period. This highly competitive party system which gives no long run advantage to the governing party is a major force stabilizing the Jamaican political system by providing orderly succession in the frequent transfers of state power from governing to opposition parties.

A third important factor is the high level of politicization of the party system which generates entrenched loyalties toward the competing parties, especially among the poorer classes. This high level of loyal support for the competing parties creates a unique situation in Jamaica in which support for the party leaders and political parties is stronger among the poorer classes than among the rich and the middle class and generates emotionally intense partisan loyalties for parties and party leaders among the most socially disadvantaged classes in the political system. These strong political loyalties among the poorer classes bind these classes to pro-system political orientations and restrain the potential to convert dissatisfactions into anti-system political behavior.

Clientism and patronage politics have been a major mechanism cementing these loyalty ties. But as the flow of party patronage declined in the 1980's and

1990's due to severe cut backs in government spending, strong loyalty toward the parties among voters has declined from a high of 87 percent in 1971 to a moderate 60 percent by the 1980's. Loyal party voting appears to have stabilized at this 60 percent level in the 1990's in spite of growing disillusionment with the failure of successive governments to deal with the problems of the high cost of living, declining working class purchasing power, high levels of unemployment and declining access to social services (health, housing and education).

TABLE 9:1
National Election Outcomes In Jamaica

Elections	Party Victorious	Whether governing or in opposition
1944	JLP	neither as party formed for the first time
1949	JLP	governing party
1955	PNP	opposition party
1959	PNP	governing party
1962	JLP	opposition party
1967	JLP	governing party
1972	PNP	opposition party
1976	PNP	governing party
1980	JLP	opposition party
1983	JLP	governing party
1989	PNP	opposition party

The high level of party politicization in the Jamaican political culture spills over into the political behavior of the security forces. The police and the army express voting choices[10] similar to the rest of the population. For example, in

1976, the police and the army voted for the PNP as did the majority of the electorate. Similarly, in 1980, both the army and the police vote shifted toward the opposition JLP, reflecting the national trend in voting choices. The fact that the political preferences of the military and the police echo the political preferences of the majority of the electorate reduces the temptation for the security forces to intervene in political life or to destabilize constitutional government. The army and police also reflect the high level of support for the party system within the political culture of the majority classes which further weakens any potential for the security forces to develop strategies to challenge or undermine civilian rule and constitutional government.

In spite of high levels of economic discontent among the poorer classes and the lower middle class, the Jamaican electorate has shown only a 2 percent level of support for the country's only Communist anti-system political party, the Workers Party of Jamaica (WPJ) led by university intellectual, Dr. Trevor Munroe. Reflecting the drift in its hardline Leninist *bourgeois* interests and has watered down its radical Marxist class position. The weak appeal of anti-system Marxist tendencies helps to reinforce the stability of Jamaica's two party system. Cynicism toward politics and party leaders among the 40 percent of the electorate which has become alienated toward the existing parties also makes it difficult for new and alternative parties and party movement to attract enough support to challenge the existing dominant parties. Ideological conservatism in a political culture heavily influenced by its small peasant, small holding social origins and Christian fundamentalist beliefs discourages support for radical anti-system ideologies.

Prospects for the Future

Jamaica and indeed the entire English speaking Caribbean fall within the international sphere of influence of the United States. Recent U.S. foreign policy has been firmly supportive of democracy and has sought to encourage the regionwide democratic movement and to undermine authoritarianism and militarism. This regionwide democratic movement which has blossomed since the 1980's has fostered a retreat of militarism and a spectacular growth of civilian led democratic regimes in Central and South America and the Caribbean. This international influence will serve to strengthen the continuity of constitutional government in the Caribbean and in Jamaica.

The most critical factor, however, guaranteeing and favoring future continuity of constitutional government in Jamaica is the country's high level of stress management and political capability in the handling of political and social tensions. A combination of factors reinforcing each other provide a foundation on which political stress management is likely to be preserved in Jamaica. These factors include political pragmatism, ideological conservatism, strong clientelistic and party-patronage systems, high levels of party loyalty among the socially disadvantaged classes, the absorption of the security forces into the mainstream loyalist political culture and the very competitive two party system which facilitates frequent and orderly transfers of power from governing to opposition parties. Jamaica is, therefore, likely to continue to be an atypical country among developing nations with an assured future of stable constitutional government under civilian rule.

Notes

1. For a detailed overview of political trends in the Caribbean, see Carl Stone, *Power in the Caribbean Basin--A Comparative Study of Political Economy*, (Philadelphia: Institute for the Study of Human Issues, 1986).

2. The global survival of liberal democracy in developing countries is extensively researched in Carl Stone, *Understanding Third World Politics and Economics* (Browns Town, Jamaica: Earle Publishers, 1980).

3. These theories are extensively discussed in Eric Nordlinger, *Soldiers in Politics: Military Coups and Governments* (New Jersey: Prentice Hall, 1977); in Samuel Huntington, *Political Order in Changing Societies*, (New Haven: Yale University Press, 1968); in Amos Perlmutter, *the Military and Politics in Modern Times* (New Haven: Yale University Press, 1978); in Abraham Lowenthal and Samuel Fitch *Armies and Politics in Latin America* (New York: Holmes & Meier, 1986); in Kenneth Ingham, *Politics in Modern Africa*, (London: Routledge, 1990); in Clive Thomas, *The Rise of the Authoritarian State in Peripheral Societies* (New York: Monthly Review, 1984); and in David collier, *The New Authoritarianism in Latin America* (New Jersey: University of Princeton Press, 1979).

4. Huntington, *Political Order in Changing Societies*, pp. 32-59.

5. See Gordon Lewis, *The Growth of the Modern West Indies*, (New York: Monthly Review, 1968).

6. See Gordon Lewis, *The Growth of the Modern West Indies*, (New York: Monthly Review, 1968).

7. See Carl Stone, *Class, Race and Political Behavior in Urban Jamaica* (Kingston: ISER University of the West Indies, 1973).

8. For detailed discussions of the 1970's in Jamaica, see Evelyn and John Stephens, *Democratic Socialism in Jamaica*, (London: MacMillan, 1986); Michael

Kaufman, *Jamaica Under Manley, Dilemmas of Socialism and Democracy* (London: Zed Books, 1985); and Carl Stone, *Class State and Democracy in Jamaica* (New York: Praeger, 1986).

9. For an analysis of the 1980 and 1989 elections, see Carl Stone, *Politics Versus Economics--The 1989 Elections in Jamaica* (Kingston: Heinemann, 1989).

10. These data are presented in Mark Figueroa, "An Assessment of Overvoting in Jamaican Elections," *Social and Economic Studies* (September 1985), pp. 71-106.

10

Institutionalizing Civilian Rule in Developing Countries: The Case of India

Sarbjit Johal

After forty-four years of independence, India's armed forces continue to operate under civilian direction. Many other developing countries, in contrast, have succumbed to military takeovers. The size of India means that a significant part of the developing world has never been under military rule.[1] This record is even more anomalous because many of the social conditions that have led to military intervention in other countries are also present in India--ethnic, linguistic, and regional differences, secessionist movements, and large-scale poverty. The Indian armed forces are an effective fighting force of 1.2 million personnel.[2] They are well-led and -equipped and could take power if they had the will to do so.

Two views emerge as possible explanations regarding the absence of a military takeover in India. One is that India is the country established under civilian rule and will continue so in the future. The norms of civilian supremacy are deeply rooted and accepted by military officers. Another is that the socio-economic conditions for military intervention are not yet present in India but may arise if present troublesome trends continue, such as secessionist movements, political instability, and the further decline in the legitimacy of civilian institutions. This study takes a middle view: the norms of civilian supremacy are powerful in India and the threshold for military intervention is high. But a military takeover is possible if the legitimacy of civilian institutions continues to decline.

Civilian-Military Relations in India

India's colonial experience had left legacies of British constitutionalism, which were to profoundly influence independent India's political and military leaders. Among the internalized British norms of constitutionalism were civilian supremacy over the armed forces, an independent judiciary, individual rights, and democratic elections.

India's civilian leaders quickly established supremacy over the military when the country became independent in 1947. This was not difficult for the armed forces were weak in numbers, leadership, and equipment. The partition of the British Indian Empire into the two independent states of India and Pakistan initially disorganized the new Indian military. Whole units of the British Indian Army were divided between the two countries, and several military bases and training establishments were lost to Pakistan. At partition, India's inheritance of military equipment and supplies was either inadequate or obsolete. The officer corps was small, lacked experience in strategic planning, and immediately after independence had to be led by British commanders. No military challenge was possible or likely because of the makeup and structure of the military leadership.

Not only was the military weak, it also faced a strong civilian leadership. Prime Minister Jawaharlal Nehru and Home Minister Vallabhai Patel mastered India's partition problems and looked beyond them to developing a democratic India under civilian rule. The Congress Party was popular. It had led the independence movement and had a national base of appeal. The military had played no role in the independence movement, unlike other independence movements such as Algeria's in the 1950s and early 1960s. The Congress further established its dominance by winning state and national elections in the 1950s. Underpinning this one-party dominance was a *Congress culture*, which was also shared by other political parties.[3] The culture emphasized economic and social development through central planning; self-reliance in defense, the economy, and technology; democratization by widening electoral participation to India's masses; and a nonaligned foreign policy, which sought to maximize India's influence in a bipolar international system.

Nehru ensured civilian supremacy by setting up a higher defense organization in which the cabinet formulated defense policy. The armed services fell under the Ministry of Defense, led by a civilian minister and dominated by civil servants. In 1955, the government abolished the military post of Army Commander-in-Chief. The post of heads of the three services was replaced by three separate chiefs of staff. Although the army was numerically the most powerful service, it now ranked equal in protocol with the other two services.

Immediately after independence, the military was preoccupied with reorganizing, reequipping, and developing defense bases, installations, and production factories. The military followed civilian direction fighting against Pakistan in the disputed princely state of Kashmir. It also helped reabsorb other princely states, such as Junagadh and Hyderabad, and quelled a communist rebellion in the Telengana region of the old Hyderabad state.

In the 1950s, the military met the goals set for it by civilians. It modernized its equipment, started its own defense industries, and contained the military power of Pakistan. Nehru concentrated on building up India's economic power and diplomatic leadership of the developing countries through nonalignment. Even when Pakistan joined a military alliance with the United States in 1954, Nehru gave the military only enough resources to match the increase in Pakistan's military power.

The army leadership disagreed with civilian leaders over China and promotions within the army. Krishna Menon, the Minister of Defense from 1957-62, became controversial for disregarding lines of authority in the armed forces and for promoting officers above their seniors. Moreover, he saw Pakistan and not the People's Republic of China as the major security threat to India. Relations between China and India deteriorated after 1957, when the Tibetans unsuccessfully revolted against Chinese occupation. The Indian government also discovered that China had encroached on territory claimed by India. The army leadership recognized that the country lacked the military power to carry out Nehru's "Forward Policy" of physically challenging Chinese encroachments. This policy, made by civilians, provoked China into launching a punitive attack on India in the Himalayas.

India's defeat by China in the border war of 1962 unnerved the civilian leadership. It quickly recovered and began a military build-up to meet potential threats from both Pakistan and China. The government rapidly expanded the army's officer corps. In 1964, the government announced a longer-range defense build-up in India's First Five Year Defense Plan (1964-69), which envisaged an expanded army of 825,000 men, made up of twenty-five divisions, including ten mountain divisions and two armored divisions.[4] India's political system thus showed resilience in recovering from a military defeat, a possible cause of military takeovers. The armed forces gained more resources and importance in national life, even though the army had been soundly beaten.

The political system showed further resilience after Nehru's death in 1964. The system successfully managed the transition from the leader of India's independence movement to his successor Lal Bahadur Shastri. Shastri, however, died in January 1966, and the Congress Party chose Nehru's daughter, Indira

Gandhi, to be the next Prime Minister. The political successions came at a time when India experienced social unrest, war against Pakistan in 1965, and a severe economic crisis in 1966-67. In the war against Pakistan, the Indian military recovered some of the prestige it had lost in the Sino-Indian War of 1962.

Under Indira Gandhi the armed forces received a priority claim on India's budgets. India's military build-up continued under the Second Five Year-Defense Plan (1969-74). The balance of military power turned decisively against Pakistan. In the East Pakistan Crisis of 1970-71, Mrs. Gandhi gave clear civilian direction to the armed forces. She accepted their professional advice on matter of readiness but herself decided the diplomatic and political initiatives of the war. India's quick defeat of Pakistan in 1971 raised the prestige of the armed forces to its highest point since independence. The armed services showed that they could cooperate in launching military operations throughout the subcontinent in theaters of operation separated by thousands of miles. Victory over Pakistan, however, raised the prestige of *both* India's civilian government and the military.

After 1971, Mrs. Gandhi built up India's armed forces and paramilitary forces. These gained an added role during emergency period, 1975-77. Mrs. Gandhi declared the emergency following widespread national discontent, which included a demand from the opposition that soldiers and the police disobey orders.[5] The opposition charged that Mrs. Gandhi and some of her hand-picked chief ministers were corrupt. To prevent the national opposition campaign from gathering momentum, Mrs. Gandhi jailed opposition leaders, suspended civil liberties, and banned extreme left and right-wing parties. Mrs. Gandhi relied upon the armed and paramilitary forces for the ultimate basis of her power. While their bargaining position had certainly increased, the armed forces remained aloof from what was essentially a conflict within India's political elite. In any case, the emergency was short-lived; it was replaced in 1977 by a democratic restoration. In the general election of 1977, a coalition of opposition parties and Congress defectors decisively defeated Mrs. Gandhi.

The military's policies under the emergency paid off; it managed to preserve its autonomy and professionalism and avoid the politicization of the armed forces. The military also adapted to the return of Mrs. Gandhi to power following the general election of 1980.

In the 1980s, the Indian military was preoccupied with containing unrest in India's northeastern and northwestern regions. The Indian army carried out "Operation Bluestar" in June 1984 to dislodge Sikh militants from the Golden Temple, the holiest shrine of the Sikhs. One result was that Sikh army units mutinied, the first mutinies in independent India's history. India's military and civilian leaders downplayed the importance of the mutinies, but the military remained uneasy about its corporate integrity. The military's civilian tasks remain unpopular, but despite the misgivings the military continues to be responsible for quelling insurgencies in the northern border regions.

The military's role in the border regions is crucial because of the dangers of foreign intervention by China and Pakistan. The Indian military feels more comfortable with handling foreign threats. The government of Rajiv Gandhi used the armed forces to intervene in Sri Lanka in 1987 and in the island republic of the Maldives in 1988. In the first intervention, India assisted the Sri Lankan government in fighting a secession by the Tamil minority; in the latter intervention, Indian forces restored the legitimate government of the Maldives after a coup.

Civilian control of the armed forces remains strong in India. Even though the armed forces have been given a greater role in domestic and external duties, civilian power is predominant. The absence of military intervention in India's political system can be accounted for by further examining socio-economic, political, military organizational factors, and international factors.

Socio-Economic Factors

India's large population, geographical size, and social diversity, all make military intervention difficult. The many centers of political and economic power mean that it is not enough to take control of New Delhi but of other cities and states as well. The populations of India's states and some cities surpass the populations of many independent countries. Indeed, a military coup in India would be equivalent to ten or fifteen coups in other developing countries. A military coup in one or two cities would risk the possibility of contercoups and resistance by other military units or Indian parties and labor unions.

The present military role in Indian politics is confined to aiding civilian authorities in maintaining law and order and fighting breakaway movements. The military has contained secessionist movements on India's periphery without difficulty. The likelihood of Kashmir, Punjab, Nagaland, or Mizoram seceding is remote, unless there is a failure of will among the civilian leadership. The civilian and military tasks of holding on to these areas have been made much easier because they are on the periphery. The heartland of India's political system (Haryana, Rajasthan, Uttar Pradesh, Bihar, Madhya Pradesh, and southern India) is secession-free.

Social discontent in the heartland based upon class will be more important to Indian political stability and to the possibility of military intervention. The social conditions for revolution are present in the rural areas but other revolutionary conditions are not: a revolutionary party, an articulated revolutionary program, support for revolution from India's intelligentsia, and a failure of will by India's present political leadership. India's political system has so far been able to contain such challenges, including the communist uprising in Telengana, the Naxalite movement, and a revolutionary Maoist uprising in Andhra Pradesh, Madhya Pradesh, Maharashtra, and Orissa.[6] Furthermore, India's other social divisions of ethnicity, religion, language, region, and caste dilute class divisions. A national revolutionary movement would have to overcome these divisions.

Since 1947, India's political system has had a successful record of economic performance, having developed agriculture, industry, science, and technology. India is agriculturally self-sufficient and has built up a self-reliant industrial base. Economic liberalization under Rajiv Gandhi in the mid-1980s spurred the economy and the growth of India's middle class. There are still many economic problems of equity, vulnerability to external oil price shocks, rigid bureaucratic control of the economy, an inefficient state sector, and a growing foreign debt. Even if there were an economic crisis, a military takeover would not be inevitable. It would depend upon the length and severity of the crisis, the legitimacy of civilian institutions, and on whether the military's corporate interests (budgets, arms purchases, autonomy) were also being damaged or threatened by the economic crisis at the same time.

Political Factors

The *Congress culture* has helped to legitimize civilian rule in India. First, it has given civilian leaders legitimacy based upon India's independence struggle against colonialism and India's contemporary needs for social and economic development. Secondly, the armed forces have been given a clear role in the *Congress culture* to protect Indian sovereignty and to ensure India's preeminence in South Asia and the Indian Ocean. There are no basic conflicts of objectives between Indian civilian and military leaders about maximizing Indian power and influence globally and regionally.

Despite the rise of a militant Hindu party (*the Bharatiya Janata Party*) and the greater use of violence in party conflict, India's party system is strong and the basis of political succession. The political parties represent India's diverse groups and provide channels of participation. They have worked within the political system by accepting the constitutional framework, maintaining national unity, and by taking part in competitive elections.

Other political institutions and devices act as barriers to a military takeover. They prevent the instability that would make a military takeover necessary. India's federal system quarantines local unrest form the national political system. The central government has several instruments to keep stability. "Presidential Rule" has been used to replace the rule of state governments with rule form New Delhi. Preventive detention (imprisoning potential lawbreakers and insurgents), paramilitary forces, and the emergency articles of the Constitution (Articles 352-60) have all been used to handle instability.

India's civilian leaders have developed the paramilitary forces to further insulate the military form India's political system. The forces are made up of thirteen separate paramilitary forces ranging from the Coast Guard to the Central Reserve Police Force and the National Security Guards. They carry out functions such as antismuggling, antiterrorism, internal law and order, border patrols, and the protection of railways and industrial establishments. The use of presidential rule, paramilitary forces, and the emergency articles of the Constitution have all been controversial. Presidential rule has been used by central governments in New Delhi to remove popularly elected state governments. Critics have charged that it is a political instrument of control by the party in power in New Delhi rather than an instrument of maintaining national stability and unity. Paramilitary forces are often badly trained and have been unable to effectively control civil conflict. During the 1980s paramilitary units themselves went on strike, and the central government sent in the regular army to crush these strikes. Mrs. Gandhi used the emergency articles of the Constitution to impose the state of emergency in 1975 on the grounds of domestic instability. Her opponents claimed that she clamped down to protect her political position after a court had found her guilty of election malpractices and had ordered her to step down from power. Nevertheless, these instruments have buttressed civilian supremacy. Without them, India's military would be far more involved in domestic duties of law and order.

The Role of the Military

Military intervention in Indian politics is also hampered by the military's internal organization and its subordinate position in the country's higher defense organization. At all levels of India's defense organization, the military finds itself in a subordinate position. At the apex, India's defense policies are made by civilians in the Political Affairs Committee of the cabinet, which includes the Prime Minister and the Ministers of Defense, External Affairs, Home, and Finance. Interposed between the Defense Minister and the chiefs of staff of the armed forces is the Committee for Defense Planning (CPD). Although the chiefs of staff are represented on the committee, it is dominated by civil servants; in particular, the cabinet secretary, the defence secretary, and other civil servants.

Even where the military has its own committees, service rivalries are present. The Chiefs of Staff Committee is made up of the heads of the three services. It has an advisory rather than operational responsibility and is chaired by the senior-most officer among the chiefs of staff. India has no position equivalent to the Chairman of the Joint Chiefs of Staff in the United States. In 1982 the Indian government rejected proposals to create a Chief of Defense Staff (CDS). The government argued that a CDS was not needed and that it would weaken civilian control of the armed forces.[7] Supporters of the CDS idea argued that a new structure would increase the effectiveness of the armed forces. Modern warfare required integrated defense planning and operations. They also argued that the armed forces had to be free from the control of bureaucrats who had little or no expertise in defense issues. The CDS proposal, they argue, would reduce bureaucratic rather than civilian supremacy.[8]

Military intervention would still be unlikely given the non-overlapping command structure of the armed forces. The army has five regional commands, the air force five, and the navy three. A military coup would require coordination between these thirteen separate commanders.[9] A coup could still occur outside the regional commands or with only some of the commands taking part. The success of a partial coup of a segment of the armed forces is doubtful and it would likely lead to countercoups.

The composition of India's officer corps is largely representative of India's population in ethnicity, religion, and class. The majority of the corps is Hindu and no one region is dominant. There is no minority dominance as there is for the Alawites in Syria. India's political leadership has reduced the representation of Sikhs in the officer corps, and this has been a factor in Sikh unrest in the 1980s. Nor is India's officer corps drawn form the country's elite. Its recruitment from India's lower middle classes has led to concerns over mediocrity in the officer corps.[10] India's civilians have further ensured supremacy by frequently changing the top military leadership. The heads of the services are not allowed to remain in their positions for very long.[11] While this reduces military effectiveness and continuity, it does prevent military leaders from entrenching themselves in power.

There is no evidence that the corporate interests of the armed forces been threatened by civilian authorities. True, the military is in a subc position and grumbles over bureaucratic control, but the military has input into defense policy, and civilians have favorably treated military budget and arms requests. The 1980s were a decade of generally increasing defense budgets in real terms.[12]

Nor are the corporate interests of the armed forces threatened in any way by India's paramilitary forces. These forces are too fragmented, serve too many specialized functions, and are too short of resources to be of any threat to the regular armed forces. They are under the authority of different ministries and are non-ideological. It is in the interests of India's civilian leaders to rationalize the paramilitary forces and to increase their budgets. In this way, the civilians can rely less upon the army in containing domestic unrest. Further involvement by the military in unpopular domestic tasks may politicize the armed forces, as they come to resent their inability to concentrate on external defense.

International Factors

The armed forces have been constantly deployed to protect Indian security from many threats. First, India has fought several wars with Pakistan. Relations with Pakistan are tense over Pakistan's nuclear program, Kashmir, and over Indian charges that Pakistan has been aiding Sikh secessionists. Skirmishes between Indian and Pakistan forces continue in Kashmir. Second, India maintains large forces on its borders with China. Attempts to negotiate the Himalayan border dispute with China have made little progress. India is also concerned by China's nuclear program and development of delivery systems. A third security threat is from the potential instability of smaller neighbors such as Bangladesh, Nepal, Maldives, and Sri Lanka. Indian governments are intent in preserving the stability of these states and in preventing foreign intervention in these states.[13] Finally, New Delhi is concerned by superpower activity in the Indian Ocean and in Southwest Asia. India's objective is to limit or end superpower military involvement in the Indian Ocean and Southwest Asia.

One implication of India's security environment is that the armed forces have been able to make a strong claim on budgets and on state-of-the-art weaponry. India's navy has been given resources to expand in the Indian Ocean. The army and air force have been given resources for fighting a two-front war against Pakistan and China. The major constraint has been other claims on India's budgets, such as industrial investment and social development. Another implication of the security environment is that India's civilian and military leaders have drawn lessons from Pakistan's history of military rule and alliance with the United States. The leaders seek to avoid a similar cycle of involvement in politics, which could destroy the morale and effectiveness of the armed forces. Indian leaders have also sought to avoid a military alliance with a foreign country, remembering that Pakistan's alliance with the United States led the Pakistani military to expand its power relative to civilian institutions and finally overthrow the civilian government in 1958.

Some observers argue that the constant security threats make it less likely that the Indian military will intervene in domestic politics. The magnitude of India's domestic and foreign challenges are such that the armed forces can only effectively concentrate on one or the other.[14] This argument assumes a necessary contradiction between the external and internal tasks of the armed forces. But it is also possible to envisage a number of scenarios where the armed forces would intervene domestically to protect their foreign mission. Political instability and budget cuts may lead to a takeover if the military felt that civilians lacked the resolve to defend India's security. The military could also develop nuclear weapons to meet external threats, reduce manpower, and then concentrate on India's domestic problems.

So far, military and civilian leaders share security perceptions, which are to meet the security threats from Pakistan and China, maintain military preeminence in South Asia, and increase India's influence in the Indian Ocean. It is unlikely that there will be a divergence between soldiers and civilians in the future over either the ends or means of foreign policy.

Conclusion

The corporate interests of the armed forces are not threatened. Military intervention will more than likely result from causes outside the military. The outlook here is not very optimistic. India's social system is divided by caste, religion, and economic cleavages. Its democratic politics have degenerated into violence and political instability. India has had a succession of weak governments since 1989. Terrorists assassinated Rajiv Gandhi during the violent election campaign of 1991. His party, the Congress, failed to win an overall majority of seats in the lower house of Parliament.

In June 1991, the Congress (I) obtained 226 seats out of a total of 545 in the *Lok Sabha*. The new Prime Minister P.V. Narasimha Rao formed a minority government. The Congress faces a major opposition party, the

Bharatiya Janata Party, which obtained 119 seats. Still the Congress remains in power with the help of the smaller opposition parties.

A number of scenarios are possible. First, one party could emerge dominant in the political system. A strong government in New Delhi could then have the power to carry out effective domestic programs. Domestic conflict would likely continue, though, regardless of how strong the government is at the center. Secondly, India could see the return of the political instability of 1967-71 or 1978-79. These periods usually ended with the return of one-party dominance by the Congress Party. Third, India's instability could tempt weak central leaders to rely more on the regular and paramilitary forces or even to declare a state of emergency using the precedent of 1975-77. The armed forces could be invited to share political power. Finally, the armed forces could unilaterally take power. For this to happen there would have to be large loss of civilian legitimacy and a threat to the corporate interests of the military. These two conditions are currently absent in India, but they could quickly arise if the political instability continues and if it threatens the military.

Notes

1. In mid-1988, India's population of 815.6 million was 20.6 percent of the population of developing countries. World Bank, *World Development Report* (New York: Oxford University Press, 1990), Table 1, pp. 178-79.

2. *Military Balance 1990-91*, (London: Brassey's for International Institute for Strategic Studies, 1990), p. 161.

3. A theoretical treatment of one-party dominance by the Congress is found in Rajni Kothari, *Politics in India* (Boston: Little, Brown, 1970).

4. Lorne J. Kavic, *India's Quest for Security: Defense Policies 1947-1965* (Berkeley and Los Angeles: University of California Press, 1967), pp. 192-93.

5. Stephen P. Cohen, "The Military," in Henry C. Hart, ed., *Indira Gandhi's India: A Political System Reappraised*, (Boulder, Colo.: Westview Press, 1976), p. 207.

6. "The Robin Hood of Orissa," *Economist* February 6, 1991.

7. Jerrold F. Elkin and W. Andrew Ritezel, "The Debate on Restructuring India's Higher Defense Organization," *Asian Survey* 24, 10 (October 1984): 1069-85.

8. See, for example, S.K. Sinha, *Higher Defense Organization in India* (New Delhi: U.S.I. of India, 1980).

188

9. Lt. Gen. Dr. M.L. Chibber, "India is Totally Safe Against a Military Coup," *Journal of the United Service Institution of India* 119, 498 (October-December 1989), p. 383.

10. Stephen P. Cohen, "The Military and Indian Democracy," in Atul P. Kohli, ed., *India's Democracy: An Analysis of Changing State-Society Relations* (Princeton: Princeton University Press, 1988), pp. 106-108.

11. From August 1947 to August 1991, the average service time for army chiefs (C-in-C and CAS) was 30.7 months, for chiefs of the naval staff 36.2 months, and for chiefs of the air staff 36.7 months. S.K. Baranwal ed. *Military Yearbook 1989-90* (New Delhi: Guide Publications, 1989), pp. 497-99; and *Asian Recorder* (New Delhi) various issues 1987-91.

12. *SIPRI Yearbook 1989* (Stockholm: Stockholm International Peace Research Institute, 1989), p. 185.

13. Devin T. Hagerty, "India's Regional Security Doctrine," *Asian Survey* 31, 4 (April 1991): 351-63.

14. Jerold F. Elkin and W. Andrew Ritezel, "Military Role Expansion in India," *Armed Forces and Society* 11, 4 (Summer 1985), pp. 500-501.

11

Civilian Rule and Abortive Coups in Sri Lanka

Angela S. Burger

Introduction

When a poor Third World country maintains democratic civilian rule for over forty years, questions are in order. Since the most frequent cause of military rule is the breakdown of order in society, the first question is whether Sri Lanka, the island off the coast of India, has enjoyed tranquility. The answer is *no*. Major ethnic riots have traumatized the island on five occasions since independence in 1947 and labor strife (especially in the capital of Colombo) has required the army to restore order on numerous occasions.

The tear-drop shaped island is barely 140 miles wide and 270 miles long, but has experienced two rather different civil wars. In the south, the extremist Sinhalese of the *Janatha Vimukti Peramuna* (JVP) attacked 156 police stations in 1971. While the revolt was put down in a few months, the army and police conducted sweeps of lower caste villages, killing about 15,000 and jailing thousands. The leader was freed by President Jayewardene, and the JVP operated as a political party until the 1983 riots when it was proscribed. The JVP estimated at 5000, turned to terrorism in 1984, assassinating high officials and threatening not only security personnel but also their families. The military, police and "death squads" killed or captured thousands of JVP suspects, in a civil war that lasted until 1990.

Meanwhile, in the north a bitter civil war has raged from 1972 to the present between the government and Tamil insurgents who want a separate state.

In 1987, concerned about reports of genocide, the Indian government abandoned its effort to negotiate a settlement and moved peace-keeping forces into the north. Indian officials saw the conflict in terms of their own historical-environmental solutions, namely, a federal system with linguistic states, provincial police forces, and elections to determine political leadership. Unfortunately, this was not the frame of reference of the most significant insurgent force, the Liberation Tigers of Tamil Eelam (LTTE or the "Tigers") who sought independence, or the government of Sri Lanka who wanted to retain a unitary state with national police force. Within a short period of time the LTTE forces were in armed conflict with the Indian troops, who suffered more losses than expected. By late 1989 a strange alliance was formed between a newly elected Sri Lankan government and the LTTE leadership, both of whom insisted the Indian troops leave. In relative calm, the Indian force withdrew in 1990. After a few months the civil war resumed, each blaming the other. The insurrection has not been limited to the north. Several attacks have occurred in Colombo, including a 1991 car bomb which killed the heavily guarded Defense Minister as well as others in the vicinity. Extended periods of violence, often related to governmental policies, then, demand that we ask a logical follow-up question.

Have the security forces attempted a coup? The answer to that is *yes*. "Operation Holdfast" was thwarted hours before the coup attempt was scheduled to begin in 1962; an alleged conspiracy of non-commissioned officers was discovered in 1966, and during the trial of the alleged conspirators, still another group of conspirators was detected. In all three instances the civilian authorities learned of the plans. Given the problems of basic law and order, how can we explain the support the government has enjoyed among the population as well as within the government and security forces, which has prevented a successful *coup d'état?*

To try to understand the Sri Lankan counter-case, we will first briefly describe the society, then systematically examine hypotheses drawn from the literature, moving from the very broad geopolitical, societal, and political factors down to more narrow hypotheses which focus on the security forces.[1]

Sri Lanka is a plural society: the Sinhalese are dominant (74%), speak Sinhala and are largely Theravada Buddhists. Population growth earlier in the century in the south and central districts resulted in very high population densities. Expansion northward, made possible by control of the malarial mosquito and extensive irrigation projects, relieved the pressure but put them in close proximity to minority areas. After independence, their use of majority rule and democratic government to promote the economic status of the Sinhalese has led to violence.[2] The Sinhalese have now acquired a disproportionate share of prestigious positions in the public and corporate sectors.[3]

The largest minority, the Tamils, speak Tamil and are largely Hindu, but are divided into two groups. The Sri Lankan Tamils (12%) have a geographic concentration on the north and east coast, with low population densities outside the major city of Jaffna. One-third of the Tamils live scattered through the island and many thousands now live abroad. The higher castes have larger representation among the Sri Lankan Tamils and at independence were overrepresented in the executive echelons in almost every category of socio-economic-political life on the island. The north is very dry, with sandy soil and no rivers which could be developed for irrigation. These conditions led the Tamils to stress education for career opportunities and upward mobility. The Indian Tamils (6%) are very low in caste (often untouchable), and were originally considered migrant labor for the plantations. Decades later, with year-round work, they could hardly be considered migrants; however, shortly after independence the new government claimed they were Indians, and not citizens of Sri Lanka. Lengthy negotiations on their status with India resulted in procedures to regularize their position. Once they gained citizenship and voting rights on the island in the 1980's, their concentration in enclaves on the tea and rubber plantations in the Sinhalese heartland made them a significant voting bloc. While they are a minority on the island, the fact that several million Tamils live in southern India means that the Sinhalese fear Tamil domination.

The Moors (7%) speak the language of the locale and are Muslim. They originally were traders form the Middle East and many are prominent businessmen. Most of the Burghers, of Dutch descent, have emigrated, and are probably only about 1% of the population. While ethnic riots pit Sinhalese against Tamils, other minorities usually suffer too. In the 1983 riots, poor Sinhalese in Colombo who believed rumors that the "Tigers" were coming, stopped people on the streets and demanded they recite a Buddhist hymn. Those who could not--which included Christians and Muslims--were usually killed.

The economy of Sri Lanka is still plantation based, with key exports being tea, rubber, and palm oil. A major textile industry for export now exists, and considerable foreign exchange is earned by people (especially women) who send remittances from their jobs in the Middle East. The island is linked by television, courtesy of the Japanese who provided production facilities and transmission lines, as well as the print media. Sri Lanka is noted for an extensive social welfare network for the poor.

What has been the effect of two civil wars? The twenty-year civil war has devastated the economy of the Tamil areas of the north. Roads were not maintained; public buildings as well as homes were severely damaged; energy supplies were unpredictable, and transport linkages were truncated. By contrast, the civil war in the south, led by educated young people often of lower castes, brought sporadic destruction of post offices and buses, and death to thousands, but did not bring the economy to a halt. New roads were built, export industries established, irrigation expanded with new settlements. Universities, however, were closed much of the time. The tourist industry declined, and with it those services and handicrafts catering to tourists. The difference between south and north in 1990 was conspicuous.

Geopolitical Factors

Is civilian rule more likely if the state in question does not have a geopolitical position of importance to Great Powers?[4] The Sri Lankan case supports such a hypothesis. The underlying rationale traces the lines of influence which a Great Power would develop with a government in general, and the security forces in particular, for any country where it had geopolitical interests. Assertions of policy positions that went counter to the preferences of the Great Power would lead that country to utilize its close ties in the military to foment a coup.

Prior to independence, undivided India was critical for British interests in the Middle East, and Sri Lanka was critical for protection of India. After independence and partition, West Pakistan became the geographic base for British and American interests in the Middle East. Particularly after the development of the Diego Garcia naval base, there was little reason for the US to develop close strategic or political ties to India or Sri Lanka. The USSR tried to develop close ties with India, but that goal necessitated a *hands off* policy toward Sri Lanka. The island is of geopolitical importance to India, which helps explain not only Delhi's intervention in the civil war, but also why India asserted its primacy regarding use of the great natural harbour of Trincomalee.[5]

Societal Factors

Sri Lanka provides support for the most common hypothesis associated with civilian and democratic rule, namely a high literacy rate. Overall literacy stands at 87% (males, over 90%; females, 82%), with the least literate being the plantation workers (60%). The literacy rate makes possible a widespread newspaper readership of 16 national daily newspapers and 12 weeklies (6 dailies and four weeklies each in Sinhala and Tamil; 4 each in English). The 862 kgs of newsprint consumption per capita is higher than the 548 for India, or the 364 for Pakistan.

However, high levels of literacy disguise the four political problems presented by language. First, English is called the *kaduwa* or sword which separates elite from mass. It has remained the language of the elite, even though less than 10% spoke it in 1953, and instruction in it declined to 1% by 1972. The 1984-1990 insurrection by the Sinhalese youth had its roots in the inability of those with a vernacular education to obtain desirable jobs.

Second, the insistence of the Sinhalese on adoption of Sinhala was in no little part due to the larger numbers of Tamils whose knowledge of English ensured both a university education and upper-middle class careers. In 1956, the militant Buddhist, S.W.R.D. Bandaranaike, led his party to victory by pledging to adopt "Sinhala only" in 48 hours. The deliberate decision not to include Tamil as one of the official languages led to bitter protests and riots. The government responded with force; it also nationalized the Christian schools, known for the excellence of their instruction in English. Many of the 1962 coup conspirators were Christians, and all were English-speaking. The conflict was not religious, as much as it was linguistic-ethnic.[6]

Third, while the society eventually moved toward use of both Sinhala and Tamil--including through the university--the policy meant Sinhalese and Tamils lost the ability to communicate with each other. A relatively small elite learned English.

Fourth, after the adoption of vernaculars for instruction, only a fraction of those eligible for the university could be admitted. In 1960, 5,277 were eligible for 1,812 places; by 1970, 30,445 were eligible for 3,471 places.[7] In an effort to open up choice career avenues for Sinhalese, policies were adopted in the 1970's to admit Sinhalese who had lower test scores than Tamils; for a few years between 30% and 100% of university admissions were based on district population. The Sinhalese pointed out that Tamils had an early advantage because Christian missionaries had set up many excellent schools in Tamil areas of the north, but very few in the south. Tamils then tended to hire and promote other Tamils, and were known to look down on the educated Sinhalese as being "lazy and foolish."[8] Tamil resentment of the closure of economic opportunity was considered the major factor in their demand for a separate state. Even those with university degrees and executive positions complained their advancement was stunted because of their ethnic identity. The high emigration of Tamils with marketable skills intensified the anger of those who remained. The high literacy rate has enabled a greater proportion of the population to participate in a debate, intimately tied to ethnic identity and upward mobility, on majority rule and minority rights, on individual versus collective rights.

The hypothesis which links civilian rule to a sizeable middle class needs modification in the Sri Lankan case. Subjectively, the middle class is considered to be the small English-speaking class. It is ironic that the strident populist appeals to Sinhalese Buddhists were made by English-speaking politicians who have maintained political control.[9]

Objectively, economic development has not operated to expand an entrepreneurial middle class. The nationalization policies under the SLFP transferred ownership to government. The privatization policies followed since 1977 have only marginally reduced the state role, while increasing that of foreign capital. The increases in defense spending, as well as damage to tourism and destruction of property in the 1980's has slowed the growth of an indigenous middle class. The President's Commission on Youth, which was given a mandate to recommend changes to prevent another Sinhalese insurrection, recommended teaching English as well as both vernaculars to the entire population.[10] Such a policy would open up the class structure and might mitigate ethnic frictions among the young, who are the chief beneficiaries. The policy may aggravate the frustrations of those between 20 and 50 for whom the change comes too late.

Politico-Governmental Factors

It is difficult for a military to take over a government which enjoys popular support and is exercising its powers effectively. On the one hand, substantial evidence supports both hypotheses in Sri Lanka. On the other hand, the government and political institutions have exacerbated tensions and generated conflict in their operation and policies. What are the critical factors of significance for the island's civilian and democratic rule?

Universal adult suffrage was instituted in 1931, barely three years after adoption in Britain. The effect in Sri Lanka was to require politicians to appeal to the masses to gain power. That is one reason why social welfare policies in education, health, and food subsidies were introduced in the 1930's. As a result, Sri Lanka enjoys one of the highest ratings on the Physical Quality of Life Index (85). The PQLI is based on life expectancy at year one (68.9 years), literacy (87%), and infant mortality (31/1000), and has continued to rise despite the two civil wars.[11] De Silva asserts that democratic survival in Sri Lanka is due to the social welfare system.[12] This is one of the few countries which has given urban squatters a land title to their domicile, introduced water and sewage amenities in those areas, and set up residents in decisional bodies to plan the layout and control ingress.

Not only have the poor benefitted by decisions of elected civilian elites, but they have turned incumbents out of power in almost every election. Furthermore, voters are accustomed to seeing electoral promises carried out--from "Sinhala only" and the nationalization of industry and estates under the Sri Lanka Freedom Party, to the privatization policies of the United National Party. What the evidence suggests is the existence of a political middle class: an issue-oriented citizen body, who read newspapers, expect performance, and know that the vote carries consequences.[13] It is a political middle class that believes in popular sovereignty.

The strength of the belief in popular sovereignty is shown in part by constitutional developments. At independence a Westminster-style government functioned as a Dominion, with a Governor-General appointed by the monarch, and a "first past the post" electoral system. In 1970, the three parties in the United Front campaigned for a mandate to revise the constitution. They won three-quarters of the seats, and did so, eliminating the Governor General. Henceforth the Prime Minister would appoint a weak President. Citizen input was sought on four occasions before adoption. When the United National Party came to power with 83% of the seats in 1977, it amended the constitution by the procedures specified in the 1972 document. The UNP adopted a Gaullist system with a strong, directly elected President, and changed the electoral system to Proportional Representation. The UNP called a referendum to permit the existing legislators to remain in power for one term under the new constitution. The referendum passed nation-wide but was defeated in the Tamil areas of the north. Citing the election verdict, those Members of Parliament (MPs), resigned their seats at the end of their original term.

The public criticized the extension of legislative tenure by referendum, because it meant a bare majority permitted the UNP to retain its 5/6 position. However, that criticism should not divert attention from the expected political consequences of the reform. The "first past the post" electoral system which existed before the 1979 constitution had two consequences. A relatively small shift of votes brought disproportionate shifts in parliamentary representation (see Table 11:1). Two, the party which won the Sinhalese vote would govern. The Sri Lankan Freedom Party (SLFP) was the first to win power by playing the ethnic card; the United National Party (UNP), whose leaders had tried to bridge the ethnic divide, discovered power could only be gained by following suit. Each felt compelled to "out-Sinhalese" the other to gain control of the government.

Since the Tamil parties could win only in Tamil areas, they had no reason to moderate their stand either. Despite solid support of the Tamil community, the Tamil parties were irrelevant to governance. When the Tamil party MPs resigned in 1982, the community lost its ability to express itself on public policy in government.

TABLE 11:1
Votes Polled And Seats Won, 1970 and 1977

Sinhalese Parties	1970		1977	
	% votes	*% seats*	*% votes*	*% seats*
S.L.F.P.*	36.9%	60%	29.7	4.8
U.N.P.	37.9	11.3	50.9	83.2
L.S.S.P.*	8.7	12.6	3.6	0
C.P.*	3.4	4.	1.9	0
Tamil Parties				
Federal Party	4.9%	8.6		
T.U.L.F.			6.75%	10.8%
Tamil Congress	2.3	2		
Ceylon Workers' Congress			1.0	.6
Independents; others	5.9	1.3	6.1	.6

*The United Front in 1970 consisted of three parties.

Proportional Representation (PR) was adopted to encourage appeals across ethnic lines, thus lessening tensions. PR also makes massive shifts in parliamentary strength less likely from one election to another. Two logical outcomes can be predicted: first, fewer changes in the basic constitutional framework; second, a diminished ability for a party in power to make sweeping policy changes because of narrower majorities.

The concern to bring ethnic groups together is also shown by an intriguing feature incorporated in a provision for popular election of the President: if no candidate receives a majority in the initial count, the "second preference votes" of those supporting minor parties will be counted. The vote of the minorities will be decisive in "second preference." In the 1988 presidential election, Premadasa won with only 50.4%.

Does popular sovereignty include support for civil rights and liberties? The record is mixed. Parties hold frequent, well-attended, assemblies, with very few disruptions. The party turnover in government has exerted a potent pressure on the police to maintain order for the rallies of all (Sinhalese) parties. The press is generally free, although one set of newspapers owned and operated by UNP family members was nationalized by the SLFP. A reasonably independent judiciary exists. Vivid reporting of trials are a regular feature in the daily press. Respect for the Bench is illustrated by the fact that the 1962 coup conspirators were freed after the Supreme Court reversed the lower court's guilty verdict, and the 1966 alleged conspirators freed after lower courts found them not guilty.

On the negative side, civil rights were removed from the Indian Tamils in the early 1950's and from former Prime Minister Srimavo Bandaranaike after the 1977 UNP victory. Reports of violence and corruption in elections increased after 1977. Even more serious, citizen liberties were curtailed by the rebel groups, the government's security forces, politicians' goon squads, and the highly politicized unions attached to the government party.[14] Political prisoners were killed in police custody and in prison. The Prevention of Terrorism Act gave such powers to the police that constitutional protections against torture were farcical. Police could hold suspects incommunicado and without charges, and could dispose of bodies secretly without an inquest or magisterial hearing. Rules were changed to permit police-extorted confessions to be accepted in the courts. Furthermore, the government set up special Boards of Inquiry which superceded the courts.

Special attention needs to be given to the orientation of the most significant Tamil insurgent force, the LTTE. After the Indian Peace-Keeping Forces established initial order, it became apparent that the Liberation Tigers of Tamil Eelam did not support civil rights and liberties, or popular sovereignty. The LTTE has been unwilling to tolerate competition of rival insurgent groups, much less open competition in electoral politics. They have made it clear they desire power on their own terms. This finding was a shock to the government of India, and to many supporters of the Tamil community, who had assumed the LTTE would welcome free elections in a setting which virtually guaranteed autonomy for the Tamil north and east.

A qualification exists in terms of the government of Sri Lanka, which has been unwilling to accept the wishes of the Tamil community for autonomy in a federal system, with community control over their own police forces. The Sinhalese authorities view majority rule in terms of an island-wide majority, and have been willing to restrict the civil rights and liberties of those who disagree. This may change over time, given the political imperatives of the new electoral system.

Over 50,000 private volunteer or non-governmental organizations exist in this population of 16 million, but tend to be confined to a single ethnic, or religious group. The press does not link ethnic groups either. While newspaper houses have papers in each of the three languages, the content differs. In addition, the President's Commission on Youth reports that young people were alienated from the political institutions of the society. They had no role in private volunteer or non-governmental organization, and felt the "traditional parties valued family over merit," and "lacked internal democracy."[15]

The parties, interest groups, and the press, then, have reinforced multiple congruent cleavages and alienated the young. Election campaigns marked by appeals to ethnic chauvinism are hardly conducive to civil peace. On the other hand, large parliamentary majorities enabled winners to carry out promises. Policies have been implemented. Ironically, the forces which aided the development of an issue-oriented political middle class also militated against a politics of compromise and civility. But executive power has not collapsed, despite the violence precipitated by governmental policies, and in the areas under government control, the administration functions very well.

Military Factors

If experiences of armed conflict predispose the military toward coups as a method of solving problems, then the relative absence of such experiences in Sri Lanka helps explain civilian rule. Historically, Major General Anton Muttukumaru, in his *Military History of Ceylon*, found that between 161 B.C. and 1505 A.D., only six kings developed significant military forces, and they relied on mercenaries from India for their armies. However, descriptions of the people as "unwarlike" is belied by centuries of defensive guerilla warfare, sufficient to prevent unification, whether under native, Portuguese, or Dutch rule. The first British attempt to conquer the inland kingdom of Kandy ended with the death of most of the British troops. In their second attempt in 1804 the British retreated with heavy losses. They finally won in 1815, but faced rebellions in 1818, 1820 (2), 1834, 1843, and 1848, against guerillas.[16] What this history shows is a defensive capability but very limited offensive tradition.

The British preferred to recruit troops for Sri Lanka from abroad, but in 1881 permitted the formation of the Ceylon Light Infantry Volunteers. This force had almost no fighting experience. During World War I and II, the defense units served on the island, and were never in combat--unless one counts experiencing two Japanese air raids.

Sri Lanka gained independence peacefully as a consequence of India's struggle, when its own nationalist movement was still in the parliamentary mode of protest. The forces have not fought a foreign war since independence; they have considered support of the civil as a routine duty, along with marching in parades, engaging in development activities, and promoting athletics (providing 90% of the National Olympic team).

The most extensive fighting experience has come in the last twenty years, with two types of ethnic conflict. In the north, hostilities began in 1972 against multiple Tamil organizations seeking independence. The Sri Lankan forces found it difficult to counter ambushes and land mines. It was also difficult to discipline their own troops, who, after all, had no tradition of fighting and dying in the army.[17] Concerns on their excesses in 1987 led to the entry of the Indian forces, technically at the invitation of the President, who needed to turn his attention to the much more serious threat to his power from the insurrection in the south. The 80,000 Indian troops were unable to defeat the approximately 2500 Tigers (LTTE), and withdrew in 1990. Hostilities resumed with each blaming the other. It must be noted that the key decision not to withdraw the Sri Lankan police force (almost wholly Sinhalese) from the north which would be replaced by an LTTE force, was made by the Sri Lankan Government, under a militant Buddhist President, who could look upon the largest security forces the country had ever had, which were better equipped and trained, and whose morale was high due to victory in the civil war in the South.

Prominent among hypotheses is one which asserts that civilian regimes are more likely if the military enjoys corporate autonomy and has a high degree of professionalism.[18] The Sri Lankan case, however, illustrates the validity of an older, depreciated, model of control. The "Wellington model" specifies that the officer corps be composed of men who owe loyalty to those in power by virtue of common class membership, ethnic origin, or political commitment. Commonality of identification is considered to be more important than professional expertise or training, in guarding against coups attempts--or ensuring detection.[19] Let us examine how closely this model fits Sri Lanka.

The Ceylon Light Infantry Volunteers was dominated by Europeans: 210 to the 156 Ceylonese. The Sri Lankans who joined were a westernized, urban, and heavily Christian elite. Burghers and Tamils were over-represented. Prestigious private schools, which instructed in English and whose students were from middle-class, westernized families housed the Cadet Corp. No Buddhist school had a Cadet Corp. The Volunteers were essentially reservists, "weekend soldiers" with little training (and who never fought).

When the Earl of Caithness created the Ceylon army after independence, he drew on the Volunteers for 154 of the initial officers. The first two Sri Lankan Commanders of the army were Oxford graduates, and members of the Bar, with scant military training. The same type of people, with similar backgrounds, initially provided leadership in the government, the United National Party, and the military.[20]

Problems began as the congruency declined. When S.W.R.D. Bandaranaike (himself English educated, upper caste and class) was elected in 1956 espousing the cause of lower middle class Sinhalese Buddhists, he insisted that two recently formed volunteer regiments be disbanded because of alleged political activities inimical to his party, and replaced Tamils in high positions with militant Buddhists. What was the reaction in the military? Resistance: during his term, the percentage of commissions granted Tamils almost doubled while that of Sinhalese declined (see Table 11:2). After Bandaranaike's assassination in 1959, his wife became Prime Minister, and further politicized the forces with her personnel policies. Reaction to those policies took the form of the 1962 coup attempt by high military and police officers, excluding the politically-appointed commander of the army and the Inspector-General of Police. The participants were westernized, urban, and Christian, with many from the artillery (who did not allow rice and curry to even be served in their mess). They disapproved of the communal policies and behavior of the militant Buddhist Sinhalese in power. These officers were caught up in the ethnic cleavages of their society and wanted to settle the conflicts on their preferred terms. Horowitz's classic analysis of motives of coup officers shows the dominance of Lofchie's "involvement" theory, as opposed to that of "aloofness from society," corporate concerns, or personal/factional concerns found in theories of Decalo, First, Thompson and Veliz.[21] However, the very attempt challenges Enloe's hypothesis that coup attempts are less likely by ethnic minority officers because of the improbability of their being able to govern.[22]

After the coup attempt there was a concerted effort to remake the security forces in the image of the dominant political elites in government. The artillery was disbanded. Almost all commissions were given to Sinhalese, although a few were given to Tamil Christians, as shown in Table II:2.

In 1965 the United National Party came to power. The UNP had been considered the haven of the westernized middle class, but had been remodeled by J.R. Jayewardene to appeal to the lower castes and classes among the Sinhalese. The second alleged coup conspiracy occurred the next year, supposedly organized

The preferred control model in Sri Lanka has provided support, however, for yet another hypothesis that stresses the importance of military participation in national security policy-making. This "fusionist" decisional model has been much easier because of family, class, and school ties in a small, unitary state.[25] The one per cent who have attended the universities have moved into top positions in the military, the police, the civil service, the political, social, and economic institutions of the society.

Here again we spot problems. In the last presidential election, Mrs. Bandaranaike of the SLFP tried to draw the extremist Sinhalese JVP sympathizers towards her party. This strategy might have raised hackles in the security forces, who had been threatened (along with their families) by the JVP, and whom they had tried to eradicate.

Two different kinds of problems have developed within the UNP. When Jayewardene was succeeded by Premadasa as President, the "security-oriented faction" lost its central position. Premadasa, a militant Buddhist of a lower-caste, has his support among members of parliament, and, in society among the lower classes, especially the members of a militant, highly politicized labor union associated with political violence.[26] He endeavored to weaken his chief rivals: Gamini Dissanayake (party organization faction) and Lalit Athulathmudali (former Minister of National Security; also the largest vote-getter in the elections). In August 1991 Gamini, Lalit and their followers joined with the opposition parties to launch an impeachment motion against the President. The President's response was to suspend the parliament, and dismiss the dissidents from their Ministerial positions and from the party. A change in party affiliation causes the seat in parliament to be forfeited, to be filled in a special election (with the President having the constitutional power to choose the party's nominee), so it was not surprising to find a few of the signatories recanting. The impeachment effort faltered (even though the dissidents kept their parliamentary seats pending their appeal in the courts). The factional fight marks a shift in civil-military relations: in the early stages both factions called on the military to intervene in their dispute "to preserve the constitution." The top leaders of the military and police did act, choosing to support the President, even though his actions nullified the impeachment provisions of the constitution. This incident marks the first time the politicians called on the military to settle a dispute among them. Then a few days later, the President confessed that he had provided arms to the insurgent LTTE in 1990 to enable them to destroy the security forces trained and equipped by the Indians to help provide security for towns and cities in the North and East. Given the losses by the security forces in recent encounters with the LTTE, there may be division within the ranks on support of the President--not to mention concern that national security policy has been made without their input or knowledge.

Conclusion

This analysis of civilian rule in Sri Lanka has inexorably pointed up countervailing trends. The evidence suggests that a Wellington model has been consciously and successfully employed in a small country which lacks geopolitical significance, and which has had a small military with--until recently--very few combat experiences. The knowledge that the civilian government uncovered and thwarted three coup conspiracies (each at an earlier stage of development), that public support was lacking in each case, that Sinhalese youth rebelled against lack of meaningful participation, comprises part of the memory of both military and civilians. When those memories are juxtaposed with the high literacy rate, a political middle class, effective governmental performance and belief in popular sovereignty, the effect is likely to be multiplicative rather than additive. And because of the Wellington model, the security forces have enjoyed an important policy-making role. That the government and military seem to share congruent perspectives on the role of the military as well as the methods to be utilized in support of the civil, provides support for continued civilian rule.

The chief qualifier may be the rapid increase in size of the security forces. The larger the forces, the more likely a critical mass can develop to challenge civilian authorities. Has the rapid expansion, plus the move to Sinhala, substantially revoked the Wellington insurance policy of the English-educated elite? Have the operational ties developed among the security forces, all in one ministry, created reactive networks for common concerns? The impact of the discovery that President Premadasa actually provided arms to the LTTE may lead to activation of such a network, and at a time when civilian politicians are asking them to intervene.

A critical concern is whether peace might present a problem for civil-military relations. Peace would mean pressures to reduce the military, which would mean sending trained and experienced soldiers out into an economy with high unemployment, and where new jobs tend to be for women. Officers who have just spent several years putting down a revolt of the unemployed might be opposed to retrenchment. Reduction in size, or cessation of conflict would likely translate into stagnation on career ladders in the security forces, which up to now have offered opportunities for advancement. Reduction of budget would be expected to lead toward concern about equipment and training. Having experienced combat, its cessation might make the more usual ceremonial, economic, or athletic duties seem less important. Peace, then, might turn standard military concerns, or normal everyday gripes, into forces which would propel members of the security forces toward a coup to change those politics.

Unlike previous involvements in cleavages of society, renewed involvement is likely to stress corporate concerns or personal/factional motives.27 The continuance of low-level conflict in the north might be one method of forestalling decisions on reduction which might arouse the ire of the military; so might be the decision to provide arms to the LTTE. (Emigration of Tamils has reduced the base for the insurgents.) That decision gives the lie to notions that larger size might mean greater participation in policy-making, and might provide incentives to officers to manipulate those civilian politicians to whom they have ties. The future might bring a greater threat of coup, this time inspired by corporate and/or personal concerns, buttressed by identification with the dominant ethnic community, and supported by factions in the major parties.

Now that proportional representation is the rule, the existence of large governing majorities may be near an end. Effectiveness of government may have been related to alternation in power with large majorities to force policy changes. A politicized and disaffected populace may not necessarily support a less effective government, unable to carry out mandates. Given the military memory of "abuse-without-penalty" of civil rights and liberties, might not the next step be to question constitutionalism itself?

Notes

1. The primary sources are Amos Perlmutter and V. P. Bennett, *The Political Influence of the Military* (New Haven: Yale University Press, 1980), Sheldon W. Simon, ed. *The Military and Security in the Third World: Domestic and International Impacts* (Boulder, Colorado: Westview Press, 1978), Donald L. Horowitz, *Coup Theories and Officers' Motives: Sri Lanka in Comparative Perspective* (Princeton, N.J.: Princeton University Press, 1980), Samuel P. Huntington, *Political Order in Changing Societies* (New Haven: Yale University Press, 1968), Lt. General M.L. Chibber, *Military Leadership to Prevent Military Coup* (New Delhi: Lancer International, 1986), Cynthia Enloe, *Ethnic Soldiers: State Security in Divided Societies* (Athens, Ga.: University of Georgia Press, 1980), Douglas A. Hibbs, *Mass Political Violence: A Cross-National Causal Analysis* (New York: John Wiley, 1973), Bengt Abrahamsson, *Military*

Professionalization and Political Power (Beverly Hills: Sage, 1972), S.E. Finer, *The Man on Horseback* (Boulder, Colo.: Westview Press, 1988).

2. Kingsly M. De Silva, *Managing Ethnic Tensions in Multi-Ethnic Societies: Sri Lanka 1880-1985* (New York: University, 1986).

3. Committee for Rational Development. *Sri Lanka: The Ethnic Conflict. Myths, Realities and Perspectives* (New Delhi: Navrang, 1984), p. 3.

4. Simon, *The Military and Security in the Third World*; Chibber, *Military Leadership*.

5. Chibber, *Military Leadership*, p. 97.

6. Robert A. Kearney, "Language and the Rise of Tamil Separatism in Sri Lanka," *Asian Survey* v. XVIII, no. 5 (May, 1978), pp. 521-534. Michael Roberts, ed. *Collective Identities, Nationalisms and Protest in Modern Sri Lanka* (Colombo: Marga Institute, 1979).

7. Satchi Ponnambalam. *Sri Lanka: National Conflict and the Tamil Liberation Struggle* (London: Zed Books Ltd, 1983), p. 175.

8. A. Jeyaratnam Wilson. *Politics in Sri Lanka 1947-74* (New York: St. Martin's Press, 1974), p. 47. A.E.H. Sanderatne. *Glimpses of the Public Services of Ceylon During a Period of Transition 1927-1962* (Colombo: n.p., 1975).

9. Kingsley De Silva and Howard Wriggins. *J.R. Jayewardene of Sri Lanka: A Political Biography* v. 1: 1906-1956 (Honolulu: University of Hawaii Press, 1988), p. 17.

10. Sri Lanka. *Report on the Presidential Commission on Youth. Summary* (Colombo, Government Press, 1990).

11. Morris David Morris. *Measuring the Condition of the World's Poor: The Physical Quality of Life Index* (New York: Pergamon Press, 1979), p. 45.

12. De Silva and Wriggins, *J.R. Jayewardene*, pp. 15-16.

13. See Finer, *Man on Horseback*, pp. 208, for the relationship between a "high level of political culture" and low danger of military coup.

14. James Manor, ed. *Sri Lanka in Change and Crisis* (New York: St. Martin's Press, 1984).

15. *Report of the Presidential Commission on Youth*, p. 10.

16. Maj. General Anton Muttukumaru, *The Military History of Ceylon* (New Delhi: Navrang, 1987).

17. T.D.S.A. Dissanayaka, *The Agony of Sri Lanka* (Colombo: Swastika Private Ltd., 1983), pp. 29-73.

18. Samuel P. Huntington, *The Soldier and the State: The Theory and Politics of Civil Military Relations* (New York: Random House, 1957), p. 81. Chibber, *Military Leadership*, p. 87. Amos Perlmutter and V.P. Bennett, *The Political Influence of the Military*, p. 4. Eric A. Nordlinger, *Soldiers in Politics* (Englewood Cliffs, N.J.: Prentice-Hall, 1977), pp. 11-15. Huntington's theory is challenged by Abrahamsson, *Military Professionalization and Political Power*, pp. 12-13.

19. See Nordlinger, *Soldiers in Politics*, pp. 115-35; Chibber, *Military Leadership*, pp. 198-200.

20. Horowitz, *Coup Theories and Officers Motives*; Muttukumaru, *Military History*.

21. Horowitz, *Coup Theories and Officers Motives*; Michael P. Lofchie, "The Uganda Coup: Class Action by the Military," *Journal of Modern African Studies* v. 10, no. 1 (May 1972), pp. 19-35. Samuel Decalo, *Coups and Army Rule in Africa* (New Haven: Yale University Press, 1976). Ruth First, *Power in Africa* (Baltimore: Penguin, 1971). William R. Thompson, The Grievances of Military Coup Makers, (Beverly Hills: Sage Professional Papers, Comparative Politics Series no. 10-174, 1973). Claudio Veliz, ed. *The Politics of Conformity in Latin America* (New York: Oxford University Press, 1967).

22. Enloe, *Ethnic Soldiers*. See her *Police, Military and Ethnicity: Foundations of State Power* (New Brunswick, N.J.: Transaction, 1980).

23. *Ethnic Soldiers*, ch. 1.

24. S.J. Tambiah, *Sri Lanka: Ethnic Fratricide and the Dismantling of Democracy* (Chicago: University of Chicago Press, 1986), p. 48. DeSilva and Wriggins, J.R. Jayewardene, pp. 32-34. Janice Jiggins, *Caste and Family in the Politics of the Sinhalese 1947-1976* (London: Cambridge University Press, 1979). Yasmine Gooneratne, *Relative Merits: A Personal Memoir of the Bandaranaike Family of Sri Lanka* (New York: St. Martins' Press, 1986).

25. Huntington, *Soldier and the State*, pp. 80-97.

26 . Rajiva Wijesinha, *Current Crisis in Sri Lanka* (New Delhi: Navrang, 1986), pp. 96-97, provides analysis of the factional alignment in the U.N.P.

27 . William R. Thompson, *Grievances of Military Coup Makers*, pp. 12-39.

12

Civilian Rule in the Philippines

Benjamin N. Muego

Civilian supremacy over the military is firmly rooted in Philippine law and tradition. As a politico-legal principle, civilian supremacy is enshrined in three of the Philippines' four constitutions,[1] and it survived nine years of martial rule (the *New Society* from 1972 through 1981) and the ensuing *New Republic*. Under the current constitution, civilian supremacy is affirmed in Article II, Section 3 which states unequivocally that "civilian authority is, at all times, supreme over the military."[2] This is further buttressed by Article VII, Section 18, which designates the President, a civilian, as the Commander-in-Chief of the armed forces of the Philippines. Likewise, the Secretary of National Defense, the principal cabinet-level official through which the president exercises control and supervision over the military, is a civilian.[3]

The rationale for civilian supremacy, including executive and legislative control over military appointments and promotions (to qualify for the rank of colonel and above in the Philippine Air Force, Army and Philippine National Police or captain in the Navy the nominee must be *confirmed* by the Commission on Appointments, a bipartisan and bicameral legislative body), oversight over all military expenditures and Congress' exclusive authority to declare war is well elucidated in the literature. Suffice it to say that in both instances the drafters of the constitution--American and Filipino--shared a fundamental distrust of the military's alleged propensity to resolve conflicts through the application of violence and of the military's putative intolerance for constitutional processes.

Some commentators have recently suggested that the spate of abortive military coups--seven so far--over a three-year period (one against Marcos and the other six against Aquino) may be indicative of an ascendant militarization of Philippine politics and parenthetically, the erosion of civilian supremacy. It will be recalled that before the Ponce Enrile-Ramos-RAM (originally, Reform the Armed Forces Movement, since renamed *Rebolusyonaryong Alyansang Makabayan* or "Patriotic Revolutionary Alliance") coup attempt in 1986, the Philippines had never before experienced an attempted military takeover. The closest to a known coup plot before 1986 was a "post-election coup" in 1953 reportedly planned by Defense Secretary Ramon F. Magsaysay and several high-ranking AFP officers who were concerned that President Elpidio Quirino "would resort to wholesale fraud and violence to retain office."[4] The issue became academic, however, when Magsaysay won the presidency in a massive electoral victory. In sharp contrast, military takeovers have become almost routine in two of the Philippines' sister ASEAN (Association of Southeast Asian Nations) states, Indonesia and Thailand, especially the latter. Thailand's most recent coup (the eighteenth since the 1932 military takeover that ended absolute monarchy) occurred as recently as February 21, 1991.

A Brief Historical Overview

An archipelago roughly the size of Arizona, the Philippines is the second most populous country in Southeast Asia[5] and one of the region's poorest in terms of per capita income and other traditional indices of economic development.[6] This is somewhat of a paradox, since the Philippines was not only the first Southeast Asian country to regain its independence from its second colonizer (the United States); it also has the region's highest level of literacy and the largest pool of skilled and college-trained professionals. The latter phenomenon is largely an upshot of over fifty years of direct American rule, during which Filipinos were taught English and the Philippines outfitted with an American-style educational system both at the pre- and post-secondary levels. The Philippines also led virtually all of East and Southeast Asia (with the exception of Japan) in industrial development until the early 1960s when it was overtaken by Hong Kong, Korea, Singapore and Taiwan.

In addition to the United States which governed the Philippines from 1898 through 1946 (albeit formal American rule did not commence until 1901), the Philippines was also colonized by Spain for over three hundred fifty years (1521-1898) and then by Japan briefly, during World War II. The restoration of Philippine independence by the United States on July 4, 1946, led to the birth of the Second Philippine Republic[7] (SPR) which lasted until September 21, 1972, when Ferdinand E. Marcos declared martial law and abolished the 1935 Constitution, the SPR's charter. The SPR (1946-72) was supplanted by the *New Society* (NS) from September 21, 1972 through January 17, 1981, when martial law was lifted, with the NS being in turn replaced by the so called *New Republic* (NR).

The *New Republic* ceased to exist when Marcos abdicated power to Corazon C. Aquino on February 26, 1986, in the aftermath of the so called "people power revolution." In essence, the Third Philippine Republic (TPR) formally came into existence on February 3, 1987, after the ratification and coming into force of the 1987 Constitution. While the SPR and the current government (TPR) are tri-partite presidential systems patterned after the United States', the NS and NR were hybrids of the English style unitary-parliamentary system and the French unitary-presidential system. Toward the end of martial rule, Marcos became enamored with the strong de Gaulle-type presidency of the French Fifth Republic and as a result, maneuvered to have the 1971 Constitution amended to make the presidency the principal locus of power instead of just a symbolic and ceremonial position.

The successor to the deposed president, Aquino, is the widow of former senator Benigno S. Aquino, Jr. who was assassinated on August 21, 1983 on the tarmac of the Manila International Airport as the latter returned to the Philippines from self-imposed exile in the United States. While the late senator's accused military assassins, including a retired flag-level Air Force officer, have since been tried and convicted for their involvement in the assassination, Aquino remains skeptical about the outcome; she is convinced that the "real murderers" have not yet been brought to justice. It is public knowledge that Aquino blames Marcos for the death of her husband, and it is primarily for this reason that she has so far adamantly refused to allow the former president's remains to be returned to the Philippines for proper burial.

With less than a year to go before the watershed general elections which will, among other things, choose Aquino's successor as president, the Philippines faces serious economic, social and political problems, e.g., high unemployment, grinding poverty, precarious peace and order conditions and a twin-insurgency problem that has dragged on for the last twenty-two years. As economic and social conditions deteriorate from bad to worse, so apparently have Aquino's standing in public opinion polls. Evidently, many Filipinos-- including some of the beleaguered president's former supporters--directly attribute the country's problems to Aquino's *lack of leadership* if not *downright incompetence*. A nation-wide poll conducted by Ateneo de Manila University in March 1990 gave the president a measly 24 percent overall *satisfaction rating*.

In the bellwether and vote-rich Metro Manila region, Aquino registered a dismal five (5) percent approval rating, a new nadir in public dissatisfaction over presidential performance. Interestingly enough, however, Aquino fared better in urban and rural Visayas (39 and 34 percent, respectively) as well as in urban and rural Mindanao where the president registered approval ratings of 38 and 32 percentage points, in that order.[8]

It is generally assumed that coups are more likely to occur in polities where the political leadership is perceived as weak or has lost much of its legitimacy. If the latter assumption is valid, and given Aquino's diminished capacity to govern and "political lame-duck" status (she has repeatedly disavowed any interest in standing for re-election)[9] it would not be at all surprising if the same Reform the Armed Forces Movement (RAM)-Young Officers Union (YOU)-Soldiers of the Filipino People (SFP) group responsible for the previous coup attempts launch yet another bid to topple Aquino from power. Or so suggests one western analyst who lived through all six coup attempts, familiar with the coup leaders and their respective bases of support within the Armed Forces of the Philippines (AFP).[10] What is the likelihood of a seventh coup attempt occurring before the end of the year, and if so, what are its chances of success? Will the majority of Filipinos react in more clear-cut fashion the seventh time around? It will be recalled that in the past, the people (perhaps consistent with the *segurista* mentality[11]) were indifferent, if slightly scared spectators, not active participants. Would a successful coup be the death knell of civilian supremacy in the Philippines?

The People and the Military Establishment

Unlike other Southeast Asian polities where the military occupies center stage and military leaders are venerated as folk heroes (except Kampuchea, Malaysia and Singapore), the Philippines has been rather indifferent, at times even hostile, to its military. Indeed, the pantheon of Filipino heroes is dominated by men of letters, humanists, artists and statesmen; men like Jose P. Rizal (the national hero), Marcelo H. del Pilar, Apolinario Mabini, Andres Bonifacio, Graciano Lopez Jaena and Juan Luna. A notable exception is General Gregorio del Pilar, immortalized in Philippine military lore for a valiant but futile rear-guard stand at Tirad Pass against superior (both in numbers as well as in weaponry) enemy forces in pursuit of General Emilio F. Aguinaldo during the waning days of the abbreviated Filipino-American war. In all fairness, it should also be pointed out that during World War II, Filipino soldiers, albeit fighting for a foreign flag, acquitted themselves very well, first at Bataan and Corregidor and later, through organized guerrilla activity against the Japanese Imperial Army. In the post-World War II era (especially during martial rule), however, the image of the Philippine military has been generally that of a "repressive" "bloated," "factious," poorly-trained and ill-equipped organization whose "professionalism" and *esprit d'corps*, are suspect. In a related context, the military is also generally perceived as an employer of last resort for what the late Morris Janowitz used to call society's "under-classes."

The indifference of the general public toward the military may be partly due to the fact that unlike other former colonies which have since become independent nation-states, the Philippine military did not play a key role in the struggle for independence; that because "the Philippines won her independence peacefully, the [military]was never really glorified as the leader of the nationalist revolution."[12] The prime movers behind the movement that eventually resulted in American recognition of Philippine independence were civilian leaders like Manuel Luis Quezon and Sergio Osmena who led separate "independence missions" to Washington, D.C. before the passage of the Tydings-McDuffie Act which set the timetable for Philippine independence. To most Filipinos, therefore, the military from its beginnings in 1901 as an "insular police force" to its present tri-service configuration is nothing more nor less that a necessary trapping of statehood; the notion that an independent nation-state must have its own armed forces.[13]

The Politicization of the Military

Magsaysay and the Civilian Bureaucracy. Except for two episodes some thirty-two years apart--when the military enjoyed virtually universal albeit brief, public acclaim--civil-military relations in the Philippines have been somewhat strained and rocky. The first episode occurred in 1954 after the much-maligned AFP successfully crushed the armed rebellion launched by the *Partido Komunista ng Pilipinas* (PKP) and its military arm, the *Hukbong Mapagpalaya ng Bayan* (*Huk* for short) against the Philippine government in 1948.[14] The success of the counter-insurgency campaign was, in large measure, due to the thorough overhaul of the military command and organizational structure and a generous infusion of funds and war matériel from the United States.

The principal vehicle through which the Pentagon and the Central Intelligence Agency (CIA) "advised and assisted" the AFP was an organization called JUSMAG (Joint US Military Advisory Group), even as a relatively unknown provincial politician, Magsaysay, then Secretary of National Defense, acted as principal point-man.[15] Combining a mailed fist policy with a generous amnesty package (including a promise of free land for all surrendered *Huks*), Magsaysay "broke the backbone" of the communist insurgency and became an instant political celebrity. A year later, Magsaysay parlayed this phenomenal celebrity status into a landslide election victory ironically over his former benefactor, incumbent President Elpidio Quirino.

Convinced that the military chain of command and organizational structure was superior to that of the civilian bureaucracy's, and "impressed with the training, efficiency, discipline and integrity of the military,"[16] Magsaysay organized his administration around a nucleus of active-duty and retired military officers, appointing a number of them to cabinet-level positions. By and large, Magsaysay's military appointees performed well, in the process vindicating his assertion that all things being equal, military men are "better administrators" than civilians. It is interesting to speculate on what else might have happened had death not prematurely cut short Magsaysay's presidency (and certain re-election) in 1957.

It was public knowledge that shortly before the tragic plane crash that claimed his life, Magsaysay was on the verge of launching a political movement of his own, rid of "traditional politicians" from the *Nacionalista* and Liberal parties. Given Magsaysay's fondness for the military and the fact that he seemed to trust his military advisors the most, it would not be far-fetched to suggest that the "militarization" of Philippine society would have continued to gain momentum. How Filipinos would have reacted to overt militarization or the perception of eventual military rule is uncertain and problematic. In any event, if any Filipino leader could have gotten away with militarization (assuming that military hegemony was Magsaysay's ultimate goal, a highly questionable proposition) Magsaysay was the only person who could have done it.

EDSA and the Military. Another high-point in civil-military relations occurred in February 1986, at a rather unlikely site--a narrow strip of real estate called *EDSA* (acronym for Epifanio de los Santos Avenue or "Highway 54," one of the principal north-south arteries in Metro Manila's tortured road system) sandwiched between Camp Crame, headquarters of the former Philippine Constabulary, and Camp General Emilio F. Aguinaldo, general headquarters of the Armed Forces of the Philippines. It was at *EDSA* where hundreds of thousands of Filipinos, partly out of curiousity and partly in response to frantic appeals from Jaime Cardinal Sin and other church officials (broadcast over *Radio Veritas*, the only operational opposition broadcast facility at the time), chose to stand up to Marcos' "loyalist forces" en route to Camps Aguinaldo and Crame presumably to flush out rebel forces led by General Fidel V. Ramos and his RAM bodyguards and supporters. The rest is now as much myth as it is history--thousands of soldiers in full battle gear, astride armored personnel carriers and light tanks, being "confronted" by unarmed civilians with the military opting to uphold "people power" instead of suppressing it.

By helping oust Marcos and install Aquino president, the military gained "both the prestige and political influence" which made it a "crucial force in Philippine politics."[17] Predictably, however, the public's rapprochement with the military which served twin roles as guarantor and enforcer of the martial law regime's edicts for fourteen years, turned out to be short-lived. Indeed, it did not take long before the general public still enamored with the notion of "people power," started calling on the military to eschew politics and revert to its traditional role of safeguarding national security and enforcing law and order. In other words, even as the public acknowledged the key role played by the military in the "restoration of democracy," the popular sentiment to keep civilian authority paramount and the "feeling that the military must 'return to the barracks' after its dramatic involvement in the February revolution remain[ed] strong."[18]

In retrospect, the expectation that the military would promptly withdraw from the political arena and "return to barracks" was unrealistic to say the least, and may well have contributed to strong anti-regime sentiment within the AFP and in military communities throughout the country[19] that in turn, helped spawn six coup attempts over a three-year period. It is noteworthy that in addition to Ramos, the bulk of AFP officers directly involved in the *EDSA* uprising, e.g., Victor Batac, Gregorio Honasan, Eduardo Kapunan, Antonio Sotelo, and Felix Turingan, held the rank of colonel or lieutenant colonel (or equivalent rank in the Philippine Navy) and were largely drawn from three graduating classes at the Philippine Military Academy (PMA). According to a recent study,[20] these graduating classes were those of 1971, 1972 and 1973, by far the most highly politicized batches to emerge from the PMA in recent years.

Politicization of the Officer Corps. The politicization of Honasan, his classmates and other PMA alumni in the AFP officer corps is traceable to the following set of circumstances or factors: (1) the addition of humanities and social sciences courses to the PMA core curriculum in the mid-1960s; (2) the influence of activist-nationalist teachers such as Colonel Dante Simbulan and sometime later, Lieutenants Victor Corpus and Crispin Tagamolila, both of whom defected to the CPP-ML/NPA in 1971;[21] and, (3) the ripple effect of parallel ideological ferment and increased political awareness in the larger national society.[22] Before the mid-1960s, the bulk of non-military offerings in the basic "Bachelor of Science" (B.S.) degree program at the PMA were engineering and hard science courses. Curricular reform not only added new courses; it also led to other pedagogical innovations like the "discussion method," a system of instruction that afforded cadets the opportunity--many for the very first time--to express themselves on controversial issues such as Phillippine-American relations, nationalism, agrarian reform, neo-colonialism, and other similar topics.

A new breed of teachers at the PMA exemplified by Simbulan and Corpus introduced cadets to the works of the great nationalist Claro Mayo Recto and encouraged them to thoroughly examine, and if necessary challenge, conventional wisdom or prevailing orthodoxies on such contentious matters as the distribution of power in the Philippines. Drawing from data he gathered for his doctoral dissertation on the Philippine "socio-economic elite," Simbulan concluded that for all intents and purposes, the Philippines was ruled by a *principalia* class of some one hundred sixty-nine families linked together in thirty-eight affinal relationships. This numerically small *principalia* class supplied a disproportionately large number of top public officials and enjoyed a monopoly of economic and political power in the Philippines, at least during the seventeen-year period (1946-63) encompassed by the study.[23]

A third politicizing influence was the ideological ferment and heightened political awareness that seemed to transform the nation as a whole in the mid- and late-1960s. The dramatic resurgence of militant student activity in the mid-1960s, relative to unresolved and long-standing problems such as parity rights for Americans, American military bases on Philippine territory, graft and corruption was such that by 1969-70, multi-sectorial protest demonstrations were almost a weekly occurrence in the Metro Manila area. Also in the mid-1960s, patriotic organizations like *Kabataang Makabayan*(KM), *Samahan ng Demokratikong Kabataan* (SDK) and the Movement for the Advancement of Nationalism (MAN) were established and their membership rolls burgeoned, especially in traditional nationalist bailiwicks like the University of the Philippines. Amidst this backdrop, it was inevitable that in spite of their isolation from their counterparts in other campuses, the cadets at the PMA would eventually get caught up in the mainstream of events and militant student behavior.

Co-optation of the Military. Ironically, Marcos' co-optation of the military into the status of "junior partner" to "ensure his (Marcos') own political dominance"[24] during the martial law period, also contributed to the overall politicization of the AFP as an organization. The impact of Marcos' decision to accord insider-participant status to the military in the *New Society* was two-pronged. On the one hand, by directly involving key military officers in political decision-making--as "temporary replacements" for civilian leaders eased out of their positions--Marcos obscured the demarcation line that had traditionally set civilian and military authorities apart. On the other, by affording ambitious military officers a taste of self and power, Marcos made it difficult--wittingly or unwittingly--for the successor Aquino government to persuade military officers who had moved from periphery to center-stage, to "return to barracks" and resume their traditional military roles. Thus it is not an over-simplification to suggest that one of the reasons Colonel Honasan and the other early putschists (RAM-Guardians) turned against Aquino is that they (Honasan and his colleagues) did not receive the rewards and recognition they felt they deserved for their key role in the *EDSA* uprising. To make matters even worse, the planners (whomever they were) of the first anniversary celebration of EDSA neglected to invite any of the RAM-Guardian group of officers who were instrumental in the success of the so called "people revolution" that catapulted Aquino from total obscurity to the presidency of the republic.

Conclusions and Observations

The Philippines is a democratizing polity whose political traditions and governmental system are closely patterned after those of the United States. Although there is ample evidence to indicate that Filipinos had a clear understanding of the centrality of civilian supremacy in a democracy before the onset of American rule in 1898, it is equally clear that it was the Americans who formally introduced and dutifully nurtured the doctrine, even as the Philippines approached *independence.* And so it was that the Philippine founding fathers incorporated the doctrine of civilian supremacy into the 1935 Constitution, the basic law of the Second Philippine Republic, for basically the same reason as the American founding fathers in 1787--because of a fundamental fear and distrust of the military[25] and the necessity of reining in the military lest the latter is tempted to grab power for itself.

But even as the doctrine of civilian supremacy is essentially western, i.e., American, it took root in the Philippines for three basic reasons: (1) it complemented the Philippines' own "strong historical tradition of military submission to civilian authority;"[26] (2) because unlike some of its Asian neighbors, the Philippines does not have a well-defined martial tradition; and, (3) the relatively low status that the military enjoys as a discrete profession or calling, relative to other civilian occupations and professions. In fine, if most

Filipinos regard military service as a less than desirable career path for themselves or their children, it stands to reason that they are not likely to opt for military leaders (as opposed to civilian leaders) either. If military hegemony is to materialize in the Philippines, it has to rest on a popular consensus which posits the paramounce of the military as a legitimizing and democratizing institution; absent such a consensus, the military will remain indefinitely on the periphery of Philippine politics.

The six coup attempts over the last three years do not indicate an erosion of the doctrine of civilian supremacy nor signal a trend toward militarization or military hegemony as in Indonesia, Myanmar (Burma) and Thailand much earlier. If anything, the widespread support these coup attempts (especially the abortive coup of December 1989) received from a large and diverse group of AFP officers[27] and men mirror the anger and frustration of Filipinos in general about the inability or unwillingness of the Aquino government to come to grips with such problems as graft and corruption, the pauperization of the middle and lower classes, deteriorating internal security conditions and the ballooning of the national debt. This observation is borne out by an opinion poll taken in the aftermath of the 1989 coup which found, among other things, that 28 percent (the largest percentage in the cluster) of the people believed that the "rebel soldiers" staged a coup because of their "discontent with the government" while 25 percent indicated that the goal of the coup was to "topple Cory [and] grab power."[28]

A closer look at the upper- and middle-echelon of the Armed Forces of the Philippines from 1986 to the present, reveals an age-centered dichotomy on the "proper role" of the military vis-a-vis the civilian government. On the one hand, most senior active-duty or recently retired officers, products of a more traditional socialization process that emphasized a "supporting role" for the military, shied away form the idea that the military should share center stage with the political leadership. In general, these officers (exemplified by Generals Ileto, de Villa, and Ramos) received their commissions in the 1940s and 1950s and attended command and staff colleges in the United States, e.g., Fort Leavenworth (in Kansas), and Fort Bragg (in North Carolina), etc., where political principles such as civilian supremacy over the military were further honed and refined. In contrast, younger officers who were commissioned in the 1970s or later, and whose formal socialization at the Philippine Military Academy or in advanced ROTC programs across the nation, coincided with the resurgence of student activism in the 1960s, tends to view military involvement in political affairs as not only proper, but under certain circumstances even imperative. According to some circles, the progressive tendency of a sizable segment of the current AFP officer corps, e.g., those who belong to YOU and RAM is an upshot of the "Indonesianization" of the Philippine Military Academy beginning in the mid-1960s.

By and large, "Indonesianization" (an allusion to the undisputed hegemony the Indonesian Army has had over Indonesian politics since independence in 1949)[29] contemplates an active role for the military in the political arena, especially in the face of a breakdown or imminent breakdown of civilian authority. The underlying rationale behind "Indonesianization" is that the military--given its professionalism, better organization, higher degree of discipline and well defined chain of command--has an obligation to intervene in order to save or stabilize democracy. In other words, deposing or helping depose an incompetent and corrupt political leader is a logical extension of, and entirely consistent with, the military's principal role as protector and guarantor of the nation's existence. Advancing the argument one step further, Filipino proponents of "Indonesianization" suggest that the AFP became both an empowering as well as a legitimizing force when it helped depose Marcos in 1986; that the military is co-equal and co-terminous with, not subordinate to, civilian authority.

After six unsuccessful coup attempts, however, it has become evident that Filipinos are not ready for military hegemony of the Indonesian, Thai, or other genre. This accounts for the absence of enthusiastic public support for any of the coup attempts so far even as Aquino and her administration received record-low approval ratings in the polls. By withholding support form the RAM-SFP-YOU rebels in their abortive bids for power, the general public seem to be saying that military hegemony (as distinguished from partial military rule--a military junta or cabal acting thorough a civilian leader or leaders) is not possible in the Philippines because it militates against most Philippine cultural traditions, political beliefs and values. On the other hand, Filipinos might support another *EDSA*-type military intervention, but only if carried out under the aegis of civilian authority, and for the sole purpose of preserving the rule of law and other democratic institutions.

The one unique occasion when Filipinos might have acquiesced to military rule, at least initially, was at the zenith of Magsaysay's popularity in 1954. Had military rule come about, however, it would not have necessarily meant the demise of civilian supremacy but rather, as a tribute to Magsaysay's personal magnetism and charisma. President Magsaysay did not only have the solid support of the masses; he also came into the political scene at a time when the Philippines' fledgling democracy was on the verge of collapse. Rightly or wrongly, therefore, Magsaysay was viewed by an overwhelming majority of

Filipinos as their nation's and democracy's savior. Interestingly enough, Magsaysay was extremely reluctant to encourage militarization, indicating this would imperil democracy and reduce the Philippines into "just another banana republic." Politically astute and savvy as he was, Marcos did not even come close to matching Magsaysay's genuine rapport with the military and the civilian population.

While there is little doubt that the new Philippine military is much more politicized than the old AFP and today's officers and men are more activist and ideological in their collective orientation, the likelihood of military rule, short of all-out civil war and a total breakdown of civilian authority, is remote and improbable. The historical and cultural underpinnings necessary to nurture military hegemony similar to that which exists in Indonesia, Myanmar (Burma) and Thailand, are simply not present in the Philippines. If anything resembling military hegemony or rule would occur, it will probably be for a temporary duration only; just long enough to hold elections and install a democratically elected leader. While one cannot absolutely rule out military hegemony, it would have great difficulty succeeding if and when it occurs, and the Filipino people are not likely to support it for very long.

Notes

1. The 1935 Constitution which governed the Second Philippine Republic (1946-72), the 1973 or "Marcos Constitution" (1973-86) and the 1987 or "Aquino Constitution" formally ratified on February 2, 1987. Although the "Malolos Constitution" of 1898 did not specifically incorporate the principle of civilian supremacy in its one hundred one (101) separate articles, there is ample evidence to indicate that the principal author of the document, Felipe Calderon, "had a mortal fear of the...military around him who, he thought, might abuse their powers." It was primarily for this reason that the Malalos Constitution established the supremacy of the legislative branch over the executive and judicial branches. For a full discussion of this and other related points, see Teodoro A. Agoncillo, "The Crisis of the Republic," in *Development of the Philippine Constitution* (Manila: National Media Production Center, 1974), pp. 2-10.

2. Article II, Section 3, of the 1987 Constitution reads: "Civilian authority is, at all times, supreme over the military. The Armed Forces of the Philippines is the protector of the people and the State. Its goal is to secure the sovereignty of the State and the integrity of the national territory."

3. As with current Department of National Defense (DND) head General Fidel V. Ramos (ret.), however, some former DND secretaries have been retired flag-

level officers, e.g., General Rafael M. Ileto or civilians with guerrilla or para-military backgrounds like Ramon F. Magsaysay and Ruperto N. Kangleon.

4. See Viberto Selochan, "Professionalization and Politicization of the Armed Forces of the Philippines," unpublished Ph.D. dissertation, Australian National University (Canberra A.C.T., Australia), 1990, especially pp. 112-17.

5. The population of the Philippines is estimated to be about 64 million in 1991 and growing at an alarming annual rate of 2.47 percent. If this rate of growth persists, the Philippines may exceed the 100,000,000-mark by the year 2010! Needless to say, such an eventuality would pose some very difficult problems and choices to the Philippine government in both the near- and long-term.

6. In 1988, the Philippines' per capita GNP was US$530; cf., Malaysia's US$1,920, Thailand's US$845, and Singapore's US$8,435 on the "high side," and Indonesia's US$485 and Vietnam's US$200, on the "low side." For other economic data on the above Southeast Asian countries, see Thomas J. Timmons, ed. and comp., *U.S. and Asia Statistical Handbook*, 1989 Edition (Washington, D.C.: Heritage Foundation), pp. 36-37, 50-51, 66-67, 68-69, 74-75 and 78-79.

7. For a brief explanation of the term "Second Philippine Republic," "New Society," and "New Republic," etc., see Benjamin N. Muego, *Spectator Society: The Philippines Under Martial Rule* (Athens, Ohio: Ohio University Press, 1989).

8. See *People's Pulse: Ateneo de Manila University Public Opinion Survey*, (Quezon City: Center for Social and Public Affairs, Ateneo de Manila University, 1990), p. 5. In fairness to Aquino, however, it should be noted that Vice-President Salvador H. Laurel fared even worse, with a "satisfaction rating" of -11 percent during the same time period (*in. loc. cit.*, p. 6).

9. While it appears that Article VII, Section 4, of the 1987 Constitution, bars an incumbent president from seeking another term, i.e., "...the President shall not be eligible for *any re-election* [italics supplied]...," supporters of an Aquino re-election bid argue that she (Aquino) is beyond the ambit of Article VII, Section 4, *supra*, since she (Aquino) became president *before* the 1987 constitution came into force. Under this line of reasoning, the injunctive intent of Article VII, Section 4, will not be operative until 1998!

10. According to Keith Richburg, who was stationed in Manila from 1986-90 while serving as Southeast Asia bureau chief of the *Washington Post*, the anti-Aquino military alliance which consists of RAM (since renamed *Rebolusyonaryong Alyansang Makabayan* or "Patriotic Revolutionary Alliance"), Young Officers Union (YOU), Soldiers of the Filipino People (SFP), Brotherhood of Guardians and so called "Marcos loyalists" led by Brig. General Jose Ma. Zumel, may be planning one last-ditch effort to topple the Aquino government, if for no other reason than to demonstrate its ability to mount a major anti-regime military effort.

11. The term *segurista mentality* refers to the tendency to be non-committal or sit on the proverbial fence until the outcome, one way or the other is virtually assured. In other words, a *segurista* is an individual who may actually play both sides of an argument or refuse to take sides until a winning side begins to emerge. At that point, the *segurista* will, naturally, cast his lot with the winning side. In the deadly and nearly-successful December 1989 coup, for example, it is generally believed that the decision of Brigadier General Marcelo Blando of the 7th Infantry Division to hold out until the last minute--as he literally watched the tide of battle turn first in favor of the rebels then to the government's--significantly affected the outcome.

12. See David O. Wurfel, "The Philippines" in George McTurnan Kahin, ed., *Governments and Politics of Southeast Asia*, Second Edition (Ithaca: Cornell University Press, 1964), p. 716.

13. For a discussion of the evolution of the present Armed Forces of the Philippines from an "insular police force" in 1901 on through the Philippine Constabulary and Philippine Scouts stages, etc., see Muego, *Spectator Society*, pp. 102-117.

14. The *Huk* rebellion is to be distinguished from the ongoing communist insurgency being waged by the Communist Party of the Philippines-ML (CPP-ML) and its military arm, the New People's Army (NPA) against the "US-Aquino dictatorship." Now virtually extinct, the PKP has a totally different sets of goals and strategies relative to the CPP-ML/NPA.

15. The American military official whom most experts identify as primarily responsible for turning the AFP's counter-insurgency campaign around is Colonel (later General) Edward G. Lansdale. Colonel Lansdale served as Magsaysay's principal military advisor on counter-insurgency matters while Magsaysay was Secretary of National Defense and reportedly became one of Magsaysay's most trusted advisors and political tacticians, after the latter became president in 1955.

16. José V. Abueva, *Ramon Magsaysay: A Political Biography* (Manila: Solidaridad Publishing House, 1971), pp. 313-14. Among some of Magsaysay's high-profile appointees were: Colonel Fred Ruiz Castro, Executive Secretary; Major Jose M. Crisol, Director of the National Bureau of Investigation; Colonel Sotero Cabahug, Secretary of National Defense; Brigadier General Eleuterio M. Adevoso, Secretary of Labor; Colonel Jaime N. Ferrer, Undersecretary of Agriculture and National Resources; Lieutenant Colonel Frisco T. San Juan, Chairman of the Presidential Complaints Action Committee; Colonel Salvador Villa, General Manager of the Manila Railroad Company; and, Colonel Osmundo Mondonedo, Director of the Agricultural Credit and Cooperative Financing Administration.

17. Felipe B. Miranda and Ruben F. Ciron, *Development and the Military in the Philippines: Military Perceptions in a Time of Crisis* (Quezon City: Social Weather Stations, Inc., 1987), p. 1.

18. Felipe B. Miranda, "The Third Public Opinion Report: A Political Analysis," in *Public Opinion Report* (Quezon City: Ateneo-Social Weather Station, October 1987), as quoted by Miranda and Ciron, *Development and the Military in the Philippines*, p. 1.

19. During the nation-wide plebiscite on the new Constitution on February 2, 1987, for example, voters in military base-areas, e.g., Camps Aguinaldo, Bonifacio, Crame and Villamor (in Metro Manila) and Fort Magsaysay in Laur, Nueva Ecija, etc., where most military dependents are domiciled, overwhelmingly rejected the draft document (roughly 85 percent voted against to only 15 percent for), the exact reverse of the overall vote count. By personalizing the ratification campaign through slogans like "a vote for the Constitution is a vote for Cory," Aquino afforded her critics in the military a dramatic opportunity to register their displeasure towards her personally, as well as towards her government.

20. See Rigoberto D. Tiglao, et al. *Kudeta: The Challenge to Philippine Democracy* (Manila: Philippine Center for Investigative Journalism, 1990).

21. Like most of the CPP-ML/NPA's top leaders, Victor Corpus was ordered released from prison by Aquino in 1986. Since his release, Corpus has rejoined the AFP and been promoted to the rank of full colonel. On the other hand, Lieutenant Crispin Tagamolila was not as lucky; he was killed in an encounter with government troops in the 1970s, and today is listed by the CPP-ML/NPA/NDF as one of the martyrs of the "national democratic struggle."

22. See inter alia, Conrado de Quiros, "Sword Over the Throne: The Armed Forces' Rise to Power," in Tiglao, *Kudeta*, p. 58; and Rigoberto D. Tiglao, "Rebellion from the Barracks: The Military as a Political Force," in Tiglao, *Kudeta*, p. 15.

23. See de Quiros, "Swords Over the Throne," p. 58. For the full text of Simbulan's dissertation, see Dante Simbulan, "A Study of the Socio-Economic Elite in Philippine Politics, 1946-63." Unpublished Ph.D. Dissertation, Australian National University (Canberra, A.C.T.), 1965.

24. Miranda and Ciron, *Development and the Military in the Philippines*, p. 5.

25. This was notwithstanding the fact that the "Armies" and "Navy" referred to in Article I, Section 8, of the United States Constitution had yet to be established, and the presence in the convention of military men like George Washington who served as president of the Constitutional Convention.

26. See Felipe D. Miranda, "The Military," in R.J. May and Francisco Nemenzo, eds., *The Philippines After Marcos* (London: Croom Helm Ltd., 1985), p. 91.

27. In the December 1989 coup, for example, as many as five hundred thirty-three (533) AFP commissioned officers were involved, e.g., eight flag-level officers (7 Army, Air Force and Constabulary Brigadier Generals and 1 Navy Commodore); nineteen colonels (13 Army, Air Force and Constabulary Colonels

and 6 Navy Captains); fifty-three lieutenant colonels (45 Army, Air Force and Constabulary Lieutenant Colonels and 8 Navy Commanders); fifty-nine majors (47 Army, Air Force and Constabulary Majors and 12 Navy Lieutenant Commanders); one hundred fifty-five captains; one hundred thirty-five first lieutenants (123 Army, Air Force and Constabulary First Lieutenants and 12 Navy Lieutenant [j.g.]); and fifteen second lieutenants (12 Army, Air Force and Constabulary Lieutenants and 3 Navy Ensigns). See Tiglao, *Kudeta*, p. 15.

28. See Center for Social Policy and Public Affairs, p. 11.

29. According to R. William Liddle of Ohio State University, a well known specialist in Indonesian politics, the principal source of legitimacy for President Suharto's *Golkar'* is the Indonesian Army.

13

Malaysia: Shared Civilian-Military Interests

*Diane K. Mauzy**

Armies[1] intervene in civil-military politics in the Third World for a variety of reasons. Often it is to defend their corporate interests; sometimes it is to "save" the nation from corrupt or ineffectual civilian leaders, or to block reformers from embarking on development projects with which the army disagrees; or it can be to defend their perceived right, based on experience, to play a political role. It can also occur when there has been turmoil and the army becomes politicized and loses its functional "professionalism," or when armies seek to put in place certain "patrons" and remove others in "palace coups."

Although it is currently popular to view the Third World generally as undergoing or about to undergo a process of democratization, signaled by a "back to the barracks"[2] move on the part of armies, the *coup d'état* and praetorian-style politics remain a prevalent form of gaining and maintaining power. In non-Communist Southeast Asia, in 1991, Thailand has experienced another coup, after ten years of apparently extricating itself from the "vicious cycle of coups"; Burma remains under despotic military rule; Indonesia's army insists on the legitimacy of its credo of *dwi fungsi* (dual functions, one of which is political); and in the Philippines, the factionalized armed forces remain dissatisfied and highly politicized after a number of failed coup attempts.

It is of significant interest, then, to try to analyze why some Third World states have not been plagued by coups and military rule. Malaysia is one such

*I would like to thank Dr. Zakaria Haji Ahmad for his helpful comments on the draft of this chapter.

225

country. Indeed, those interested in civil-military relations often criticize researchers of Malaysian politics for ignoring or barely mentioning the role of the military.[3] Cynthia H. Enloe explains the apparent omission thusly: "One reason that the military-ethnic connection has gone unanalyzed for so long by generations of political scientists may be that political scientists, like ordinary observers, tend to devote attention to those conditions that achieve a certain level of political saliency."[4]

There has never been a coup attempt (or even a credible coup rumor) in Malaysia. The socio-political conditions thought to be conducive to coup behavior--conditions leading the army to believe that it must save or reform the nation, or protect its corporate interests--have generally been absent. At one point, the Malaysian Armed Forces (MAP) did have the opportunity to intervene, a necessary but not sufficient condition. The MAF had a clear opportunity to seize power in May 1969 when it was called in by the civilian government to restore order amidst serious ethnic rioting and confusion, but did not. Instead, having pacified the country, the top military chiefs temporarily shared power with civilian leaders, at the latter's behest, as members of the ruling National Operations Council under a state of emergency. In 1971, when parliamentary rule was restored, the military leaders quietly returned to their professional, apolitical, functions. For a number of historical, ethnic, socio-political, economic, and familial reasons, the army has stayed in the barracks.

Peaceful Transfer of Power at Independence

Malaya was granted independence in 1957 in a transfer of power that evidenced very little friction between the departing British governors and the incoming Malayan elites. The same was true when Malaysia was formed in 1963, with the addition to Malaya of the British Borneo territories of Sabah and Sarawak, and, until mid-1965, the island of Singapore.

The impetus for increased self-rule and gradual progress toward independence began in earnest after World War II, starting with constitutional reform (the establishment of the Federation of Malaya in 1948), and the introduction of local elections in the early 1950s, followed by a federal election in 1955. The British, possibly as a result of the shocking experience of the partition of India, had made it clear that they would not hand over power to one ethnic group alone. Malaya was divided almost equally between the Muslim Malays, and the predominantly non-Muslim Chinese, Indians and Others (known collectively as the "non-Malays").

Until World War II, the British had tacitly acknowledged Malay claims that, as the indigenous people and "sons of the soil" *(bumiputra)*, the Malays should be considered the primary race in the country. The British coopted the Malay aristocracy and "protected" the mass of Malay peasants and their rural way of life with "special rights" (civil service quotas, land reservations, job reservations, etc.). The British also had previously actively recruited immigrant labor from China and India when it was found that the Malays would not readily work for wages away from their villages in the tin mines and on the rubber plantations, nor were there enough Malays performing necessary urban entrepreneurial tasks. However, the British considered the immigrants to be "birds of passage," and there were no immigration quotas until the 1930s, when the ethnic mosaic was already a fact.

The end of World War II was accompanied by serious ethnic clashes that left corrosive group memories and suspicion and distrust between the races in their wake. With the realization that Malaya was in fact a multi-ethnic society, the British tried to establish a constitutional system that would give the various ethnic groups equal political rights (the ill-fated Malayan Union). This galvanized Malay nationalism, and, in the face of civil service work stoppages and mass demonstrations by the Malays, the British backtracked to a position of viewing the Malays as *primus inter pares*, with special rights, under the 1948 Federation Agreement. With tight citizenship regulations, the Malays guaranteed themselves political dominance after independence. However, to obtain independence, they needed to demonstrate to the British that the ethnic groups could cooperate and live together peacefully. An attempt to forge a multi-ethnic political party failed (the Malays would not support it), but a *coalition* of ethnic parties (the Alliance, under the leadership of the United Malays National Organization (UMNO), led by Tunku Abdul Rahman) showed that the ethnic elites could compromise to resolve their ethnic differences and still win votes. This accomplished, the British handed over power to the Alliance under the Tunku as Prime Minister. At independence, the Malays were politically dominant, but were also the least advanced group economically and educationally.[5]

The army during this period of transition was small, mostly Malay, and it was trained and officered by the British. From 1948 it was preoccupied with fighting a (mostly Chinese) Communist guerrilla insurgency in the jungle along with British forces and paramilitary police units ("The Emergency," 1948-1960). The army remained non-political, and it did not become associated or identified with the Malay nationalist movement as the civilian nationalists responded to perceived ethnic political threats prior to independence. Likewise, the civilian political elites issued no calls to the army to assist their political cause. The civilian political elites were Anglophiles who never really doubted that they would be granted independence peacefully as a result of dialogue (and the occasional demonstration). Beyond this, the country was engaged in a guerrilla war with a known enemy--Communists, who were also overwhelmingly Chinese--and dependent on the help of British officers and forces.

It is important to Malaysian civil-military relations that the army remained non-political and uninvolved in the nationalist movement, and that the transfer of power was peaceful. As a result, the army could not claim that it saved the "independence revolution," as it could in Indonesia; that its leaders forged the country's independence, as in Burma; or that it gave the people a constitution, as it helped to do in Thailand when the absolute monarchy was toppled. In Malaya/Malaysia, alone among these countries, the civilian political elites could claim full credit for political advancements, and the army leaders in turn had no legitimate claim to be nation founders and saviors rivaling the civilians.

The Colonial Legacy

Although the British had established a partly local police force and civil service soon after becoming involved in the affairs of the peninsula in the 1870s (the British Forward Movement), it was not until 1933 that the first twenty-five-man army contingent was established at the urging of the Malay "Rulers."[6] This was the Malay Regiment Experimental Company, later the Royal Malay Regiment (RMR).[7] While various small state paramilitary units had existed before 1933, this was the first pan-Malayan force. The beginning of the MAF is officially recognized as from this date. The ranks were entirely Malay, and they were trained and led by British officers and non-commissioned officers (NCOs). The RMR fought against the Japanese advance in Singapore in late 1941 and early 1942, and only remnants survived the war.

Unlike the situation in some parts of Southeast Asia (Indonesia and Burma, for example), the Japanese forces which occupied Malaya did not set up an indigenous auxiliary military force[8] and did little to stimulate nationalism in the peninsula during the occupation, although they did successfully play the races off against one another.

After the war, the process of building an indigenous army began again, and the RMR was reformed, although its numbers were initially small. In response to the "hearts and minds" campaign promoted by the Emergency, and in preparation for independence, General Sir Gerald Templer, the British High

Commissioner, in the early 1950s initiated a number of moves significantly affecting the development of the MAF.[9] First, he established a multi-ethnic Federation Regiment (later merged with another regiment to become the Federation Reconnaissance Corps), which meant that the MAF was no longer exclusively Malay, and therefore better exemplified a "national" army. Other small multi-ethnic technical units were subsequently formed (signals, engineers, transport). However, in keeping with the political realities of Malaya, the RMR remained the premier corps of the army infantry, and by the late 1950s numbered seven battalions.

Templer also enacted a new policy of "Malayanization" of the MAF officer corps, with the deliberate creation of a hand-chosen local officer corps (which was multi-ethnic). The Federation Military College was opened for officer training, and the best officer cadets were sent to Sandhurst for further training. The Malayanization of the MAF officers proceeded slowly and gradually, extending well beyond independence, at the request of the Malayan government. In 1963, nearly 200 high-ranking British officers were still serving in the MAF.[10]

Throughout this formative period, the "British model" guided the MAF, and many British military norms, procedures, and traditions survived the Malayanization of the MAF. Most important among these are the ideals of professionalism and political subservience to civilian authority.[11] These values are reinforced by many professional and service-related required courses, for officers and the ranks, which serve to socialize the soldier to take great pride in his duty to his profession and technical effectiveness as a servant of the state. According to Zakaria Haji Ahmad, more than 90 percent of all regular officers have studied at the Sungei Besi Royal Military College or overseas in Britain or other Western countries. For promotion, all middle-level officers must take a formal course at the Armed Forces Staff College, and more senior officers are sent for courses at the Armed Forces Defence College (established in 1981).[12] There are also military regulations prohibiting officers from engaging in political activities.

The Historical Development of the MAF

Three important historical factors have helped shape civil-military relations in Malaysia and have contributed to the subordination of the MAF to civilian authority. First, the numerical growth of the MAF has been gradual and slow. Second, the army has been, until very recently, a non-conventional force. Third, the MAF's roles, duties, and limits have been clearly defined in the Constitution and through regulations, and the MAF has been subjected to tight political/bureaucratic control from the beginning.

The expansion[13] of the MAF was a deliberately slow process until 1970, although since that time it has been more rapid. In 1963, the MAF numbered only 14,000 personnel.[14] There were two basic reasons why MAF expansion was gradual. First, the newly independent state was protected by the Anglo-Malayan Defence Agreement, and then, from 1971, against external aggression, by the Five-Power Defence Arrangement. Second, Prime Minister Tunku Abdul Rahman chose to spend the country's limited national revenues on economic development rather than on supporting a large military force, attractive to many decolonized Third World leaders for symbolic and prestige purposes.[15] The British met their defense commitments by helping to subdue the Communist insurgents during the Emergency and by defending newly-created Malaysia against Indonesia's armed confrontation in the mid-1960s.

The importance to civilian-military relations of the small size and gradual growth of the MAF rests not just with the enhanced capability afforded to civilian control, but to the fact that until the 1980s, the federal police, including para-military forces (the Police Field Force), represented a larger force than the army (during the Emergency, army expansion was temporarily halted and attention was turned to expanding the federal police). Hence the MAF did not enjoy a monopoly over the weapons of violence.

Another factor that may have influenced the MAF not to intervene in politics was the army's development, until the late 1970s, as a non-conventional force. The army was designed for counter-insurgency deep in the jungle, a task which emphasized the role of the infantry. This role has meant that, first, until recently, much of the army has been preoccupied with jungle tasks, rather than sitting idly in its barracks near the seat of government.[16] (Although the Emergency was declared officially over in 1960, the insurgency continued until 1990, on a smaller scale). Second, it meant that the army had no need for, and did not acquire, hardware such as main battle tanks, although in the mid-1980s an armored corps of a cavalry regiment with light tanks and armored vehicles was created. Elsewhere, there have been coups without tanks, but, since coups must be rapid to be successful, it is a prime tactic of coup groups to move quickly through the capital city streets in intimidating tanks, and then surround the palace and/or key government buildings. Third, since the Emergency was a conflict that created a law and order problem, and stressed intelligence and hearts-and-minds operations, much of the responsibility rested with the federal police rather than the army, and both forces were coordinated by civilian overlords.[17]

This gave the army experience in taking orders from civilians on basic security matters and working with the police, and it prevented the army from developing an attitude that it alone had saved the country and was solely responsible for its internal security and well-being.

Another factor influencing civil-military relations in the historic development of the MAF, is that the MAF's role has always been clearly defined and its actions subject to strong political/bureaucratic control from the onset. The formal notion that the MAF's "role should be functional in terms of the profession of arms and services and that it should be an instrument of the state subservient to the government in power" is clearly stated in the constitution (Article 132).[18] The Armed Forces Act (1962), and other legislation and statues, further define the role and responsibilities of the MAF. To be sure, constitutions have sometimes been rendered meaningless by coups, but legal restraints accompanied by socialization to professional norms puts the onus on the coup leaders to find extra-legal justification to legitimize their actions. Interestingly, in Malaysia it has been the MAF officers rather than civilian authorities who have publicly expressed worries about a corrosion of professionalism in the military. In 1977, the theme of the Senior Officer's Conference was "The Challenge to Military Professionalism." Concern was expressed about a growing overlap between military strategy and politics and about a conflict in responsibilities. The undercurrent of the conference was that the MAF did not want to be used politically, where it might be "highly non-functional."[19]

In Malaysia the chain of command is clearly stipulated. The Commander-in-Chief is the *Agung* (King), of symbolic importance, especially to the Malays. In fact, it would be difficult for many Malays to act against the *Agung*. The heads of each branch of the service are responsible to the Ministry of Defence (MINDEF), as is the Chief of the Armed Forces Staff (CAFS), now known as Chief of Defence Forces (CDF), the overall MAF commander. MINDEF is a large parallel civilian bureaucracy, with a preponderance of Malay civil servants, headed by a secretary-general whose position is considered equivalent to the overall commander. MINDEF, in turn, is under the direction of the Defence Minister, who is always a Malay and also a senior UMNO politician. One of the Minister's and MINDEF's tasks is to exercise tight supervision of the MAF and also to monitor the activities, as well as look after the interests, of the ex-servicemen. Interestingly, there is not only a division of functions between the MAF and the police, but additionally the two security forces are responsible to separate ministries. The police are responsible to the Home Minister, who is always a key Malay UMNO politician. This portfolio is currently held by

Prime Minister Dr. Mahathir bin Mohamad, which may indicate the pre-eminent role of the police in domestic issues.

Additionally to MINDEF supervision, the Tunku in 1956 set up a joint civilian-military Armed Forces Council, which functions something like a Public Services Commission. The Tunku saw this as providing "a measure which will ensure that the armed forces of an independent federation will stand in proper relationship to the Head of State and the government of the day."[20]

The MAF's Corporate Interests

The military, like all organizations, seeks to safeguard and even expand its interests. Unlike other organizations, however--except perhaps the police--the military has the armed means at its disposal to remove political leaders it deems to be trampling on its interests.

In Malaysia, there appear to be few frustrations in terms of budgetary allocations, symbolic rewards, perquisites, pay, promotions, and retirement benefits. Salaries, working conditions, and terms of service in the all-volunteer armed forces are comparable to civil sectors. Budgetary allocations are comparable to some of Malaysia's neighbors in the region, thus reducing the occasion for envy, although the MAF officer corps is well aware of the prestige, status, and perquisites enjoyed by the politicized militaries of Thailand and Indonesia. However, by virtue of its armed power, manpower size, and the huge resources invested in it, the MAF is one of the most important pressure groups in the country, while at the same time remaining politically detached in its tasks.

As has been noted, the MAF expanded slowly, and initially its resource allocations were relatively small. Economic development was the top priority, and the civil service enjoyed, and continues to enjoy, top consideration in budgetary decisions and allocations.[21] However, Malaysia is a comparatively rich Third World country with substantial revenues (derived from natural resources, such as oil and gas, timber, palm oil and tin, and a large export manufacturing sector), and the MAF has been given enough to steadily expand its size, equipment purchases, and operating expenditures.

The first major expansion of the MAF took place in 1969-70 as a result of the May 13th civil disturbances, and also because the British had given notice of their intention to withdraw from military commitments "East of Suez." During this period, the MAF expanded from nine to sixteen battalions. This expansion coincided with the full Malaysianization of the MAF. Another substantial expansion occurred from the late 1970s through most of the 1980s. This was a military expansion program known as PERISTA, which had the aim of converting the MAF from a counter-insurgency force (since the threat from Communist guerrillas had declined, and was ended by formal agreement in 1990), to a conventional military designed to protect the country against external aggression. During this period, the MAF increased in manpower to 113,000 in 1988.[22] This was accompanied by sharp budgetary increases for buying new military hardware, including a new weapons system purchased in September 1988, stores, operational expenditure, and by construction of new military bases, such as the Lumut naval base, and an expensive (about $2.3 billion) and sophisticated new military complex in Gemas, Johor.[23]

Over the years, there has been some grumbling over the year-end promotions and posting orders, mostly related to the elevation of some officers with links to the political elite, and there have been controversies over the awarding of some defense contracts,[24] the implication being that political favoritism or kickbacks determined the sale (but criticism is muted because the disclosure of most pertinent facts and data would contravene the Official Secrets Act). However, on the whole, the MAF gives the impression of being an organization that is satisfied that its corporate interests are being protected.

Familial Ties and Agreement on the Goals of Government

Those who analyze the MAF usually comment on the familial connections between the ruling elite and senior MAF officers. Zakaria states that observers (including some military men) believe that a significant reason why the MAF did not seize power in May 1969 was because the Chief of Armed Forces Staff was General Tunku Osman Jewa, the nephew of Prime Minister Tunku Abdul Rahman.[25] Succeeding Prime Ministers have also had relatives and/or in-laws at the top of the MAF pyramid, including the present Prime Minister. Beyond strictly familial ties, there also exist strong personal bonds between many of the senior officers and the UMNO political elite as a result of relationships between their families, and shared experiences, such as having gone to school together, belonging to the same religion and speaking the same language, and sharing common ethnic memories and aspirations. As a result, there are many close friendships and mutual trust between a number of the top MAF officers and senior UMNO politicians. In a deferential system that is percolated with patron-client ties, these bonds filter down through the officer corps.

However, perhaps the single most important reason why the army has stayed in its barracks in Malaysia is that there is a coincidence of interests and substantial agreement between the Malay civilian and military leaders on the political rules of the games and the conduct of the exercise of power.[26] There is agreement on the constitutional and legal parameters, which allow for the exercise of limited democracy, while safeguarding political stability, state security, and Malay political hegemony. The civilian political process is viewed as being strong and functional; there is no political void. There is also basic agreement on state ideology, developmental goals and policies, and on ethnic preferences which favor Malays in tertiary education enrollment, employment, government contracts, etc. Further, as Enloe has noted, there has not been a major disruption to the ethnic status quo in terms of political roles[27] (unlike their ethnic counterparts in Fiji and Lebanon, the political hegemony of the Malays has not been seriously challenged). The Malays have--and have always had since independence--political hegemony, although they enforce it more openly and fully nowadays. The New Economic Policy, which was begun in 1970 and continues, now as the National Development Policy, designed to uplift the Malays economically, confirms this dominance. Beyond this, demographic changes favor the Malays, who are winning the "numbers game" (indeed, some Malay economic planners see the day, perhaps optimistically, when ethnicity will no longer be of prime concern).

What all of this means for civil-military relations, is that the senior Malay MAF officers, already tied closely to the Malay political elite by familial links which engender trust and loyalty, and having few--if any--disagreements over the symbols, goals, and operation of government, would find it very difficult to justify and legitimize a military take-over. In the absence of a political threat, they cannot pose as saviors; in the absence of an abrupt shift of policy, they have no threats to block; in the absence of a Nasserite-type socialist zeal, they have nothing which they want to reform.

The Ethnic Equation: The Role of the Royal Malay Regiment (RMR)

There are no precise data available on the ethnic breakdown of the Malaysian military.[28] However, the rough figures released occasionally make it clear that there is more non-Malay representation in the officer corps than in the ranks, which are overwhelmingly Malay; that the top echelon of the officer corps is solidly Malay; and that the Malays are preponderant in the combat services, while the non-Malays are concentrated in the technical services.

The MAF as a whole is dominated by the army, of which the infantry units are the core. The premier corps is the RMR, which is entirely Malay. Another, smaller, infantry unit is the Rangers, which is multi-ethnic, but has a significant Malay representation. The third unit is the Special Service Regiment, a commando-style strike force, which is 99 percent Malay.[29] There are no entirely or predominantly non-Malay units in the MAF. The dominance of the RMR is apparent in its traditional control of the Army Staff Division at MINDEF and the top command of the MAF. Practically all of the indigenous CAFS (now CDFs), the post of Army Chief, and the Chief of General Staff have been held by officers who are or were with the RMR. According to Chandran Jeshurun, there is practically no one at the rank of Major-General or above who does not have a RMR background.[30] Thus, Malays from other corps and all non-Malay officers face great handicaps in moving up the military pyramid.

Since the military is directly identified with the legitimacy of the exercise of state authority, the government proclaims and reiterates that it is policy that the military be a "national," not ethnic, force, and that the skewed composition is due to historic and economic reasons (e.g., the historic dislike of the Chinese for military service, and the ease with which Malays become recruits for reasons of upward mobility). It is also true, however, that UMNO has resisted as unnecessary calls from its Chinese coalition partner (the Malaysian Chinese Association) and a mainly Chinese opposition party (the Democratic Action Party), for compulsory national service. Likewise, the UMNO politicians have rejected outright, and often with emotion and vehemence, any notion--regarded by the Malays as provocation--to convert the RMR into a multi-ethnic force. In 1971, Prime Minister Tun Razak stated in Parliament that, while it was government policy that the MAF should, as far as possible, reflect the multi-ethnic society, "it needs to be remembered that because of the original purpose of its formation the Royal Malay Regiment is reserved for the Malays only and this situation is preserved in Article 8 (5) (f) of the Constitution."[31]

It appears that the UMNO politicians, the Rulers who serve as honorary officers, and probably most Malays, regard the RMR as the chief defenders, not only of the King and government, but also of the Malays' native land, culture, and religion. There is a belief that the RMR can protect the Malays if necessary.[32] Its role is not seen as a national arbiter in civil disturbances, but as the law enforcer for a Malay-led government. It was the RMR which was called out in May 1969 to put down the ethnic violence (a move that created some controversy temporarily, especially after complaints were lodged of ethnic bias on the part of some of the soldiers). From this time on (although some would contend earlier), the RMR emerged as an important symbol of Malay state security and national power. For the non-Malays, the RMR symbolizes the ultimate weapon of Malay political hegemony.

It is clear that, if there were going to be a military take-over in Malaysia, only Malay units could carry it out successfully, and the concurrence, at least, of the RMR--the most loyal and most trusted corps--would be necessary.

The Royal Factor

In Malaysia, there are hereditary heads of most of the states (all those except for the former Straits Settlements of Penang and Malacca and the two Borneo states), who are known collectively as the Rulers. Every five years they vote, from among themselves, on a new constitutional monarch for the country (the honor rotates, in fact, by state). The *Agung* (King) has a number of ceremonial and constitutional duties, among which is serving as Commander-in-Chief of the MAF. The Rulers are responsible as constitutional heads but exercise real influence, for those powers reserved to the states (religion, land administration, etc.). Most Rulers are honorary officers of MAF regiments and/or battalions.

This "feudal" system, as it has evolved, means that most Malays still strongly identify with the state of their birth and the Ruler, to whom they feel deference and allegiance, and seek guidance on and protection for religious and cultural matters. Urban, well-educated (especially Western-educated) and cosmopolitan Malays naturally feel less of a bond. The non-Malays, especially the Chinese, while not experiencing a feudal loyalty, generally support the institution of royalty as a conservative force making for moderation. The *Agung*, a position created at independence and one which is pan-Malaysian, has only very slowly gained some of the prestige and aura possessed by the Rulers.

Nonetheless, the *Agung* and the Rulers are highly pertinent symbols of Malay political control and the existing constitutional framework. As such, so long as there is harmony between the Rulers and the government, they represent a strong deterrent to Malays, especially the rank-and-file in the MAF, against taking any armed actions against the government of the day, since such action would be viewed not only as being illegal, but as being disloyal and traitorous to the Rulers and the *Agung*.

International Factors

For Malaysian civil-military relations, there is little on the international scene to provide any complications. The country is politically stable and economically prosperous, its borders are secure, it has no important grievances with its neighbors (and no militarily weak neighbors) and, in fact, is tied to them through the Association of Southeast Asian Nations (ASEAN), a trading, cultural exchange, and "quasi-security"[33] arrangement. Neither the government nor the military seem inclined toward external aggression or military adventurism (even given the possible irredentist situation of ethnic Malays, with some grievances, in southern Thailand). The government proclaims strong ties to the Islamic world, but in fact its orientation is also basically pro-Western, a posture that suits the MAF's interests. Malaysia has cordial relations and trading relationships with most states (except Israel, South Africa and a couple of others).

The one international factor which could be considered a concern is the example of military involvement in politics among its Southeast Asian neighbors (Thailand, Burma, Indonesia, and, to a certain extent, the Philippines). However, military intervention in these countries has provided a number of negative lessons: it has not solved the problems of corruption, slow economic growth, and political instability, and it has contributed to military factionalism, increased corruption, and declining professionalism. Consequently, as far as international factors are concerned, the MAF has little to feel envious or jittery about.

The Future of Civilian-Military Relations in Malaysia

Thirty-four years after independence, with unbroken civilian rule and sustained political institutionalization, it seems improbable that the MAF would now attempt to intervene. Yet, because the MAF--or more specifically, the army--has the capacity for seizing power by force of arms, certain problem areas and hypothetical scenarios should be discussed.

First, the MAF is changing. The large expansion in the 1980s, which some contend was too rapid,[34] means that Malaysia now has a large, conventional war machine (not yet with main battle tanks, but with light tanks and armored fighting vehicles) which is relatively idle and for which the huge expenditures are hard to rationalize. Coupled with this is a generational change that will take place in the 1990s, that will see locally-trained (Royal Military

College (RMC)) officers and a small group trained in the Indonesian staff colleges assume top command. Jeshurun writes that there is more "uncertainty about the future" concerning the socialization and commitment to established tradition of the younger Malay officers who are more "indigenous," being products of an exclusively Malay language education. He writes that it will be "critical for the first batch of the RMC leadership of the MAF...to exercise the appropriate degree of control and influence over these younger officers in order to ensure the continued stability of civil-military relations."[35]

Second, there has been talk during the last fifteen years among academics and observers of strains of Islamic fundamentalism permeating sectors of the MAF rank-and-file and NOCs (although apparently there have been no published studies on this sensitive topic). The fundamentalists in the country seek the establishment of an Islamic state, perhaps a republic, with laws based on the *Quran* and *Hadith* to replace what they view as a Western secular state system currently in existence. Radical fundamentalists in the army, to the extent that they exist and if they could form a coup group (presumably requiring that they entice some officers to their cause), could justify the use of force as being necessary to further Islamic goals.

The government, MAF, and police are not unaware of the fundamentalists, especially the more radical fringe groups, in the country. Thus far, successful efforts have been made to control and monitor the movements of these groups and to placate religious Malays by government patronage and concessions as part of an Islamization policy. In the MAF, for example, a "Religious Corps" was established in the mid-1980s to cater to "Islamic needs." The Islamic *doa selamat* is read at parades, facilities and time-off for prayers are provided, and Islamic strictures concerning food and drink in canteens is observed. There are no publicly known links between the MAF and the opposition Islamic party, PAS (*Partai Islam Se-Malaysia*).

Third, as the percentage of Malays in the population has risen, the spectre of the Malays somehow losing political control has receded. In the next century, the ethnic challenge will likely be one of dealing with a clear minority rather than confronting a dangerous ethnic foe. As such, the political saliency of ethnicity ought to decline. This has political and military ramifications. The Malays have always closed ranks against perceived threats to race, culture, and religion, and the Royal Malay Regiment has been the ultimate weapon.

With the threat from the non-Malays diminished, the Malays have predictably begun to indulge in intra-Malay disagreements. In fact, in the 1980s, the ruling party, UMNO, split, and the Malays have been polarized politically since. There were some fears that the UMNO split would spill-over to the MAF and that Kelantanese officers (the "k-factor") would be more loyal to the Sultan of Kelantan and his uncle, Tengku Razaleigh--Dr. Mahathir's chief political rival--than to the government. However, the MAF as an organization has thus far been able to remain non-aligned in Malay politics, although it is subjected to some pressures. In 1990, Dr. Mahathir won a convincing electoral victory over his Malay detractors (although UMNO lost badly in Kelantan). The key question of who Dr. Mahathir's successor will be, and how he handles the intra-Malay polarization and the year-end MAF promotions, could directly affect civilian-military relations in the future.

Finally, with abundant rumors of alleged official corruption and reports of government scandals--a new phenomenon in Malaysia--there is always the possibility of younger Malay MAF elements becoming dissatisfied with the political situation and attempting a coup in order to cleanse and reform the system (not much is known about the orientation of the younger officers). However, as long as the economy prospers, the government appears effective, upward mobility in the MAF is sustained, and the prospect of good job opportunities for ex-officers remains, it seems unlikely that alleged corruption will spur the creation of a coup group.

In conclusion, there are hypothetical situations where one could imagine that in the future a disgruntled Malay army group might attempt to seize power. However, Malaysia's political system features accepted and institutionalized norms and procedures governing the exercise of power, including strong political/bureaucratic control of the military and the substantial persuasion exercised over Malays by the King and the Rulers. The civilian political process is strong and working. The MAF in turn has its own professional tradition of non-involvement in politics, and it gives the appearance of being an organization that is satisfied. In the absence of turmoil arising in the country, or a radical and threatening departure from government policies, it is highly improbable that the army would leave its barracks.

Notes

1. Although the term "military" is often used, the branch of the armed forces associated with coup activity and praetorian politics is typically the army. It is very difficult for the air force or navy to mount a coup without the involvement of the army, since it is necessary physically to seize key government buildings and sometimes members of the government. On the other hand, even a faction of the army can seize power unilaterally.

2. See, for example, the special issue on the military in the *Third World Quarterly*, vol. 7, no. 1 (January 1985), especially Peter Lyon, "Introduction: Back to the Barracks," pp. 9-15, and S. E. Finer, "The Return to the Barracks," pp. 16-30. Also see Constantine P. Danopoulos, (ed.), *From Military to Civilian Rule* (London: Routledge, 1991).

3. See Chandran Jeshurun, *Malaysian Defence Policy*, Kuala Lumpur: Penebit Universiti Malaya, 1980, xv-xix.

4. Cynthia H. Enloe, *Police, Military and Ethnicity: Foundations of State Power* (New Brunswick: Transaction Books, 1980), p. 69.

5. For a political history of Malaysia, see R.S. Milne and Diane K. Mauzy, *Politics and Government in Malaysia* (Singapore: Times Books International, rev. ed., 1980); Gordon P. Means, *Malaysian Politics*, 2nd ed. (London: Hodder and Stoughton, 1976); and K.J. Ratnam, *Communalism and the Political Process in Malaya* (Kuala Lumpur: University of Malaya Press, 1965).

6. The variously-titled hereditary heads of the Malay states are known officially as the Rulers. Most but not all have the individual title of sultan.

7. The Malay Regiment was given the honorific of "Royal" in 1958 by the *Agung* (King). It is known as the RMR in English and the Rejimen Askar Melayu Di Raja (RAMD) in Bahasa Malaysia.

8. See Zakaria Haji Ahmad, "Malaysia," in Zakaria Haji Ahmad and Harold Crouch (eds.), *Military-Civilian Relations in Southeast Asia* (Singapore: Oxford University Press, 1985), p. 123; and Means, *Malaysian Politics*, pp. 44-46. The Japanese did set up one indigenous unit but it did not function as a military force and played no post-war role (unlike the Japanese-initiated armies in Indonesia and Burma). See Joyce Lebra, *Japanese-Trained Armies in Southeast Asia* (Hong Kong: Heinemann Asia, 1977).

9. The Malayan Naval Force was reestablished in 1948 and renamed the Royal Malayan Navy in 1952 in recognition of its distinctiveness from the British Royal Navy. The Royal Malayan Air Force was formed in June 1958.

10. Chandran Jeshurun, "Development and Civil-Military Relations in Malaysia: The Evolution of the Officer Corps," in J. Soedjati Djiwandono and Yong Mun Cheong (eds), *Soldiers and Stability in Southeast Asia* (Singapore: Institute of Southeast Asian Studies, 1988), p. 262.

11. Zakaria, "Malaysia," pp. 126-27.

12. *Ibid.*, pp. 128-29.

13. It is the official policy of the Malaysian government not to release any detailed information concerning military manpower, ethnic percentages, weapons, and equipment, even to Parliament. The possession or dissemination of such information is prohibited by the Official Secrets Act, which allows for the imprisonment of violators.

14. Enloe, *Police, Military and Ethnicity*, p. 76.

15. Zakaria Haji Ahmad, "The Military and Development in Malaysia and Brunei, with a Short Survey on Singapore," in Soedjati and Yong (eds.), *Soldiers and Stability in Southeast Asia*, p. 235.

16. The army was given the responsibility for "framework operations" in the jungle. See R. Clutterbuck, *Riot and Revolution in Singapore and Malaya, 1945-1963*.(London: Faber and Faber, 1973).

17. See Richard Stubbs, *Hears and Minds in Guerrilla Warfare: The Malayan Emergency 1948-1960* (Singapore: Oxford University Press, 1989).

18. Zakaria, "Malaysia," p. 120.

19. Jeshurun, "Development," p. 268.

20. Quoted in *Ibid.*, p. 262, from the *Straits Times*, September 14, 1956.

21. Zakaria, "Malaysia," p. 119. For a neo-Marxist interpretation, see Lim Mah Hui, "Contradictions in the Development of Malay Capital: State, Accumulation and Legitimation," *Journal of Contemporary Asia*, vol. 15, no. 1 (1985), p. 59.

22. *Far Eastern Economic Review*, November 24, 1988, pp. 23-24.

23. *The Star*, November 3, 1989.

24. The large acquisition order of Air Force fighter planes and possibly submarines from Britain became controversial in 1989, when a British newspaper alleged that the deal involved kickbacks to Malaysian politicians. Later, several Malaysians were arrested under the Internal Security Act for allegedly passing on information about the deal to one of Malaysia's neighbors (unnamed). See the *Far Eastern Economic Review*, December 21, 1989, pp. 20-21.

25. Zakaria, "Malaysia," p. 119. Also see Enloe, *Police, Military and Ethnicity*, p. 81.

26. See Stanley Bedlington, *Malaysia and Singapore* (Ithaca: Cornell University Press, 1978), p. 166-67. He writes that there is little likelihood of any military takeover because of the absence of any important tensions between the MAF and the political elite.

27. Enloe, *Police, Military and Ethnicity*, p. 82.

28. The government released some basic figures after May 1969 in its publication, *The May 13 Tragedy* (Kuala Lumpur: National Operations Council, 1969).

29. Zakaria, "Malaysia," p. 129.

30. Jeshurun, "Development," pp. 261 and 263, and Zakaria, "Malaysia," p. 125.

31. Quoted in Jeshurun, *Malaysian Defence*, p. 66, from parliamentary records for 19 March 1971 (PD/DR 1/16, col 2054).

32. See Jeshurun, *Malaysian Defence*, pp. 50-67.

33. Officially ASEAN is not a security pact. However, a number of bi-lateral security arrangements exist among the ASEAN member states.

34. Zakaria, "The Military," p. 242.

35. Jeshurun, "Development," p. 269. Also see M.G.G. Pillai, "King and Ministers, Malaysia's Army In the Middle," The *Statesman* (India), October 19, 1988.

14

The Future of Civilian Rule and Democracy in a Changing World

Constantine P. Danopoulos

Beginning with the early 1970 s, an increasing number of Southern European, Asian, Latin American and, more recently, African countries joined the list of developing societies experimenting with civilian rule and even democratization. Military regimes withdrew from the levels of authority making room for civilian led governments. Sensing the reverberations of this trend, Myron Weiner declared in 1987 that "few issues are more likely to seize world attention for the remainder of this century than the question of whether authoritarian countries in the Third World will make a transition to democratic civilian rule."[1] The trend toward democratization was accelerated with the collapse of Soviet communism and the end of the Cold War prompting an increasing number of totalitarian, authoritarian or semi-authoritarian countries (some discussed in this volume) to move toward market economics, privatization of the means of production and democratic politics. Samuel Huntington refers to this phenomenon as "a global democratic revolution" and deems it "probably the most important political trend in the late twentieth century."[2] Democracy is generally accepted to include secret balloting, universal and adult suffrage, regular elections, partisan competition, executive accountability, and associational recognition and access.[3] Terry Karl correctly identifies another dimension of democracy important to the developing world: civilian control of the military.[4]

Democratization is not exactly a novelty. In Huntington's mind the present is the "third wave" of democratization that the world has seen in the nineteenth and twentieth centuries. The first wave began in the 1820s, lasted until the

1920s, and resulted in "the widening of the suffrage" in the United States and almost 30 other countries. The rise to power of Mussolini in Italy marked the beginning of a reversal. By the early 1940s, the number of democracies had been reduced to twelve. The victory of the Allies in World War II spurred a second era of democratization, lasting for less than two decades. During this period a total of 36 countries were governed democratically. But the second wave was also reversed. By the time the present wave began in the early to mid 1970s, the number of democracies in the world had dropped to 30.[5] In terms of numbers, the current wave appears the strongest, encompassing until now 40 or more countries. Is the present era of democratization likely to suffer the same fate as its predecessors? This essay will seek to assess the nature of the ongoing transition to democracy and speculate on its future.

The Nature of the "Third Wave"

Huntington identifies five "major factors" as being responsible for the present wave of transitions to civilian rule and democracy: legitimacy deflation on the part of authoritarian regimes, largely due to less than spectacular performance; widespread economic growth in the 1960s and 1970s which led to increases in education and urbanization, improving living standards, and bestowing middle class expectations; the Vatican's shift away from supporting authoritarianism and in favor of expanding democracy; changes in the policies of the two superpowers (U.S. and U.S.S.R.) and the appearance of the European Economic Community (EEC); and finally, "snowballing" i.e., the spread of democracy in one place generated similar demands in other places.[6]

While all encompassing and well thought out, Huntington's democratization factors appear designed to explain the shift away from authoritarian politics in Southern Europe, Latin America and possibly some East European countries where Catholicism was a significant force and there was considerable economic growth and other attributes associated with economic development and modernization. Democratization movements in African countries and, in many respects, the former Soviet Union were little affected by the change of heart in the Vatican. Instead, the chronic, deep and incurable state of the Soviet Union's economy encouraged Gorbachev and his associates to consider *perestroika* and *glasnost*. Likewise, abysmal economic conditions and steadily deteriorating standards of living in most African countries prompted a significant number of African dictators to join the democratization revolution and to allow for multipartyism and competitive politics.

Unlike previous democratization waves, the current one is economically driven. It is rooted in the failure of closed regimes (both authoritarian and totalitarian) to solve the economic ills of their societies; and it is fuelled by unprecedented western cultural penetration of the Third World and even the former Soviet bloc. The dismal performance of closed regimes undermined the argument that single partyism and state intervention in the economy constituted the best hope of nation-building and freedom from neocolonial domination in Africa and other parts of the developing world. Similarly, stagnation in the Eastern bloc destroyed the possible appeal of the command economy model advocated by the Soviet Union. Western, and primarily American, cultural penetration through television, radio, films and other forms of entertainment exposed the suppressed and often destitute peoples of Africa, Latin America and the former Eastern bloc to the "sweet fruits" of freedom and free enterprise, and made them even more aware of their misery and backwardness. Often masking its own economic problems, the West managed to convince the peoples of the developing and communist worlds alike that its own "economic [and] material improvement" constituted the best "advertisement for capitalism" and political democracy.[7]

In other words, the recent democratization wave is based on the belief that political democracy and free enterprise are inseparable and one cannot exist without the other.[8] Giuseppe Di Palma underscores the indivisibility of the free enterprise-democracy dyad saying that "[n]o transition from dictatorship has successfully done away with the market without doing away with the prospects for democracy."[9] Evidence of this can be seen in the widespread and often hasty privatization program undertaken by recently democratizing or redemocratizing countries. Taking their cues from experiments in France and Spain, the elected governments of Peru, Brazil, Bolivia, Mexico and Argentina inaugurated often far reaching privatization programs. President Carlos Saúl Menem of Argentina, for example, dramatically reversed his campaign promises and "went to the heart of Argentina's statist and stifled economy." The government "privatized" the country's economy "in haste, and has auctioned state assets to the best positioned, without much concern for details or monitors."[10]

Post-communist regimes in Poland, Czechoslovakia, Hungary, and, more recently, in Russia under President Boris Yeltsin, are pursuing privatization and democratization. The "rush to capitalism" and political democracy in communist countries, according to Deborah Milenkovitch, is attributed to the fact "[t]he three pillars of socialism--state ownership of production, central planning, and central management of the economy--were completely discredited."[11] Bartlomiej Kaminski echoes this conclusion, stating that the collapse of state socialism, or the "syndrome of withdrawal" as he phrases it, "is the result of a response to a cumulative process of economic deterioration."[12]

African countries displayed similar patterns.

> Economically bankrupt [African regimes] faced fiscal paralyses, never ending budgetary crises, financial constraints on development, mushrooming public debts, greater dependency relationships vis-a-vis external donors, and no scope for political maneuverability....Trapped in a free-fall to economic oblivion African authoritarian rulers had no choice but to respond to calls for economic privitization and democracy.[13]

Jon Kraus' assessment of democratization in Africa is even more direct. He states that

> Benin's dramatic decision to allow multiparty elections in March 1991, flows from economic and political collapse. And in Congo, the ruling Congolese Workers party renounced Marxism and adopted a social democratic platform because of severe economic weakness and externally supported economic liberalization.[14]

A recent article in *The Economist* supports this view as well.

> Africans have at last lost patience with their rulers. They are particularly angry about declining living standards, but also about arbitrary and bad government, corruption and a breakdown of law and order. They have decided that multipartyism [and] free enterprise policies are their most likely salvation.[15]

The trend toward democracy and free market economies has also received considerable prodding from the West and international financial institutions. Privatization and political pluralism have been among the requirements demanded by the U.S. and other Western countries, the World Bank, and the International Monetary Fund (IMF) as prerequisites for financial assistance and loans to countries in Africa and East Europe and states comprising the newly formed Commonwealth of Independent States. In spite of the conservative and often militaristic rhetoric, the Reagan administration proclaimed the so-called "Reagan Doctrine" and established the National Endowment for Democracy, a quasi-governmental institution, aimed at promoting democratic institutions and market economics around the world. The Bush administration is following a similar line. Visiting Secretary of State James Baker, for instance, told Albanian officials that "further U.S. assistance would be made conditional on Albania's taking concrete steps toward democracy and a market economy."[16] The British Foreign Secretary, Douglas Hurd, echoed Baker's remarks saying:

> Countries which tend towards pluralism...and market principles should be encouraged. Governments which persist with repressive policies, corrupt management and wasteful, discredited economic systems should not expect us to support their folly.[17]

Michel Camdessus, the IMF's Managing Director, struck a similar theme stating "[g]ood economics is good politics, and vice versa."[18] He echoed a similar line during a recent visit to Lima, telling the Peruvian President that Peru "cannot continue to receive foreign aid" unless it proceeds with immediate and deep economic reform.[19] Faced with abysmal and deteriorating economic conditions, Third World governments have little choice but to accept the conditions set forth by international lending institutions. Even radical populists of the Jerry Rawlings type were forced to compromise. With Ghana's economy "barely extant [Rawlings] had to submit to IMF guidelines in order to acquire the foreign banking necessary in order to keep the economy afloat."[20]

Will the "Third Wave" Survive?

What we see unfolding before our eyes is a process of democratization and not necessarily the existence of democracy. Democracy and democratization, though related, are not synonymous. Military disengagement and democratization refer to a process that may or may not lead to to the establishment and consolidation of civilian rule and democracy. The question, therefore, should not be whether democracy will survive, but instead whether democratization will lead to the birth of a healthy child (democracy) or complications will abort the pregnancy.

As mentioned earlier, the present democratization wave is driven by the abysmal failure of closed regimes to address severe economic deficiencies. In other words, democratization has spurred expectations on the part of the citizenry. The survivability of democratization, then, is likely to depend on the extent to which new regimes perform to expectations. Terry Karl is on the mark when she states that

[p]atterns of greater economic growth and more equitable income distribution, higher levels of literacy and education, and increases in social communication and media exposure may be better treated as the products of stable democratic processes rather than the prerequisites of its existence.[21]

Can the mere existence of democratic institutions, however feeble, deliver the goods and thus pave the way for economic improvement and political democracy?

In a seminal article Philippe C. Schmitter and Terry Lynn Karl argue while democracy is associated with citizen participation, political competition, majority rule, public cooperation and representative government, democracy is not a miracle cure. By attaining democracy a society will not necessarily resolve "all its political, social, economic, administrative, and cultural problems." Despite widespread sentiments to the contrary, democracies are not economically and administratively more efficient than other forms of government, or more capable to handle social conflict and to provide for orderly stable and consensual government than autocracies. Finally, democracies may lead to "more open societies and polities---but not necessarily [to] more open economies."[22]

Although it may be too early to pass judgement on the long term success of newly democratizing regimes, there is evidence pointing to worsening economic conditions, particularly with regard to income distribution and allocation of wealth. Privatization policies so far have widened the chasm between the rich and the poor. While the more educated, westernized, wealthy and well connected minorities have benefitted significantly from privitization, those in the middle or lower part of the socio-economic pyramid are experiencing a steady and profound deterioration of living standards. State withdrawal has often been associated with the removal of safety nets which, however inefficient and corrupt, meant the difference between subsistence and starvation, underemployment and unemployment, crammed housing and rooflessness.

In Menem's Argentina, for example, "[o]ne third of the population has been left outside the system. Poverty spreads while wealth is concentrated in fewer hands."[23] To qualify for low interest loans in 1987 the Mozambican government implemented an austerity program required by the IMF and other international lending institutions.

These economic measures have hit poor urban dwellers hardest. An estimated 60 percent of the population lives in absolute poverty...Unemployment has also increased, the number of civil service employees is being reduced, and state-owned enterprises are for sale.."[24]

David P. Werlich paints an equally grim picture for Peru following the imposition of President Fujimori's shock treatment, known as "Fujishock."[25]

Eastern Europe and the former Soviet Union show similar patterns. Well placed former communist party *apparatchiki* used their connections and knowledge to take advantage of privatization programs, and in many cases, to acquire substantial wealth in very short time. As in Third World countries, the gap between the haves and the have nots is becoming wider and substantial portions of the population (50 percent or more) now live in poverty. Unemployment is high and rising, crime is on the increase. Production has fallen dramatically, government coffers are empty, and the new private entrepreneurs "tend not to pay taxes." *The Economist* recently reported that economic reform in Poland, considered one of the "bravest" and "boldest," is "in jeopardy" and its major architect, Finance Minister Karol Lutkowski, resigned in frustration.[26]

Elections, multipartyism and more open and competitive politics have not necessarily brought about government stability and administrative efficiency. A myriad of political parties entered the fray making it difficult for political majorities to emerge. In Russia, for example, there are at least 250 known political parties and the list is growing. A total of 29 electoral lists appeared in last November's parliamentary elections in Poland, and none of them received more than 13 percent of the vote. In Benin, a country of four million, 1800 candidates and 26 political parties struggled to fill the 64 seats in the country's legislative assembly. "The picture," says a seasoned observer of African politics, "is repeated across the breadth of Africa, reaching its nadir in Zaire where 96 parties have requested registration to date" (early 1992).[27]

This type of hyperpolitics reflects social, economic and, above all, ethnic fragmentation. Political openness and freedom have accentuated these divisions, further complicating the process of coalition building and jeopardizing government stability. In some situations, social fragmentation has led to voting along ethnic lines and even prompted break away movements. Coalition governments may be more representative and democratic but are generally weak and often unable to tackle pressing and difficult problems. In addition, structural difficulties such as opposition from established bureaucracies, lack of know-how, uncertainty and absence of infrastructures have combined to slow down privatization and the establishment of market economies. Under the circumstances, administrative efficiency, social tranquility, political harmony and economic growth are likely to be the victims, at least in the short run.

The immediate difficulties of democratizing regimes is also compounded by the inability or unwillingness of the West, and particularly the U.S., to provide much needed economic and technical assistance. Although encouraging democratization and free market economies, the Bush administration has done little to help the new democratic regimes. America's response, in the words of former President Richard Nixon, has been a "penny-ante game" and "pathetically inadequate."[28] Constrained by an economic recession, a worsening budget deficit, and "a coalition of forces and interests that offer no political basis for economic support of the international trends favored by the United States,"[29] the Bush administration "asked for only partly sums to assist the fledgling democracies of Europe."[30] No "peace dividend is in the offering for Africa" either.[31] The conservative, "American first" challenge mounted by Patrick Buchanan against President Bush for the Republican nomination for President made it even more difficult for the administration to come out in favor of aid to the struggling economies of Russia and other former Soviet republics. If America "fails to address its more fundamental domestic needs...," warns David Gergen, "[the] window of opportunity for constructive internationalism [and] the will and the capacity to undertake new commitments...will diminish sharply."[32] Washington and other Western countries finally came out in favor of a $24 billion package; it remains to be seen whether Congress will approve funding and whether the proposed amount will be sufficient to address the severe economic difficulties facing the Commonwealth of Independent States. In general, however, foreign policy issues and assistance to democratizing regimes so far have been almost totally left out of the 1992 presidential campaign.

Failure to address economic and social problems which led to the "political exhaustion" and "loss of legitimacy" of closed regimes, and, in turn, created the expectation that "democracies can now be expected to govern effectively and efficiently" may well backfire.[33] Unless the new democratizing regimes are able to tackle immediate issues and perform better than their authoritarian predecessors, they may also face public disenchantment and deprive themselves of the time, space and popular acceptance needed to survive long enough to become consolidated. "Experience has shown," Schmitter and Karl reminds us, "that democracies too can lose the ability to govern."[34]

Extremist movements of the left or the right seem to still possess some muscle and certainly the willingness to present a threat to democratizing regimes. Right wing movements in Russia, Bulgaria, Poland and elsewhere have mushroomed. Their presence is augmented by comparable ultranationalistic political parties in France, Italy, Austria and other countries of the democratic world. The traditional left, on the other hand, though wounded and in disarray, still possesses enough strength to be a political factor. The "cold turkey" privatization program in Poland, for example, created enough popular discontent to give leftist parties over 30 percent of the vote in last November's parliamentary elections. Ex-communists had similar successes in Albania, Romania and Bulgaria. The now defunct Soviet Communist Party is still able to stage sizeable public demonstrations protesting price increases and to demand a return of the old regime.

By far the greatest threat against democratization, however, comes from the armed forces which, in spite of failures and less than enviable records as political governors, command the means and the organizational structure to supplant the new regimes and stop democratization in its tracks. In Venezuela (February 1992), a group of army officers, unhappy with President Perez's austerity program and concerned about their country's economy, attempted a coup against the popularly elected government. The Haitian military overthrew President Aristide last August when it became apparent that he planned to take steps to reduce the army's autonomy and political power.

Yet the "third wave" of democratization may fare better than the previous two. People learn from experiences and travails and may be less inclined to support efforts to bring back old and unsuccessful schemes. The failure of the Venezuelan would-be praetorians to enlist the support of other units in the armed forces and to attract any popular following not only led to the failure of the coup but provided evidence that democracy, in spite of all its faults, is preferable to autocratic rule. The Venezuelan military appear to have also concluded that staying in the barracks may be the best way to protect the institution's corporate interests. A similar point can be made about Argentina where a number of attempts to overthrow President Alfonsin and his successor, Carlos Menem, ended in failure. Such a unified front by civilians and the military is without precedent in that nation's troubled history.

In other words, democratization is a process that does not always follow a straight path, but a force that surges forward despite reversals, difficulties and barriers. It arrives through a lengthy process during which other forms of government are tried and eliminated. And it has a contagious quality to it. Richard Sklar states that democracy has "developmental effects. It comes to every country in fragments or parts; each fragment becomes an incentive for the addition of another."[35] Thus the present democratization wave can be seen as a delayed continuation of previous ones. And even though it may be reversed, the long term future of democracy is brighter not necessarily due to its ability to deliver the goods, but because, as Winston Churchill said, it is the worst form of government, except for all others.

Notes

1. Myron Weiner, "Empirical Democratic Theory and the Transition from Authoritarianism to Democracy," *Political Science*, vol. 20:4 (Fall 1987), p. 806.

2. Samuel P. Huntington, "How Countries Democratize," *Political Science Quarterly*, vol. 106.: 4 (1991-92), p. 579.

3. Democracy as a "procedural minimum" is attributed to Guillermo O'Donnell and Philippe C. Schmitter, *Transitions from Authoritarian Rule: Tentative Conclusions about Uncertain Democracies* (Baltimore: The Johns Hopkins University Press, 1986), p.8.

4. Terry Lynn Karl, "Dilemmas of Democratization in Latin America," Comparative Politics, vol. 23:1 (October 1990), p.2.

5. Samuel P. Huntington, "Democracy's Third Wave," *Journal of Democracy*, 2:2 (Spring 1991), p.12.

6. *Ibid.*, pp. 13-17.

7. Eric Hobsbawn, "Harder Times Ahead for Capitalism," *The Guardian*, November 30, 1991, p. 27.

8. Charles E. Lindbloom, *Politics and Markets*, (New York: Basic Books, 1977), pp. 116-117.

9. Giuseppe Di Palma, *To Craft Democracies--An Essay on Democratic Transitions*, (Berkeley, Los Angeles, Oxford: University of California Press, 1990), p. 91.

10. Juan E. Corradi, "The Argentina of Carlos Saúl Menem," *Current History*, (February 1992), pp. 81-82.

11. Deborah Milenkovitch, "The Politics of Economic Transformation," *Journal of International Affairs*, vol. 45:1 (Summer 1991), p. 152.

12. Bartlomiej Kominski, *The Collapse of State Socialism*, (Princeton, N.J.: Princeton University Press, 1991), p. 162.

13. Samuel Decalo, "The Process Prospects and Constraints of Democratization in Africa," *African Affairs*, vol. 91 (January 1992), pp. 14-16.

14. Jon Kraus, "Building Democracy in Africa," *Current History*, (May 1991), p. 210.

15. *The Economist*, February 22, 1992, pp. 17-20.

16. Elez Biberaj, "Albania at the Crossroads," *Problems of Communism*, vol. 40:5 (September-October 1991), p. 13.

17. *The Economist*, February 22, 1992, p. 20.

18. *Ibid.*, p. 20.

19. *Times of the Americas*, March 4, 1992, p. B2.

20. Victor Azarya and Naomi Chazoan, "Disengagement from the State in Africa: Reflections on the Experience of Ghana and Guinea," *Comparative Studies in Society and History*, vol. 29:1 (January 1987), p. 113.

21. Karl, "Dilemmas of Democratization," p. 5.

22. Philippe C. Schmitter and Terry Lynn Karl, "What Democracy Is...and Is Not," *Journal of Democracy*, vol. 2:3 (Summer 1991), pp. 75-88.

23. Corradi, "The Argentina of Carlos Saúl Menem," p. 82.

24. Virginia Curtin Knight, "Mozambique's Search for Stability," *Current History*, (May 1991), p. 220

25. David P. Werlich, "Fujimori and the Disaster in Peru," *Current History* vol. 90 (February 1991), pp. 82.

26. *The Economist*, February 22, 1992, p. 41.

27. Decalo, "Democratization in Africa," pp. 30-31.

28. *Time*, March 23, 1992, p. 29.

29. Michael Mendelbaum, "The Bush Foreign Policy," *Foreign Affairs*, vol. 70, No. 1 (1991), p. 20.

30. David Gergen, "America's Missed Opportunities," *Foreign Affairs*, vol. 71, No. 1, (1992), p. 4.

31. Decalo, "Democratization in Africa," p. 30.

32. Gergen, "America's Missed Opportunities," pp. 18-19.

33. Schmitter and Karl, "What Democracy Is...And Is Not," p. 86.

34. *Ibid.*, p. 86.

35. Richard L. Sklar, "Developmental Democracy," *Cooperative Studies in Society and History and History*, vol. 29, No. 4 (October 1987), p. 74.

Index

256

Association of Southeast Asian
Nations (ASEAN), 210, 237,
241(n33)
Athulathmudali, Lalit, 203
Auma-Osolo, Agola, 90
Austria, 251
Averbury, Lord, 80
Avirgan, Tony, 113, 121(n48)
Al-Awdah, Sheik (Saudi Arabia), 61

Baghdad Arab summit (1978), 29
Baker, James, 247
Bamenda Congress (Cameroon), 94
Bandar, Prince (Saudi Arabia), 57
Bandaranaike, Sirimavo, 197, 203
Bandaranaike, S.W.R.D., 193, 200
Bangladesh, 11, 185
Bank of Zambia, 150
Banque des Etats d'Afrique Centrale,
99
Barotse people, 150
Bataan, 213
Batac, Victor, 215
Bedouins, 24, 25, 29, 55-56, 68(n6)
Be'eri, Eliezer, 55-56
Bell, M.J.V., 118
Bemba people, 150
Benin, 246, 249
Berbers, 44
Berlin Conference (1884-1885), 108
Bharatiya Janata Party (India), 182,
187
Bienen, Henry S., 111, 113
bin Shaker, Zeid, 30
Bishops' Manifest for Peace
(Guyana), 82
Biya, Paul, 10, 97, 98, 99, 101
political liberalization under, 94,
100, 102
Black, Yondo, 102
Black Power movements, 165, 167
Bolivia, 245
Bonifacio, Andres, 212
Borneo, 226
Botswana, 142
Brazil, 12, 73, 122-123(n65), 245
Briand, 101

British East Africa, 108. *See also*
Tanzania
British Forward Movement
(Malaysia), 228
British Indian Army, 178
Brotherhood of Guardians
(Philippines), 217, 221(n10)
Brotherson, Festus, 81
Buchanan, Patrick, 250
Buddhists, in Sri Lanka, 190, 194,
199-200, 201, 203
Bulgaria, 250, 251
Burger, Angela, 7, 11
Burghers, 191, 199, 201(table)
Burma, 218, 220, 225, 228, 237,
240(n8)
Burnham, Forbes, 14, 74-75, 84,
86(n15)
control of Guyana Defense Force
by, 16, 75-76, 77, 78, 79, 80
and Nyerere compared, 85
Burnham, Viola, 80
Bush administration, 247, 250

Cabahug, Sotero, 222(n16)
CAFS. *See* Chief of the Armed
Forces Staff
Calderon, Felipe, 220(n1)
Camdessus, Michel, 247
Cameroon, 63(table), 89-90, 93-
104, 142
economy of, 97-99, 101-102, 103
and France, 10, 99, 101-102,
103-104
leadership style in, 14, 95-97,
100-101
mechanisms of civilian control
in, 6, 16, 93-96, 100-102
Cameroon National Union (CNU), 6,
93-94.
See also Cameroon People's
Democratic Movement
Cameroon Organization to
Fight for Democracy (COFD),
99, 102